SHERLOCK HOLMES OF BAKER STREET

If it is permissible sometimes to reconstruct biography on the basis of the known proclivities of one's hero . . .—RICHARD D. ALTICK, THE SCHOLAR ADVENTURERS.

Perhaps the reader should be warned that, when I retell a tale, my version may not be well rounded; it may be designed to emphasize latent elements, for reasons which should be discernible from the context.—HARRY LEVIN, THE POWER OF BLACKNESS.

"Behold the fruit of pensive nights and laborious days . . ." —SHERLOCK HOLMES, "HIS LAST BOW."

"Has anything escaped me? . . . I trust there is nothing of consequence which I have overlooked?"—JOHN H. WATSON, M.D., THE HOUND OF THE BASKERVILLES.

SHERLOCK HOLMES OF BAKER STREET

A Life of the World's First Consulting Detective

BY WILLIAM S. BARING-GOULD

BRAMHALL HOUSE · NEW YORK

ACKNOWLEDGMENTS

Baker Street Irregulars everywhere have helped to make this book. I am deeply grateful to all of them, but in particular I would like to acknowledge my indebtedness to these, and their publishers:

Rolfe Boswell, author of "Sarasate, Sherlock and Shaw," in *The Baker Street Journal*, January 1952.

The late Gavin Brend, author of *My Dear Holmes*.

The Marquess of Donegall, for his editorship of *The Sherlock Holmes Journal*.

James Keddie, Jr., editor of *The Second Cab* (Boston: Stoke Moran, 1947).

Robert Keith Leavitt, author of "Annie Oakley in Baker Street," in *Profile by Gaslight: An Irregular Reader about the Private Life of Sherlock Holmes* (New York: Simon & Schuster, 1944).

A. Carson Simpson, author of *Simpson's Sherlockian Studies* (Philadelphia: International Printing Company, 1953–60).

The late Edgar W. Smith, for his editorship of *The Baker Street Journal* and for his many writings.

Rex Stout, for creating a certain very special person.

Dr. Julian Wolff, the present editor of *The Baker Street Journal*.

Ernest Bloomfield Zeisler, author of the *Baker Street Chronology: Commentaries on the Sacred Writings of Dr. John H. Watson* (Chicago: Alexander J. Isaacs, 1953).

The author wishes to express his gratitude to the late Sir Arthur Conan Doyle, but for whom this book could never have been thought of, let alone written; he also wishes to thank his Estate, and John Murray, the publishers of the Sherlock Holmes books and stories, for permission to make use of copyright material and quote from it so liberally.

This book is for
the woman
in my life—
CEIL

THE PLAYBILL

The year '87 furnished us with a long series of cases . . . of which I retain the records.
            —JOHN H. WATSON, M.D.

"That's genius, Watson. But if I am spared by lesser men our day will surely come."
            —SHERLOCK HOLMES.

. . . it is only natural that I should dwell rather upon his successes than upon his failures. . .
            —JOHN H. WATSON, M.D.

"There is something devilish in this, Watson."
            —SHERLOCK HOLMES.

"What do you make of it, Watson?"
            —SHERLOCK HOLMES.

"I am not sure that of all the five hundred cases of capital importance which I have handled there is one which cuts so deep."
            —SHERLOCK HOLMES.

*"I never saw a case yet that Holmes could not throw a
light upon."*
—INSPECTOR ATHELNEY JONES.

*After my marriage and my subsequent start in private
practice, the very intimate relations which had existed
between Holmes and myself became to some extent
modified. He still came to me when he desired a companion in his investigations . . .*
—JOHN H. WATSON, M.D.

*It is with a heavy heart that I take up my pen to write
these the last words in which I shall ever record the
singular gifts by which my friend Mr. Sherlock Holmes
was distinguished.*
—JOHN H. WATSON, M.D.

*(The) public . . . has shown some interest in those
glimpses which I have occasionally given them of the
thoughts and actions of a very remarkable man . . .*
—JOHN H. WATSON, M.D.

*"Your son . . . has carried himself in this matter as I
should be proud to see my own son do, should I ever
chance to have one."*
—SHERLOCK HOLMES.

*"I travelled for two years in Tibet, therefore, and
amused myself by visiting Lhasa and spending some
days with the head Lama. You may have read of the remarkable explorations of a Norwegian named Sigerson, but I am sure that it never occurred to you that
you were receiving news of your friend . . ."*
—SHERLOCK HOLMES.

The crime was of interest in itself, but that interest

was nothing to me compared to the inconceivable sequel . . .
　　　　　　　　—JOHN H. WATSON, M.D.

No characters in this book are fictional, although the author should very much like to meet any who claim to be.

WILLIAM S. BARING-GOULD

I. THE GENTEEL GYPSIES: 1854–64

Travel, in the younger sort, is a part of education.
FRANCIS BACON.

It was the year in which Henry David Thoreau wrote *Walden*.

It was the year in which the Republican party was born in Ripon, Wisconsin.

It was the year in which the Doctrine of the Immaculate Conception of the Blessed Virgin was adopted by the Roman Catholic Church.

These are the events *The World Almanac* lists as "memorable" for the year 1854.[1]

Unaccountably, the *Almanac* fails to list perhaps the most memorable event of that same memorable year. It was the birth, in the early hours of the morning of Friday, January 6, of a third and last son to Siger and Violet Holmes at their farmstead of Mycroft[2] in the North Riding[3] of Yorkshire, England, a district famous for its horse-breeding stables and its wind-swept—"wuthering"—heights.

But let us go back ten years, to 1844.

---

[1] The year 1854 also saw "The Charge of the Light Brigade," one of the most heroic episodes in British military history, in which some 670 men of an English light cavalry brigade, fighting in the Crimean War, charged a heavily protected Russian artillery post at Balaklava, eight miles away from besieged Sevastopol.

[2] "My croft!" a remote Holmes ancestor had once exclaimed to a visitor, and Mycroft the house and lands had become. The holdings gave their name both to Siger Holmes's elder brother and to his second son.

[3] Yorkshire folk will tell you that a *riding* measured the distance that a Saxon overlord could go riding in a day, but the true meaning is not so picturesque. A riding is only a thriding, or thirding, a division into three parts. There is, of course, no *South* Riding of Yorkshire. The three are the North, the East, and the West.

In the early spring of that year, a young cavalry lieutenant in the services of the East India Company—uniform blue and gold —had offered, one evening, to drive a friend home from the company mess. Perhaps the dinner had been an exceptionally good one. Certainly both the cavalry lieutenant and his friend were heavy men, each weighing in the neighborhood of fourteen stone.[4] In any case, it followed that the dogcart shortly turned over. The friend fell upon his companion, the cavalry lieutenant. The friend was unhurt, but the hip of the cavalry lieutenant was dislocated, and he was invalided home without delay.

He landed in England a month later, and limped off the Indiaman at Portsmouth jetty to be greeted by the news that his elder brother Mycroft had been killed in a fall from a horse. As the only surviving son, the ex-cavalry lieutenant was now the Squire of Mycroft, a wealthy and important man.

Siger Holmes, the new Squire of Mycroft,[5] promptly did two things. First, he grew a beard. Then he set out to find a wife.

He found her in Violet Sherrinford, daughter of a quite celebrated soldier, naturalist, and explorer, Sir Edward Sherrinford, and one of four daughters in a family distinguished in many directions. Violet's mother was a sister of Emile Jean Horace Vernet (1789–1863) and a daughter of Antoine Charles Horace, commonly called Carle, Vernet (1758–1835), both French artists of distinction.

The courtship was brief. The bearded, limping, very dark, very tall suitor who had appeared so suddenly from nowhere was not only a man of wealth and position, he was also a man of spirit and a handsome man. Indeed, his personality at times was little short of overpowering.

No portrait of Siger Holmes of Mycroft remains to us, but we are told that Siger's nephew, his sister's son, George Edward Challenger, closely resembled his uncle Siger, and we have a journalist's, one Malone's, description of the nephew, himself to become a famous explorer and zoologist:

It was his size [Malone writes] which took one's breath away—his size and his imposing presence. His head was enormous, the largest I have

---

[4] Americans would say that each man weighed about 196 pounds.

[5] There are many Scandinavian place names in the North Riding, and it seems certain that Siger Holmes, like his brother Mycroft and his second son Mycroft, had been named by his parents for the place of his birth.

ever seen upon a human being. I am sure that his top-hat, had I ventured to don it, would have slipped over me entirely and rested on my shoulders. He had the face and beard which I associate with an Assyrian bull; the former florid, the latter so black as almost to have a suspicion of blue, spade-shaped and rippling down over his chest. The hair was peculiar, plastered down in front in a long, curving wisp over his massive forehead. The eyes were blue-grey under great black tufts, very clear, very critical, and very masterful. A huge spread of shoulders and chest like a barrel were the other parts of him which appeared above the table, save for two enormous hands covered with long black hair. This and a bellowing, roaring, rumbling voice made up my first impression of the notorious Professor Challenger.[6]

Siger Holmes married Violet Sherrinford at St. Sidwell's, Exeter, on May 7, 1844. Sherrinford Holmes, their first-born, named, of course, for his mother's family,[7] came into the world in 1845. Their second son, Mycroft, arrived in 1847, their third son, Sherlock, not until seven years later.

Siger Holmes insisted that the boy should be named William Sherlock, for the father had long been an admirer of that seventeenth-century theologian and author (1641–1707), and quoted often from his famous *Practical Discourse Concerning Death*.

The boy's mother favored calling him Scott—Sir Walter was her favorite author.

At last, a compromise was arrived at. The boy was baptized William Sherlock Scott Holmes.

Sherlock—the name in the old Anglo-Saxon means "fair-haired" or "shining," for little Sherlock resembled his mother—*Holmes*.

That is the name we know him by today. It is a name that has spread to every corner of the globe. To millions, he is the master detective of all time. We know him best, perhaps, through the writings of the doctor who was his friend and devoted companion for seventeen of the twenty-three years in which Sherlock Holmes of Baker Street was in active practice.

And the picture that Dr. John Hamish Watson, late of the Army Medical Department, has given us of Mr. Sherlock Holmes is, in many ways, an inspired one.

---

[6] *The Lost World;* London: Hodder and Stoughton; New York: Doran, 1912.

[7] Again, this is a place name. "Sherrinford" derives from "Shearing-ford," a shallow section of a stream where sheep were sheared of their wool.

But Dr. Watson, for a multitude of reasons—often simply the deep and gentlemanly desire not to wound some living man or woman who had played an innocent part in one of the cases that the doctor was about to lay before the public—was all too frequently forced to mask a date, a place, a person, even an entire event, in his published version of a Holmes adventure.

Often, in his writings, Dr. Watson begs the reader to excuse him if he conceals a date or any other fact that might enable an astute observer to trace the actual occurrence. Again and again he mentions a case in which Holmes played a prominent role—only to tell us that the world is not yet prepared to hear the details. One at once recalls the *Matilda Briggs,* not the name of a young woman but the name of a ship, associated with the adventure of the giant rat of Sumatra.

Now, in 1962, with the announcement that Sherlock Holmes's long-awaited *The Whole Art of Detection* will soon be given to the world, would seem to be a fitting time to present the first full investigation of the public and the private life of a man whom many of us, like Dr. Watson, will always consider to be one of the "best and the wisest" that the world has ever known.

With the birth of his third son, a restlessness settled upon the ex-cavalry lieutenant.

Siger Holmes was still young. He was a man of parts. In India he had enjoyed the company of cultured persons. And now, in Yorkshire, he found himself surrounded by clods. Shooting and fishing did not appeal to him. He tried study.

That was in the May of 1854. More than a year later, exasperated beyond further bearing by his life of studious domesticity, Siger Holmes led his entire family aboard the steamship *Lerdo* on July 7, 1855. They were bound for Bordeaux, across the Bay of Biscay. From Bordeaux they traveled to Pau, and there they wintered, taking a flat in the Grande Place.

What Siger Holmes did with himself during that winter of 1855–56 we do not know. But he and his family were persons of consequence, representatives of a dominant race. And the exchange was much in their favor. Thus it was not so difficult, or even expensive, for the Squire of Mycroft in Yorkshire to have a flat in the Grande Place, or to buy his own carriage, as Siger Holmes did that winter.

They stayed at Pau until May of 1858, until Sherlock was four. Then the whole family removed to Montpellier, where many of Mrs. Holmes's maternal relatives, the Vernets, had settled.

The coach was brought out, the horses hitched up, the family put in. They jingled over the plain.

They took a snug and pretty little house in the best part of town. There was a pleasant flower garden, with a goldfish pool to delight Sherlock and his brothers. There was even a Promenade in Montpellier, the finest in France. It looked toward the Pyrenees, and in the south the Mediterranean glinted. Here Violet Holmes strolled with her French cousins.

It was all very pleasant. They could have stayed there forever had not Sir Edward Sherrinford fallen ill. His daughter and her family returned to England to be near him. Then in the autumn the old knight died. His son-in-law was free to whisk his family abroad once more, and this he promptly did. In October 1860 they crossed to Rotterdam. Two months later this wandering family, these genteel gypsies, pitched tent in Cologne.

The Rhine in that winter of 1860–61 was frozen over, and the whole family had several months of peace during which Siger Holmes continued his studies. But when the ice began to break and whirl down the stream, the restless Yorkshireman got out his carriage and was off again.

This kind of Continental travel was not uncommon at the time. The era of the great wars had not yet arrived. Bismarck was ahead, Napoleon was behind, as the Holmes family wandered over Europe, the father on the box of the carriage, urging on the horses, his great black beard flying in the wind; the mother within; the boys looking with relish through the carriage windows at the Continent's wonderful things.

Darmstadt, Karlsruhe, Stuttgart, Mannheim, Munich, Heidelberg—the carriage covered thousands of kilometers over bad roads, in all weathers and temperatures, the baggage piled on top, the family jostling within.

Heidelberg to Berne, Berne to Lucerne, Lucerne to Thun by October—on and on the rumbling carriage rolled, beyond the cities, into villages and towns and wild corners of Europe where few English families had ever been before, where few for many years were to follow. They visited Italy, they traveled to the Tyrol and to Salzburg, they went to Vienna and thence to Dresden. They arrived in Saxony, and later stayed for a time at Mann-heim.

The journey lasted almost four long years, and had a lifelong influence on young Master Sherlock Holmes. He developed an enviably intimate knowledge of Europe. He became to some extent a European, that civilized being whom the Western world has not yet succeeded in turning out in quantity. Unaware of a boy's ordinary interests, always in the company of his brothers and his parents—who were, in their separate ways, great lovers of all that was beautiful and sublime—the whole bent of his char-acter was formed at this time.

It was a highly unusual childhood, but Sherlock was a highly unusual boy, destined to become a highly unusual man.

And then, in 1864, the Holmes family of Yorkshire left Ger-many and returned to quite different scenes.

II. OLD SHERMAN, WINWOOD READE, MAÎTRE BENCIN, AND PROFESSOR MORIARTY: 1864–72

A season of mental anguish is at hand and through this we must pass in order that our posterity may rise.
WINWOOD READE.

They were, by contrast, depressing scenes for a boy accustomed to the slow unrolling of the landscape of Europe across a carriage window.

Siger Holmes leased a house in Kennington—one of those solid, middle-class villas that, in the 1860's, abounded in this once-pleasant suburb of London.

A man of strong character, Siger Holmes had fixed notions on how his sons should now be educated. These notions included three theories. The first was that every child's mind was a blank, on which could be written whatever the parents desired. His second theory was that nothing should be learned by heart, a process which, he maintained, encouraged a parrot mind. Even stranger was the father's hostility to imagination. It had to be suppressed, because he disapproved of it. How all this may have benefited Sherlock and his brothers—and how, perhaps, handicapped them—is a matter for interesting speculation.

Sherrinford, Siger Holmes decreed, should enter Oxford at once. As the eldest of the three brothers, he would, of course, inherit the family holdings in Yorkshire. His future, so far as Siger Holmes was concerned, was settled—Sherrinford was simply to be a country squire.

Mycroft, Siger Holmes decided, might well audit the books in one of the Government departments, for the boy seemed to have quite an extraordinary faculty for figures. Mycroft, too, should go to Oxford—in 1865, when he would be eighteen.

Sherlock his father desired to make, after thorough mathematical training, an engineer.

Meantime, he sent his younger sons to a board school. It was a dim, ill-defined place, where the gas was always burning in the basement passage which led to the classroom. The school was extremely ugly in all respects, possessing not even a playing field, but only a sad, asphalted square, bounded by high brick walls.

It is a pity that we do not know more about the two years Sherlock spent there.

Sherrinford never went to school. Mycroft had one year. Sherlock in his life had altogether only three years of ordinary English schooling. So how they acquired the rudiments of learning, as the restless carriage rolled across Europe, is a mystery. We can only conclude that their mother must have taught the children their letters and their sums while the wheels turned, and Siger Holmes cracked his whip upon the box.

Sherlock was a day boy at the board school. He did not flourish there, but he gained a deep respect for it.

Years later, whirling up to London in a Portsmouth train, Holmes said to Watson, as they passed Clapham Junction:

"It's a very cheering thing to come into London by any of these lines which run high and allow you to look down upon the houses like this."

Watson thought he was joking, for the view was sordid enough.

"Look at those big, isolated clumps of buildings rising up above the slates, like brick islands in a lead-colored sea," the detective went on.

"The board schools," Watson replied.

"Lighthouses, my boy! Beacons of the future! Capsules, with hundreds of bright little seeds in each, out of which will spring the wiser, better England of the future."[1]

There was in the life of Sherlock Holmes in these days one great consolation.

He discovered, in Pinchin Lane, in Lower Lambeth, the shop

[1] "The Naval Treaty."

where lived and worked old Sherman, the naturalist and bird stuffer.

Young Sherlock, thrown much upon his own resources, and with an insatiable curiosity, loved to frequent the curious little shop. We can picture him now, a thin, eager youth helping the old man with the skinning, making impressions of bird and animal tracks in plaster of Paris, bursting with questions about the poisonous effects of vipers and swamp adders.

In the winter of 1865–66, Sherlock was ill, spending months in the attic-bedroom which was his dormitory.

When he was convalescent, his father, by an odd chance, gave him to read *The Martyrdom of Man,* by Winwood Reade (1838–75), traveler, novelist, and controversialist, as well as a nephew of Charles Reade.

It is a sad work, and its conclusions may well have depressed young Sherlock.

In any case, he never forgot the book, and recommended it to Watson in 1888 in the strongest possible terms.[2]

Seemingly recovered from his illness, which was very severe, Sherlock was taken by his parents to the farmstead of Mycroft in Yorkshire. There for a year he was a day boy at the grammar school in the neighboring town, an ancient, quiet place.

These were comparatively happy days.

Then, in the winter of 1867–68, the boy's health worsened. He was growing fast, and thin. In order to settle the matter, in the summer of 1868, he was taken to London to see an eminent specialist, Sir James Smith.

Having examined the child, Sir James pronounced him delicate. Perhaps Sir James was right, but his patient throughout many years worked with an energy which would surely have ruined any but the strongest of constitutions. Only twice, in later life, did the health of Sherlock Holmes ever fail, and then under none but the most remarkable of circumstances.

"It was some time," Watson wrote,[3] "before the health of my friend, Mr. Sherlock Holmes, recovered from the strain caused by his immense exertions in the spring of '87. . . . His iron constitu-

---

2 *The Sign of the Four.*
3 In "The Reigate Squires."

tion . . . had broken down under the strain of an investigation which had extended over two months, during which period he had never worked less than fifteen hours a day, and had more than once, as he assured me, kept to his task for five days at a stretch. The triumphant issue of his labours could not save him from reaction after so terrible an exertion, and at a time when Europe was ringing with his name, and his room was literally ankle-deep with congratulatory telegrams, I found him a prey to the blackest depression. Even the knowledge that he had succeeded when the police of three countries had failed, and that he had outmanoeuvred at every point the most accomplished swindler in Europe, was insufficient to rouse him from his nervous prostration."

Again, in the spring of the year 1897, Holmes's iron constitution showed signs of giving way in the face of a long period of constant work of the most exacting kind. Dr. Moore Agar, the Harley Street specialist, ordered a complete change of air and scene, and Holmes was induced at last to journey to Poldhu Bay on the Cornish peninsula. Curiously enough, as we shall see, the "period of rest" prescribed by Dr. Moore Agar was to bring Holmes the strangest case he was ever called upon to handle, as he himself once said.[4]

However, in 1868, the verdict was given: the boy was delicate, and his formal education was to be abandoned. More immediately exciting, and certainly of more pressing import to Siger Holmes, the decision was taken to go abroad once more. Sir James, pursing his lips, recommended the South of France for the boy's health, and so, accordingly, it was Pau again for the Holmes family.

Siger, Violet, and Sherlock Holmes sailed in September 1868, from Plymouth to St. Malo, taking a leisurely month over the rolling miles southward, resolutely halting wherever they chanced to be each Sunday to attend the church that meant so much in the life of Sherlock's mother.

They arrived at Pau in October 1868, thus beginning the last Continental visit Sherlock Holmes was ever to make with his parents.

From it, Sherlock was to get two benefits that would stand him

---

[4] "The Adventure of the Devil's Foot."

in good stead for many years to come. To "toughen" the boy, Siger Holmes himself volunteered to teach him boxing. The father also had the son enrolled in the most celebrated fencing school in Europe, the salon of Maître Alphonse Bencin.

The wiry little Frenchman with the fierce military mustaches eyed the tall, thin, quiet English boy curiously.

"*Bien*," he said at last. "We begin at the beginning. This is the *tirer au mur,* the stroke at the wall. You must learn it before I teach you the simplest parry at tierce. Bah! Do not hit! *This* is no boxing fight! Body and arm are one, moving together . . ."

Strangely enough, Sherlock proved himself to be a marvelous pupil to both his teachers.

"His cross-punch under the jaw!" his father chuckled, rubbing his own jaw. "And his straight left! I'll make a bruiser of him yet, Violet. You should see us at work."

Sherlock Holmes's mother shuddered.

By the spring of the year 1871, Siger, Violet, and Sherlock Holmes were back in England.

One cause of their return was a bad farming season in Yorkshire, so that the tenant farmers of Siger Holmes found difficulty in paying their rents. In any event, the family settled down at Mycroft.

For Sherlock, the year 1871 was ideal.

He had a pony. And now within easy reach of the winding, climbing lanes lay the utterly fascinating expanses of the moorland, a sea of enormous heather-covered waves, where in the summer the tors shimmered in the haze and where at all seasons a baffling mist could quickly enshroud the whole. It was one of the last genuine wildernesses left in all England. It was easy to get lost in it, and Sherlock and his pony often spent a night in the open. Years later, as he briefly made a neolithic hut on the moors of Devonshire his home, Sherlock Holmes was to be grateful for those experiences in Yorkshire.

Siger Holmes, with characteristic obstinacy, made one final attempt to pour his youngest son's mind into the mold of the engineer he still desired him to be. His method of effecting this was to employ, during the summer of 1872, a most extraordinary tutor.

Professor James Moriarty was extremely tall and extremely thin, with shoulders rounded from much study and a forehead that domed out in a white curve. Then only twenty-six, he had hair that was already gray, and his eyes were cavernous holes deeply sunk in his head. He had a solemn way of talking, he was clean-shaven, pale, and ascetic-looking, as all good scholars should be. But the impression of dignity that might otherwise have been conveyed was marred by the fact that his face protruded forward, and was forever oscillating from side to side in a curiously reptilian manner.

At the age of twenty-one—in 1867—this remarkable man had written a treatise on the binomial theorem which had a European vogue. On the strength of it—and because of certain connections his West of England family possessed—he won the mathematical chair at one of the smaller English universities.

There he soon produced his magnum opus—a work for which, despite his later infamy, he will be forever famous. He became the author of *The Dynamics of an Asteroid*.

As the late Edgar W. Smith (1894–1960), Professor Moriarty's most perceptive biographer, has written:

"This monumental work, incomprehensible to the scientific critics of the time, ascended to such rarefied heights of pure mathematics that we can only now begin to guess at the profundities it may some day be found to hold. The element of most striking moment in its philosophical concept is the relationship it adumbrates between the celestial and the atomic systematic structures. Postulated in its primary stages upon the dynamics of one of the small planets having its orbit between Mars and Jupiter, the equations are integrated by an intricate sequence of extrapolations to embrace the solar system in its totality, and the hypothesis is boldly advanced, on the basis of the derived analyses, that this cosmic atom clustered around its nuclear sun is inherently unstable, and hence susceptible not only to spontaneous disintegration but also to induced fission. It would be going too far to say that Moriarty anticipated Albert Einstein in the construction of the formula $E = mc^2$; but, as bearing upon the trend of his thinking along these revolutionary lines, deep significance must be attributed to the conclusions he reached with respect to the immanence of energy in the phenomenon of mass, and to the frequent introduction into some of his more abstruse calculations of a factor correlated with the speed of light. Such formulae as he did actually set down were built, admittedly, upon the structures and behaviors of the macrocosms, but when these are interpreted in the light of his insistence upon the prevalence of perfect mathematical parallels in the instance of the microcosms, we cannot fall to recognize the magnificent vision Moriarty possessed of energy potential within the atom, and of the practicability of its release through fission. His purely theoretical speculations in this pioneering field of human thought, which are only now, after seventy years, receiving empiric application, are perhaps not fully comprehended or appreciated even today."[5]

Between Sherlock Holmes and Professor James Moriarty there flared up instant hatred.

The profesor could teach the boy nothing, and he soon left Mycroft to return to his academic calling.

As for Sherlock, he went happily back to his pony and the moors.

But now the time was approaching when a wider world was to make its call upon him.

In the October term of the year 1872, Sherlock Holmes took up residence at Christ Church, like his brothers Sherrinford and Mycroft before him—a first-year man at Oxford.

[5] "Prolegomena to a Memoir of Professor Moriarty," *The Second Cab*, edited by James Keddie, Jr.: Boston: Stoke Moran, 1947, pp. 61–2.

III. OXFORD AND CAMBRIDGE: 1872–77

I had often endeavoured to elicit from my companion what had first turned his mind in the direction of criminal research, but I had never caught him before in a communicative humour.

JOHN H. WATSON, M.D.

Not until he entered Oxford did Holmes discover that others found remarkable his faculty of observation and his facility for deduction.

The discovery amazed him. He had thought that *all* men observed and deduced as he and his brothers had always done, for Mycroft, at least, possessed these qualities in an even greater degree than did Sherlock.

Years later, in an article addressed to those who would improve their powers of deduction and analysis, Sherlock Holmes wrote:[1]

. . . let the inquirer begin by mastering . . . elementary problems. Let him, on meeting a fellow-mortal, learn at a glance to distinguish the history of the man and the trade or profession to which he belongs. Puerile as such an exercise may seem, it sharpens the faculties of observation and teaches one where to look and what to look for. By a man's fingernails, by his coat-sleeve, by his boot, by his trouser-knee, by the callosities of his forefinger and thumb, by his expression, by his shirt-cuffs—by each of these things a man's calling is plainly revealed. That all united should fail to enlighten the competent inquirer in any case is almost inconceivable.

[1] "The Book of Life," *The Fortnightly Magazine*, Vol. XXI, No. 3, March 1881, pp. 18–23.

Very tall, unhandsome enough to be exceedingly interesting-looking, no scholar or athlete, but a speaker of six languages with a head filled with lore picked up in a childhood of Continental travel, Sherlock Holmes at the age of eighteen was something quite outside the ordinary run of Oxford undergraduates—in 1872 or in 1962.

He was a very lonely youth. The special nature of his childhood had kept him from ordinary friendships, the lack of school background from any associations to take on to the university.

Yet, during his first year at Oxford, Holmes made one friend.

The man was a figure of fascination to Holmes from the first time the undergraduate set eyes on the don who lectured on mathematics and logic.

Charles Lutwidge Dodgson, then forty, was, like Holmes, a resident of Christ Church, the college that had been his own alma mater.

He was a man of moderate height, slim, with one shoulder higher than the other and a smile that was slightly askew. He carried himself stiffly erect, walked with a peculiar jerky gait, and was afflicted with both deafness in one ear and a decided stammer.

Passing Dodgson as he walked through Peckwater[2] one morning, Holmes noted telltale signs of acid stains and flash-powder burns on the don's right hand.

"Excuse me, sir," Holmes said, "but I see that you are interested in photography."

The don's mild blue eyes took on a look of childlike wonder.

"However did you guess that?" he cried.

"No, no," said Holmes. "I try never to guess. It is a shocking habit—destructive to the logical faculty."

Briefly, Holmes explained his deduction. The don was delighted.

"Come to my study for five-o'clock tea, if you have a mind to," he said. "I will show you my equipment and some of the photographs I have so far taken."

That afternoon Holmes was there on the dot. Soon he was being shown an extraordinary collection—family photographs,

2 One of the two large quadrangles at Ch. Ch. Tom's Quad is of course the other.

photographs of poets and painters and scientists and divines—and dozens and dozens of photographs of little girls of Dodgson's acquaintance whom he called his "child friends."

Less interested in the photographs—though they were composed with remarkable taste and skill—than he was in the man himself, Holmes by shrewd questioning soon discovered some amazing things.

This prim, fussy, cranky man—this man whom Holmes had previously thought so dull—was in fact a man who dabbled in sleight-of-hand and in paper-folding tricks. He enjoyed games of all kinds. He had invented ingenious mathematical and word puzzles—and ciphers, to Holmes's great interest—and even a system for memorizing *pi* to seventy-one decimal points. He was an enthusiastic patron of both the opera and the theater, and a long-time friend of the great actress, Ellen Terry.

Most telling of all to the mischief-loving Holmes, the Reverend C. L. Dodgson had perpetrated two incomparable literary jests. Under a name not his own, he had published, in 1865, a marvelous book called *Alice's Adventures in Wonderland*, and, published that very year, an even more wonderful sequel, *Through the Looking-Glass and What Alice Found There*.

Holmes saw much of Dodgson in the winter and spring that lay ahead. Their arguments were many, for both were men of strong opinions. Dodgson often grew very excited in his wrangles with Holmes, but never angry—he too much admired Holmes's logic for that. As Stuart Dodgson Collingwood was to write, in his *Life and Letter of Lewis Carroll* (London: T. Fisher Unwin, 1898): "The war of words, the keen and subtle conflict between trained minds—in this [Dodgson's] soul took delight, in this he sought and found the joy of battle and of victory. Yet he would not allow his serenity to be ruffled by any foe whom he considered unworthy of his steel; he refused to argue with people whom he knew to be hopelessly illogical."

Then, during his second year at Oxford, Holmes made another friend.

"You never heard me talk of Victor Trevor?" he asked Watson one night during the winter of 1887–88, as they sat on either side of the fire in the old room at Baker Street. "He was one of the only friends I made during the two years I was at Christ

Church.[3] I was never a very sociable fellow, always rather fond of moping in my rooms and working out my own little methods of thought, so that I never mixed much with the men of my year. Bar fencing and boxing, I had few athletic tastes, and then my line of study was quite distinct from that of the other fellows,[4] so that we had no points of contact at all."

Trevor, against all rules of the university, kept a dog—a bull terrier—within the college grounds. Early one morning, as Holmes was going down to chapel, the animal froze onto his ankle. The bite was deep and painful, and Holmes found himself confined to his rooms for ten days. Trevor was deeply disturbed by what his pet had done, and he came over to inquire about Holmes on each of the ten days. A hearty, full-blooded young man, full of spirit and energy, he was nonetheless as friendless as Holmes. His visits, which consisted at first of only a minute's chat, soon lengthened as the two young men found subjects in common. Before the end of the term they were close friends.

Trevor's father was a widower, and Victor was his only son. They lived at Donnithorpe, in Norfolk, and Trevor, late in June, invited Holmes to visit him for a month of the long vacation.

Holmes accepted. On Sunday, July 12, 1874, he rode in a dog-cart up the wide, lime-lined avenue that led to the old-fashioned, wide-spread, oak-beamed, brick building Victor Trevor called home.

From the start of the visit, Trevor's father interested Holmes extremely. A strong man, both physically and mentally, he knew few books but had traveled far, and what he had seen of the world he had remembered.

They sat, one evening shortly after Holmes's arrival, over a glass of port after dinner. Soon young Trevor began to talk about Holmes's ability to observe and infer. The father listened carefully to the son's description, but it was very plain that he thought the young man was exaggerating.

"Come, now," he said with a laugh. "I should make an excel-

---

[3] In his published account of the first case in which Holmes was ever engaged, Watson saw fit to render this line as, "He was the only friend I made during the two years I was at college."

[4] For the present, Siger Holmes's obstinacy had won out. Holmes was getting the thorough mathematical training which his father hoped would make the young man an engineer.

lent subject for your talents, Mr. Holmes. What can you deduce from me?"

Sherlock Holmes sipped his port. "Not very much, I'm afraid," he said at last. "But I might suggest that during the last year or so you have gone about in some fear of a personal attack."

The laugh faded from the old man's lips, and he turned to his son in great surprise.

"Why, that's true enough, Victor," he said. "You'll recall that I wrote you how Sir Edward Hoby and I had recently broken up a poaching gang. The members got out of gaol some months ago. One night, in the taproom of the Bull and Pheasant, the landlord heard them swear to knife us. Since then, Sir Edward has actually been attacked, and I've kept carefully on guard. But unless you've told Mr. Holmes something of this, I've no idea how he knows it."

Young Trevor shook his head. "I'm sure I said nothing about it. How *did* you know, Sherlock?"

"Your father carries a handsome stick," Holmes said, leaning across the table and picking it up. "The inscription tells me that it was presented to him in June of last year. It is very heavy. You can see that he has recently gone to some work to bore the head of it and then to pour melted lead into the hole. The stick is now a formidable weapon. I reasoned that your father would not take such precautions unless he had some danger to fear."

"Very good!" old Trevor cried. He clapped his hands as though he were applauding an actor in a play. "Now, what else can you tell me?"

"You boxed a good deal in your younger days."

"Right again. Did you know it by my nose?"

"No, by your ears. I am a boxing man myself, and I have observed how the sport can flatten and thicken the ears."[5]

"Anything else?"

"By the callosities on your hands, I should say that you have

---

[5] Holmes was later to write two short monographs on the subject of the human ear. ("On the Variability of Human Ears," *The Anthropological Journal*, Vol. XL, Nos. 8 and 9, pp. 672–76, 712–19.) See his mention of these monographs in Watson's account of the gruesome adventure of "The Cardboard Box."

done a great deal of digging."[6]

"I made my money in the gold-fields."

"You have been in New Zealand and you have visited Japan."

"True."

"And you have been closely associated with someone whose initials were J.A. It is someone you were afterwards eager to forget."

To the amazement of both young men, old Trevor fixed his eyes on Holmes with a strange, wild stare, then pitched forward across the table in a dead faint. Quickly, Victor and Sherlock undid his collar and sprinkled water over his face. In a few minutes, the old man gasped, sat up, and forced a smile.

"I hope I didn't frighten you," he said. "Though I look strong, I have a weak heart, and it doesn't take much to knock me over. I don't know how you manage this, Mr. Holmes, but it seems to me that all the detectives of fact and of fancy would be children in your hands. That's your line of life, sir, and you may take the word of a man who has seen something of the world."

"And that recommendation," Holmes later told Watson, "was, if you will believe me, the very first thing which ever made me feel that a profession might be made out of what had up to that time been the merest hobby."

Holmes continued in his conversation with old Trevor, "I hope I have said nothing to pain you."

"Well, you certainly touched upon a rather tender point," the old man said. "How do you know, and how much do you know?" He spoke now in a half-joking way, but a look of terror still lurked at the back of his eyes.

"You'll remember," Holmes explained, "that the other day we were all three of us out on the lake with the boat. You bared your arm to draw in a fish, and I saw that the letters 'J.A.' had been tattooed in the bend of the elbow. The pink pigment used is peculiar, known only to Japanese artists.[7] The letters are still

---

[6] Holmes was later to write "a curious little work" which he called *A Study of the Influence of a Trade upon the Form of the Hand;* London: Privately printed, 1886. See *The Sign of the Four.*

[7] Holmes was later (1878) to write upon the subject of tattoo marks also. He mentioned his monograph in 1887 during his investigation of The Red-Headed League.

perfectly legible, but an attempt has obviously been made to obliterate them with acid."

"What an eye you have!" old Trevor cried. "It is just as you say. But let's talk of something else. The ghosts of old loves die hard."

Holmes spent a restless night. To continue with his mathematical studies, after the train of thought started by old Trevor's "recommendation," seemed to him quite impossible.

The next day he wrote to his father in Yorkshire.

He had decided, he told Siger Holmes, to make of himself, not an engineer, but the world's first consulting detective.

Siger Holmes was furious.

"I will provide for you an allowance that seems to me to be reasonable," he wrote to his son at Donnithorpe. "But I wish never to set eyes upon you again."

Holmes knew that as long as his father lived he could never return to the house and lands in Yorkshire. He telegraphed to his brother Mycroft in London. "Please find me London rooms. Enter my name for study of organic chemistry, Bart's. Explain all when we meet. Sherlock."

The study of organic chemistry, Holmes had decided, was one of the many studies he must now undertake to fit himself for the role he was determined to play in life. He would begin in the laboratories at St. Bartholomew's Hospital, London, that mighty institution affectionately known to its students as "Bart's."

It is curious that Mycroft Holmes, at twenty-seven a rising young Government clerk, busily enrolling his brother Sherlock as a student at Bart's, may well have passed, in its gloomy corridors, a burly man some five years younger than himself.

Had Mycroft Holmes asked, he would have been told that the man's name was John H. Watson.

And who was John H. Watson?

A Hampshireman, it seemed, who had spent most of his boyhood in Australia. And a graduate of Wellington College. Now that he had chosen to follow the career of an army doctor, he was a student at the University of London Medical School, training in surgery at St. Bartholomew's . . .[8]

During the next few days, there was a touch of suspicion in the senior Trevor's manner toward Holmes. Then, one afternoon, a sailor who called himself Hudson had appeared. Thin and brown and crafty, the seaman had demanded that his "old friend" Squire Trevor take him in. An hour later, when Sherlock and Victor entered the house, they found old Trevor stretched dead drunk on the sofa in the dining room.

The whole incident left a most ugly impression upon Holmes. He felt that his presence was a source of embarrassment to his friend. He decided to leave Donnithorpe the next day, and went up to London and the rooms that Mycroft had found for him.

For seven weeks Holmes worked industriously on his first experiments in organic chemistry. One day, however, when autumn was far advanced, and the long vacation was drawing to a close, he received a telegram from Victor, begging him to return to Donnithorpe. Holmes dropped everything and set out for Norfolk at once.

Dr. John H. Watson has written of the message which struck old Trevor dead with horror when he read it: "The supply of game for London is going steadily up. Head-keeper Hudson, we believe, has now been told to receive all orders for fly-paper, and for preservation of your hen pheasant's life." He has told how Holmes solved the riddle by reading every third word in the message, beginning with the first: "The game is up. Hudson has told all. Fly for your life."[9] He has told of the statement drawn up by Victor's father, with its explanations of the remarkable past for which Hudson was blackmailing old Trevor.

And so ended Holmes's first case, the extraordinary case that Watson was later to call that of "The *Gloria Scott*."

Though he had not yet attained a degree at Oxford (and,

[8] Medical men other than John H. Watson who were associated with St. Bartholomew's include: Dr. William Harvey, personal physician to Charles I, who discovered the circulation of the blood; Percivall Pott, who, having cured himself of an unusual type of broken ankle, gave his name to the "Pott's fracture"; John Abernethy, the brusque, independent, brilliant surgeon whose lectures were so well attended that the lecture hall had to be enlarged to accommodate his listeners.

[9] As Holmes tells us in "The Adventure of the Dancing Men," he was later (1896) to write "a trifling monograph" upon the subject of secret writings. In it he analyzed 160 separate ciphers.

indeed, was never to attain a degree), Holmes now decided that Cambridge offered a greater opportunity to study all the branches of science. Accordingly in the late autumn of the year 1874, he entered Gonville and Caius College, famous for its associations with medicine and with the natural sciences.

Here Holmes led a very different life from that he had led at Oxford.

"During my last years at Cambridge University,"[10] he told Watson, "there was a good deal of talk there about myself and my methods."

And he made many friends, among them Reginald Musgrave, an undergraduate in the same college.

Musgrave was not generally popular at Caius, although it always seemed to Holmes that what was objected to as his pride was really an attempt to cover extreme natural diffidence. In appearance, Musgrave was exceedingly aristocratic—high-nosed and large-eyed, with languid and yet courtly manners. He was indeed a scion of one of the oldest families in the kingdom, though his branch was a younger one which had separated from the more celebrated northern Musgraves in the early years of the sixteenth century, and had at length established itself in West Sussex, where Hurlstone, the manor house of the Musgraves, was said to be perhaps the oldest inhabited building in the county. Something of his birthplace seemed to cling to the man. Holmes could never look at him without thinking of gray archways and mullioned windows.

Now and again Holmes and Musgrave would drift into talk, and more than once Musgrave expressed a keen interest in Holmes's methods of observation and inference.

It was an important acquaintanceship for Sherlock, for only four years later he was to handle the strange case of the Musgrave Ritual, a chain of events so singular that it was the first to arouse national interest in Holmes as a solver of mysteries.

But between his last talks with Musgrave, in 1875, and the case of the Musgrave Ritual, in 1879, many other adventures lay in store for young Mr. Sherlock Holmes.

---

[10] Watson saw fit to change "Cambridge University" to "the University" when he published his account of the adventure of "The Musgrave Ritual."

IV. MONTAGUE STREET: 1877-79

". . . there I waited, filling in my too abundant leisure time by studying all those branches of science which might make me more efficient. Now and again cases came in my way . . ."
SHERLOCK HOLMES

When young Mr. Sherlock Holmes came up to London from Cambridge in the spring of the year 1877, he took rooms on Montague Street, just round the corner from the British Museum.

There, in the Reading Room,[1] he acquired that knowledge of sensational literature which Watson called "immense." "He appears," Watson wrote in *A Study in Scarlet*, "to know every detail of every horror perpetrated in the century."

Among the many works that Sherlock Holmes must have studied at this time, we must surely include *The Newgate Calendar . . . from . . . 1700 to the Present Time* (London, 1773) as well as the later *Newgate Calendar: Containing the Lives . . . of . . . Housebreakers, Highwaymen, Etc.*, by an Old Bailey Barrister (London, 1840?). Holmes read, remembered, and in later life made frequent use of his knowledge of the annals of crime, from Jonathan Wild (1682?–1725), to whom Holmes once compared Professor Moriarty,[2] to Thomas Griffiths Wainewright (1794–1852), whom Holmes cited as having been no mean artist, as well as a poisoner.[3] But Holmes showed himself equally familiar with the exploits and methods of fictional detectives—

---

[1] Then open to students, thanks to the recent introduction of the electric light, until 8:00 P.M. in winter and 7:00 P.M. in summer.

[2] In *The Valley of Fear*.

[3] In "The Adventure of the Illustrious Client." It is interesting to note that Oscar Wilde (1854–1900), born in the same year as Holmes, was of the same opinion. See Wilde's essay, "Pen, Pencil, and Poison."

Poe's Dupin and Gaboriau's Lecoq, for example. (Dupin, in Holmes's opinion, was "a very inferior fellow" and Lecoq was "a miserable bungler.")[4]

Nor was Holmes's instruction in crime drawn only from books.

One day the reader at the next seat, a fat man with a large brown beard, looked up from his statistics of the minute wages earned and the vast profits made in the Lancashire cotton industry, and noticed Holmes's peculiar line of reading.

"You are interested in assassinations?" he asked in a thick Prussian accent.

"Yes," Holmes admitted.

"Then you must meet my friends the Anarchists."

Holmes was delighted to meet anyone who could enlighten him about criminal methods and the criminal mind. The Anarchists proved to be very well informed about assassination, though still eager to study new information on the subject in the Reading Room. There were three of them who could be found there regularly: Stepan, Ivan, and Sviatoslav. Stepan was a jovial man with red cheeks and a black beard. He adored children and dogs and had already accounted for two grand dukes, accosting the first in a crowded street while disguised as an officer in the Imperial Guard, striking up a conversation before stabbing His Highness with a butcher's knife and then nobly tending to the dead aristocrat until the hue and cry had died down and he could make his escape. The second assassination was carried out with equal dash, Stepan leaping onto the duke's moving droshky, leaping off before it could stop, and disappearing into a lane where he had already hidden a disguise. He walked out in a large hat and heavy overcoat as his pursuers dashed past him.

Ivan was a morose and moody man who spent his time reading about explosives, while the gnomelike, chuckling Sviatoslav devised infernal machines of ever-increasing ingenuity.

The firsthand knowledge that Holmes picked up from these men was to prove invaluable to him, years later, when he was summoned to Odessa to solve the Trepoff murder. For Stepan, Ivan, and Sviatoslav, the detective always had a sneaking liking. But the bearded scholar who had introduced him to the Anarchists no longer interested him; indeed he found the man's

4 Holmes so expressed himself in *A Study in Scarlet.*

disquisitions on economics most tedious, and having, as Watson later remarked, only a "feeble" knowledge of politics, the name Karl Marx meant nothing to him.

Holmes wrote, as well as read, in the Montague Street days; certainly it was during this period of "too abundant leisure" that he composed many of the literary works that can now be identified as having come from his pen.

There was "Upon the Dating of Documents," which saw publication in *The British Antiquarian* in its issue of September 1877. Holmes showed a wistful pride of authorship in his first published monograph when he assumed, in 1888, at the time of the Baskerville case, that Dr. James Mortimer might have read it.

There was *Upon the Tracing of Footsteps, with Some Remarks upon the Uses of Plaster of Paris as a Preserver of Impresses.* Holmes showed a copy of this work to Watson in 1888, and in all probability there was also an edition in French, since it is mentioned among the books and pamphlets that François le Villard of the Sûreté was translating at that time.[5]

Most important, there was Holmes's *Upon the Distinction Between the Ashes of the Various Tobaccos: An Enumeration of 140 Forms of Cigar, Cigarette and Pipe Tobacco, with Coloured Plates Illustrating the Difference in the Ash.* It is apparent that Holmes took particular pride in the authorship of this monograph, for it is the only one of Holmes's many works which Watson quotes the great detective as mentioning more than once.[6]

It was also during the Montague Street days that Holmes acquired one of his most treasured possessions.

Walking along Tottenham Court Road one afternoon, after a frugal lunch in Soho, he spied in the dusty bow window of a pawnshop a violin which his expert's eye at once told him was a Stradivarius. To Holmes's amazement and delight, he found that the proprietor had no idea of the violin's true value. Holmes was able to purchase it for a mere fifty-five shillings.[7] It was worth two hundred times what he paid for it. He ever afterward

[5] *The Sign of the Four.*
[6] In *A Study in Scarlet, The Sign of the Four,* and "The Boscombe Valley Mystery."
[7] "The Cardboard Box."

kept it carefully in its case in a corner of his room.[8] Only once, if we can believe Watson, did he treat it carelessly; at a time when his spirits were certainly ruffled, he flung it down.[9]

Holmes's mother had taught him to play the violin in that pleasant summer of 1871. Now, the owner of a Stradivarius, he devoted himself to the instrument. By 1881 he had become an accomplished performer.

"Do you include violin-playing in your category of rows?" he asked Watson anxiously at the time of their first meeting.[10]

"It depends on the player," Watson replied. "A well-played violin is a treat for the gods—a badly played one . . ."

"Oh, that's all right," Holmes cried with a merry laugh.

"I see," Watson wrote (he is speaking of a time a few weeks later), "that I have alluded to [Holmes's] powers upon the violin. These were very remarkable, but as eccentric as all his other accomplishments. That he could play pieces, and difficult pieces, I knew well, because at my request he had played me some of Mendelssohn's Lieder, and other favourites. When left to himself, however, he would seldom produce any music or attempt any recognized air. Leaning back in his arm-chair of an evening, he would close his eyes and scrape carelessly at the fiddle which was thrown across his knee. Sometimes the chords were sonorous and melancholy. Occasionally they were fantastic and cheerful. Clearly they reflected the thoughts which possessed him, but whether the music aided those thoughts, or whether the playing was simply the result of a whim or fancy, was more than I could have determined. I might have rebelled against these exasperating solos had it not been that he usually terminated them by playing in quick succession a whole series of my favourite airs as a slight compensation for the trial upon my patience."[11]

"Look here, Watson, you look regularly done," Holmes said

---

8 "The Adventure of the Empty House."
9 "The Adventure of the Norwood Builder."
10 *A Study in Scarlet.*
11 Watson's wording here ("trial upon my patience") has been taken to mean that the "series of my favourite airs" were from the works of Sir William Schwenck Gilbert (1836–1911) and Sir Arthur Seymour Sullivan (1842–1900), especially *Trial by Jury* and *Patience.*

to the doctor in 1888.[12] "Lie down there on the sofa and see if I can put you to sleep."

Watson tells us that "he took the violin from the corner, and as I stretched myself out he began to play some low, dreamy, melodious air—his own, no doubt, for he had a remarkable gift for improvisation."

The passing years served to enhance Watson's admiration for Holmes as a musician. "My friend was an enthusiastic musician," he wrote in "The Red-Headed League," "being himself not only a very capable performer, but a composer of no ordinary merit."

Yes, scraping on his violin, as Watson put it, was always, for Holmes, a favorite occupation.

Now and again cases came Holmes's way.

We know that the adventure of the Musgrave Ritual was the *third* of these, and, thanks to the researches of two great Sherlockian scholars, Mr. Robert Keith Leavitt and the late Edgar W. Smith, we can identify the first and second as well.

"As the student will discover by reading the *Proceedings* of the [British] Rifle Association for 1877, 1880 and 1881," Mr. Leavitt writes,[13] "there was a scandal in that organization in the years 1877 and 1878 concerning alleged cheating by collusion between shooters and scorers during the course of rifle matches, and it became so notorious that the Association went to the trouble and expense of retaining counsel and agents to collect 'voluminous evidence against persons suspected of fraud at the matches.' "

Consulting the *Proceedings* for 1879, Mr. Leavitt found, in the records of one of the biggest matches, the Alexander, of the preceding year, 1878, that ninth place with a prize of £10 was won by *Corporal Holmes of the 19th North Yorkshires*. In the same year, the same Holmes had taken forty-eighth place in the match called the St. George's for a prize of £6.

Note that Corporal Holmes's unit was the 19th North Yorkshires, recall that Sherlock Holmes was born and, to some extent,

---

[12] *The Sign of the Four.*
[13] "Annie Oakley in Baker Street," *Profile by Gaslight: An Irregular Reader about the Private Life of Sherlock Holmes,* edited by Edgar W. Smith; New York: Simon & Schuster, 1944, pp. 230–42.

reared in the North Riding of Yorkshire. Obviously, Sherlock Holmes was the agent retained to gather the evidence of fraud. Naturally, he would have gathered that evidence in the guise of a competitor.[14]

"This scandal, known as 'The Mullineaux Case,' " Mr. Leavitt concludes triumphantly, "occupied Holmes over three months [according to the *Proceedings*] but was handled by him with such competence and discretion that [as in so many of his cases] legal proceedings were avoided and the details never became public, though as late as 1880 members of the Association who were in the know were clamoring for information—and being shut up for their pains."

If Holmes's first case, in the Montague Street days, was perhaps somewhat prosaic, his second case of the time was exotic enough to delight the most romantic writer.

It will be remembered that Holmes, in the spring of the year 1887, was able to be of some service to one who called himself Wilhelm Gottsreich Sigismond von Ormstein, Grand Duke of Cassel-Falstein and hereditary King of Bohemia.[15]

But was 1887 Holmes's *first* meeting with this mysterious personage? Not at all, Edgar W. Smith suggested.[16]

"I shall not lament the loss of my incognito, for it enables me to thank you with the more authority."

These words, Mr. Smith noted, might well have been addressed to Sherlock Holmes by "the hereditary King of Bohemia" in that spring of 1887.

But they were not.

"They were . . . addressed," Mr. Smith wrote, "in 1878 to a certain Brackenbury Rich, a dashing lieutenant in Her Majesty's forces who had greatly distinguished himself in one of the lesser Indian hill wars, by one who called himself Prince Florizel. And as authority for their utterance we have the testimony not of John H. Watson, M.D. . . . but of Robert Louis Stevenson,

---

14 Mr. Leavitt suggests that Holmes was brought into the case by one Lieutenant Backhouse of the 6th Lancs. Presumably he came by his knowledge of Holmes's remarkable talents as a neighbor of the Holmes family in the North Riding.

15 "A Scandal in Bohemia." The true identity of Bohemia's "hereditary King" will be investigated in a later chapter.

16 "A Scandal in Identity," *Profile by Gaslight, op. cit.,* pp. 262–73.

who chronicled, in his *New Arabian Nights,* the doings of this royal blade.

"Yet we cannot doubt," Mr. Smith continued, "on the strength of the evidence available in the two accounts that Gottsreich and Florizel were one being and the same. However carefully the two narrators may have tried to give their heroes individuality, the likeness of their propensities, their characters, their very persons, shines with the clarity of a beacon through the pages in which their deeds are told. . . .

"We know, of course, to whom the embattled Gottsreich turned when blackmail reared its ugly head and ruin loomed upon the horizon. . . . But we are not told who it was, [nine] years earlier, who had engineered the escape of Florizel from the equally imminent, but purely physical terrors of the Suicide Club. 'All has been managed by the simplest means,' the faithful Colonel Geraldine reported. 'I arranged this afternoon with a celebrated detective. Secrecy has been promised and paid for.' Who could have merited the trust of Florizel's entourage in this previous hour of royal need? Who could have been brought to share the sacred confidence of this differently dangerous escapade? Who, indeed, but that same Great Man who was to serve the smitten Gottsreich so discreetly and so well in [the year 1887]?"

And so, for his second case, the struggling young detective with rooms in Montague Street was called upon to intervene in the reckless, not to say the lethal, goings-on a propos the Suicide Club.

On the morning of Thursday, October 2, 1879, Reginald Musgrave walked into Holmes's rooms on Montague Street.

He had changed little physically since Holmes had known him as a fellow-undergraduate at Caius College, Cambridge. He was dressed like a young man of fashion. His manner was as quiet and suave, his bearing as aristocratic, as those which had formerly distinguished him.

The two shook hands cordially.

"I hope all has gone well with you, Musgrave," Holmes said.

"You probably heard of my poor father's death," Musgrave replied. "He was carried off about two years ago. Since then I have, of course, had Hurlstone to manage. I am member for my district as well, so my life has been a busy one. But you, Holmes—is it true that you are turning to practical ends those powers with which you used to amaze us?"

"Yes," Holmes answered. "I have taken to living by my wits."

"I am delighted to hear it, for your advice at present would be exceedingly valuable. We have had some very strange doings at Hurlstone, and the police have been quite unable to throw any light on the matter. It is really the most extraordinary, the most inexplicable business."

"Please let me have the details," cried Holmes eagerly.

Lighting a cigarette, Reginald Musgrave told Holmes his story.

Of the seven house servants at Hurlstone (the garden and stables of course had a separate staff) the one who had been longest in the service of the Musgraves was the butler, Brunton. He was a young schoolmaster out of a place when he was first taken up by Reginald Musgrave's father, twenty years before, but he was a man of energy and character, and he soon came to be invaluable in the household. Yet this paragon had one fault. He was a bit of a Don Juan. A few months before, he had become engaged to Rachel Howells, the second housemaid, but then he had thrown her over and taken up with Janet Tregellis, the daughter of the head gamekeeper.

On the Thursday morning preceding his visit to Holmes, Reginald Musgrave—unable to sleep—had risen at two o'clock in the morning and gone to the billiard room to pick up a novel he had been reading. Seeing a glimmer of light coming from the open door of the library, he had suspected burglars, picked up a battle-ax from the wall, and crept on tiptoe to the library door.

Brunton, the butler, was in the library. He was sitting, fully dressed, in an easy chair, with a slip of paper, which looked like a map, upon his knee, and his head sunk forward upon his hand in deep thought. Suddenly, as Reginald Musgrave looked on, Brunton rose from his chair, walked to a bureau at the side of the room, unlocked it and drew out one of the drawers. From this he took a paper, and returning to his seat, flattened it out beside the candle on the edge of the table, and began to study it with close attention.

Reginald Musgrave took a step forward. Brunton sprang to his feet, thrust into his breast the chart-like paper he had been originally studying.

"So!" Musgrave cried. "This is how you repay the trust we have placed in you. You will leave my service tomorrow."

The butler bowed with the look of a man who is utterly crushed, and slunk past Musgrave without a word. Musgrave turned to the paper which Brunton had taken from the bureau. To his surprise it was simply a copy of the questions asked and the answers given in a quaint old observance called the Musgrave Ritual—a sort of ceremonial peculiar to his family, which each Musgrave for centuries past had gone through upon his coming of age.

Musgrave relocked the bureau and turned to go, when he was surprised to find that the butler had returned and was standing before him.

"Sir," he cried, in a voice which was hoarse with emotion, "I can't bear the disgrace. If you cannot keep me after what has passed, then for God's sake let me give you my notice and leave in a month, as if of my own free will."

"A month is too long," Musgrave replied; then, after the butler begged for a fortnight, said, "Take yourself away in a week, and give what reason you like for going."

For two days after this, Brunton was most assiduous in his attention to his duties. On the third morning, however, he did not appear after breakfast to receive his instructions for the day. They searched the house from cellar to garret, but there was no trace of him.

On the third night after Brunton's disappearance, Rachel Howells apparently drowned herself. Dragging the lake, Musgrave discovered a linen bag which contained a mass of old rusted metal and several dull-colored pieces of pebble or glass.

"This strange find," the young aristocrat concluded, "was all that we could get from the mere, and although we made every possible search and inquiry yesterday, we know nothing of the fate of either Rachel Howells or Richard Brunton. The county police are at their wits' end, and I have come to you as a last resource."

"I must see that paper, Musgrave," Holmes said. "The paper

your butler thought it worth his while to consult, even at the risk of the loss of his place."

"It is an absurd business, this ritual of ours," Musgrave answered, "but at least it has the grace of antiquity to excuse it. I have a copy of the questions and answers here, if you would care to run your eye over them."

These were the questions and answers on the paper he now handed to Holmes:

"Whose was it?"

"His who is gone."

"Who shall have it?"

"He who will come."

"What was the month?"

"The sixth from the first."[17]

"Where was the sun?"

"Over the oak."

"Where was the shadow?"

"Under the elm."

"How was it stepped?"

"North by ten and by ten, east by five and by five, south by two and by two, west by one and by one, and so under."

"What shall we give for it?"

"All that is ours."

"Why should we give it?"

"For the sake of the trust."

That same afternoon saw Holmes and Musgrave at Hurlstone.

As to the oak, there could be no question at all. Right in front of the house there stood a patriarch among oaks, one of the most magnificent trees that Holmes had ever seen. It had stood there, Musgrave said, since the time of the Norman Conquest.

Of the elm, there remained only a stump—the tree had been struck by lightning in 1869. But Musgrave knew its height, which

---

17 It should be noted here that, from the fourteenth century until the year 1752, the legal beginning of the year in England was March 25. The seventh month—"the sixth from the first"—would therefore be the month of September 25–October 24 at the time that the Musgrave Ritual was originally composed (Reginald Musgrave tells us that it was written in handwriting of the "middle seventeenth century").

was sixty-four feet—his old tutor had used the tree as part of an exercise in trigonometry.

Musgrave was reminded of something: Brunton, too, had asked about the height of the elm only a few months before.

When the sun was just clear of the oak, Holmes went with Musgrave to his study and whittled a peg. To this he tied a long string, with a knot at each yard. Then he took two lengths of a fishing rod that came to just six feet, and went back to where the elm had stood. He sank the rod into the ground, marked out the direction of the shadow, and measured it. It was nine feet in length.

The calculation was of course a simple one. If a rod of six feet threw a shadow of nine feet, a tree of sixty-four feet would throw a shadow of ninety-six feet, and the line of one would be the line of the other.

Holmes measured out the distance, which brought him almost to the wall of the house, and thrust a peg into the spot. From this starting point he proceeded to step. Ten steps with each foot took him along parallel with the wall of the house. Then he carefully paced off five and five to the east and two and two to the south. This brought him to the very threshold of a low, heavy-linteled door in the center of the oldest part of the house. Two steps to the west meant now that he was to go two paces down the stone-flagged passage, and this was the place indicated by the ritual.

"And under!" Musgrave cried.

They went down a winding stone stair. At the bottom lay a large and heavy flagstone, with a rusted iron ring in the center, to which was attached a thick shepherd's check muffler.

The county police were summoned. Then Holmes, with their aid, succeeded in raising the flagstone. There, in a small chamber, lay a squat, brass-bound wooden box—and the figure of a man, the missing butler.

Holmes soon reconstructed the midnight drama. Brunton had discovered the secret chamber, just as Holmes had done. With the help of Rachel Howells, he had raised the flagstone. The butler in the pit had unlocked the box, passed up its contents. And then—the slab had come crashing down into its place. With the muffled screams of her faithless lover ringing in her ears, Rachel Howells had then thrown the linen bag and its contents into the mere.

But what had been in the box?

"Let me see the contents of the bag you fished from the mere!" Holmes cried.

They ascended to the study, and Musgrave laid the debris before him.

"This rusted metal," said Holmes, "is nothing less than the crown of the Kings of England."

"The crown!" Musgrave exclaimed.

"Precisely. There can, I think, be no doubt that this battered and shapeless diadem once encircled the brows of the Royal Stuarts!"

V. ON STAGE AND OFF IN ENGLAND AND AMERICA: 1879–81

"In your case, Holmes, what the law has gained the stage has lost."

OLD BARON DOWSON on the night before he was hanged.

You and I would have found the London of the late 1870's a ridiculously inexpensive place in which to live. Not so did Holmes, on the allowance his father regarded as "reasonable."

So alarming did the state of his finances become that he soon realized (like Watson two years later) that he must either leave the metropolis or choose to make a complete alteration in his style of living.

On the very day that he had come to this conclusion, he was walking through Piccadilly Circus, when there came a tap on his shoulder, and, turning, he recognized one who had been an undergraduate in Holmes's own college during his days at Cambridge.

"Lord Peter!" Holmes exclaimed.

"Please, no titles," said the strange, languid young man who had stopped him. "I prefer to be know these days by my professional name—Langdale Pike."[1]

"Your professional name?" Holmes said, raising an expressive eyebrow.

Langdale Pike bowed. "Langdale Pike, the actor," he explained.

Holmes burst out laughing. Like Reginald Musgrave, Lord

[1] The Langdale Pikes are, in fact, two hills in Westmorland overlooking Wordsworth's Grasmere. It is obvious that Lord Peter was a north-countryman, probable that Holmes had made friends with him at Cambridge for this reason.

Peter—"Langdale Pike"—was a scion of one of the oldest families in the kingdom.

"Indeed," said Langdale Pike, "my father has disinherited me for it."

"Well," Holmes replied, "not that it means as much, but I'm the next thing to being disinherited myself."

"Capital!" said Langdale Pike. "Come lunch with me at my club and tell me all about it."

Holmes accepted the invitation eagerly. The chef at Langdale Pike's St. James's Street club[2] enjoyed a reputation that was international.

"I have had a most brilliant idea," said Langdale Pike, as they sat over a bottle of port a few hours later. "You're not a bad-looking fellow, Holmes—at least you're tall enough—and you have a voice that should carry well over the footlights. There's a small part open in *Hamlet*—we mostly do Shakespeare, you know. Why don't you come round to the theater with me and read for it? Old Sasanoff's not a bad sort, as actor-managers go. By the way," he added, "can you act at all?"

"I really don't know," Holmes said. "I haven't tried yet."

Holmes took as his stage name "William Escott," derived from his Christian names William S. (for Sherlock) Scott.

And critics are generally agreed that "William Escott" made an amazing success as an actor. This was partly due to Holmes's impressive figure and to his face: the high forehead, set off by strongly marked and exceedingly flexible eyebrows, the large, positive nose, the narrow, sensitive lips, the strong, thin jaw, the keen and piercing gray eyes—and, to crown all, the thick, slightly wavy, dark brown hair, which Holmes as an actor wore rather long.

But Holmes also became a devout student of the theater. He devoured books on stage history and manuals of acting technique as he had previously devoured the annals of crime. He spent hours experimenting with make-up and with costumes. He even took a deep and intellectual interest in the problems of stage

---

2 Although most theatrical people of course belong to the Garrick Club —*not* in St. James's Street—"Langdale Pike" in his true identity would be a member of Boodle's, White's, or Brooks's.

lighting and the construction of sets. No task was too arduous, no drill too exhausting, no expenditure of time or effort too great for the indefatigable Holmes.

Yet it would not be true to say that Holmes was ever very popular with his fellow players—not even with Langdale Pike. It would be easy to attribute this to their jealousy at his meteoric rise in a profession at which many of them had worked for years, but the easy explanation is not the whole one.

Said Michael Sasanoff, when he set out to write the story of his long life in the theater,[3] "So much absorbed was Sherlock Holmes in his own achievements that he was unable or unwilling to appreciate the achievements of others. At this time, at least, it was never any great pleasure to him to see the acting of others."[4]

Holmes's first role of importance was that of Cassius in *Julius Caesar*. So well was this production received in London that "old" Sasanoff—he was, in reality, only forty-eight at this time—turned his eyes westward to that land of opportunity, America.

Many European actors and actresses had received and were receiving a warm welcome in New York and Boston and other great U.S. cities in the late 1870's. Adelaide Ristori, the Italian actress, had made a great hit in *Medea* as early as 1866. The English actress Lilian Adelaide Neilson had made no fewer than four successful American tours—in 1872, 1875, 1877, and 1879. Tommaso Salvini, who had enjoyed the advantage of early training in Ristori's company, came to the U.S. for the first time in 1873, and gave one of the greatest performances of all time as Othello, not in the least handicapped by the fact that he had to play the role *in Italian*, while all his fellow-actors replied in English. In 1878 Modjeska had triumphed in *Camille* at the Fifth Avenue Theatre in New York. When Bernhardt made her first appearance in America, in 1880, Booth's Theatre was blocked with people hours before the performance on the opening night.[5]

So it was that Holmes, with the rest of the company, sailed for the United States on November 23, 1879, on the White Star liner *Empress Queen,* and landed, ten days later, in New York.

---

[3] *Seventy Years a Showman;* London: Stodder & Houghton, 1923.

[4] It is interesting to note that Ellen Terry in her autobiography said much the same thing about her great co-star, Sir Henry Irving.

[5] November 9. The play was *Adrienne Lecouvreur*.

Sasanoff chose *Twelfth Night* as his first American production, and it has been said that Holmes's Malvolio offered the most adequate presentation of that character that America had ever seen up to this time.[6]

The run in New York was a long one, and the troupe went on to give one hundred and twenty-eight performances in many of America's principal cities.

In the American theater then, as now, there were invariably two weekly afternoon performances, one on Saturday, the other on Wednesday. But on the five other days of the week, Holmes, who never required more than a few hours of sleep a night, even at times of prolonged activity, was left much to his own resources, and it is not to be thought that his enthusiasm for the stage diminished in any way his intense interest in criminal activities.

In New York, Holmes met Wilson Hargreave, who was later to become important in the police department of that city.[7] Hargreave, then, like Holmes, a private agent, was currently engrossed in the case of Vanderbilt and the yeggman.[8] It was Holmes who pointed out to him that the glass of the conservatory door must have been broken from the *inside,* not from the outside, a fact that eventually led to the unmasking of a Vanderbilt footman as the "yeggman" who had rifled the safe.

In Philadelphia, a shotgun bought as a prop for the play the company was then performing gave Holmes an opportunity to observe the mark of the Pennsylvania Small Arms Company, a piece of information which was to prove important to him during the curious investigation that Watson later chronicled under the title of *The Valley of Fear.*

In Baltimore, Holmes acquired a taste for oysters,[9] and on one

---

[6] Other roles in which Holmes scored notably were Mephistopheles in *Faust,* Shylock in *The Merchant of Venice,* Mercutio in *Romeo and Juliet* (where his swordsmanship was a tremendous asset), and, most memorably, as Macbeth. But *Twelfth Night* was always Holmes's favorite play. It is clear from Watson's writings that Holmes quoted Shakespeare frequently, yet *Twelfth Night* is the only play that Holmes appears to have quoted *twice.* This was partly because of his success in the role of Malvolio, but it was also due in no small measure to the fact that his own birthday was January 6—Twelfth Night.

[7] "The Adventure of the Dancing Men."
[8] "The Adventure of the Sussex Vampire."
[9] *The Sign of the Four.*

hot summer day, at the invitation of the local police, solved the mystery of a supposedly "locked room" murder by noting the depth to which the parsley had sunk into the butter.[10]

In Chicago, the detective-actor made his first acquaintance with organized gangsterism.[11]

The troupe even crossed the great Western plains, an exciting journey during which the train was once halted by a great migration of buffalo across the tracks. It was a sight Holmes never forgot. "If a herd of buffaloes had passed along there could not have been a greater mess," he complained to Watson during his investigation of the murder of Enoch J. Drebber of Cleveland.[12]

Indeed, the only parts of the United States to which Holmes's travels did not take him in 1879 and 1880 were the South and the Southwest. In spite of the American Encyclopedia that later stood on its shelf in the Baker Street sitting-room, Holmes did not know which was the Lone Star State.[13]

Everywhere the company went it found houses packed with enthusiastic audiences, and it is beyond question that Holmes ever afterward had a very special affection for and interest in the United States.

In later life he praised American slang, quoted Thoreau, showed his knowledge of the price of cocktails, and (among many other instances that might be mentioned) uttered his famous sentiment: "It is always a joy to me to meet an American . . . for I am one of those who believe that the folly of a monarch and the blundering of a minister in fargone years will not prevent our children from being some day citizens of the same world-wide country under a flag which shall be a quartering of the Union Jack with the Stars and Stripes."[14]

Holmes returned to England in the summer of 1880.

---

[10] Holmes later told the story of this case to Watson, referring to it as "the dreadful business of the Abernetty family" (not to be confused with the Abergavenny murder—an entirely different affair). Holmes was reminded of the Baltimore case during the adventure of the Six Napoleons.

[11] "My knowledge of the crooks of Chicago . . ."—"The Adventure of the Dancing Men."

[12] *A Study in Scarlet.*

[13] "The Five Orange Pips."

[14] "The Adventure of the Noble Bachelor."

He had lived sparingly in America; now the time had come to invest his savings in studies that would make him yet more proficient in the profession he still loved best. He returned to the Reading Room of the British Museum and the laboratories at Bart's. There were law, anatomy, botany, geology to be studied, more chemistry to be learned.

But now, too, the name of Sherlock Holmes, the detective, was beginning to be known. Day after day, client after client climbed the steps to his rooms in Montague Street. The cases they brought him were not all successes, as he admitted later,[15] but there were some pretty little problems among them.[16]

Meantime, half the world away, all unbeknownst to Sherlock Holmes, an event took place, on July 27, 1880, without which we today would have been left largely in ignorance about the career of the greatest detective who ever lived.

John H. Watson, an Army surgeon attached to the Berkshires (66th Foot), serving at the fatal battle of Maiwand, was struck on the shoulder by a jezail bullet. He would surely have fallen into the hands of the murderous ghazis had it not been for the devotion and courage shown by his orderly, Murray, who threw him across a pack horse and succeeded in bringing him safely to the British lines.

[15] "The Musgrave Ritual."
[16] See Appendix I: The Chronological Holmes.

VI. EARLY DAYS IN BAKER STREET: 1881–83

"By Jove! If he really wants some one to share the rooms and the expense, I am the very man for him."

JOHN H. WATSON, M.D.

Alone in the laboratory at Bart's, Holmes worked and brooded.

The rooms he had seen on the day before would suit him well, but the rental was prohibitive. If only he could find someone congenial to share them—and the monthly payment to Mrs. Hudson, the landlady. Well, he had mentioned the matter to young Stamford, and perhaps something would come of it.

Suddenly Holmes's full attention was absorbed by the test tube on the broad, low table before him. Then he heard footsteps and glanced around.

Standing in the doorway of the lofty chamber was young Stamford. With him was a middle-sized, strongly built man, with a square jaw, thick neck, mustache.[1]

"I've found it! I've found it!" Holmes shouted to young Stamford, springing to his feet and running toward him with the test tube in his hand. "A reagent which is precipitated by hemoglobin, and by nothing else!"

"Dr. Watson—Mr. Sherlock Holmes," said Stamford, introducing them.

"How are you?" Holmes said, gripping Watson's hand with a strength for which the doctor should hardly have given him

---

[1] See "The Adventure of Charles Augustus Milverton," with the possible exception of "His Last Bow," the only account of a Holmes case in which Watson allowed a description of his own physical appearance to creep in.

credit. Holmes thought to himself: "Here is a gentleman of the medical type, but with the air of a military man. Clearly an Army doctor, then. He has just come from the tropics, for his face is dark, and that is not the natural color of his skin, for his wrists are fair. He has undergone hardship and sickness, as his haggard face clearly says. His left arm has been injured. He holds it in a stiff and unnatural manner. Where in the tropics could an English Army doctor have seen much hardship and got his arm wounded?"

"You have been in Afghanistan, I perceive," said young Mr. Sherlock Holmes.

"How on earth did you know that?" the doctor cried in astonishment.

"Never mind," said Holmes, chuckling to himself. "The important thing now is the hemoglobin. Of course you see the significance of this discovery."

"Chemically it is interesting," Watson answered cautiously, "but practically—"

"Why man, it is the most practical medicolegal discovery in years. It gives us, at last, an infallible test for bloodstains. Come over here."

Holmes seized Watson by the coat sleeve and drew him over to the table at which he had been working.

"We'll need some fresh blood," he said, and dug a long needle into his finger, drawing off a drop of his own in a chemical pipette. "Now, I add this small quantity of blood to a litre of water. The mixture looks like pure water—the proportion of blood cannot be more than one in a million. But I have no doubt that we shall obtain the characteristic reaction." He threw a few white crystals into the vessel, then added some drops of a transparent fluid. In an instant the contents of the vessel took on a dull mahogany color, and a brownish dust was precipitated at the bottom of the jar.

"Beautiful!" Holmes cried, clapping his hands and looking as delighted as a child with a new toy. "What do you think of it?"

"It seems a very delicate test," the doctor replied.

"It is certain to replace the old guaiacum test, which was very clumsy and uncertain."[2] Holmes said. "And the microscope examination for blood corpuscles is worthless if the stains are a few hours old. Now, this test appears to act as well whether the blood is old or new. Had it been invented earlier, there are hundreds of men now walking the earth who would have paid the penalty for their crimes long ago."

Holmes's eyes glittered as he spoke, and he put his hand over his heart and bowed as if acknowledging the applause of a crowd conjured up by his imagination.

"You are to be congratulated," Watson said.

"There was the case of Von Bischoff at Frankfort last year. He would certainly have been hanged had the Sherlock Holmes test been in existence. Then there was Mason of Bradford, and the notorious Muller, and Lefevre of Montpellier, and Samson of New Orleans . . ."

Young Stamford laughed. "You seem to be a walking calendar

[2] "The guaiacum or lignum vitae tree is native to the West Indies and northern South America. Both bark and resin have been used much in pharmacy. In testing for the presence of blood a tincture of 1 part resin to 6 parts alcohol was used. This was added to a smaller quantity of the liquid under examination, and shaken together with a few drops of hydrogen peroxide in ether. The ether dissolves the resin, and if hemoglobin is present the mixture turns bright blue. *V. Encyclopedia Britannica,* 1880 edition."—Christopher Morley, *Sherlock Holmes and Dr. Watson: A Textbook of Friendship;* New York: Harcourt, Brace & Co., 1944.

In *The Shadow of the Wolf,* by R. Austin Freeman, we read this description of the guaiacum process: ". . . He [Dr. John Thorndyke] poured a quantity of the tincture [of guaiacum] on the middle of the stained area. The pool of liquid rapidly spread considerably beyond the limits of the stain, growing paler as it extended. Then Thorndyke cautiously dropped small quantities of the ozonic ether at various points around the stained area, and watched closely as the two liquids mingled in the fabric of the sail. Gradually the ether spread towards the stain, and, first at one point and then at another, approached and finally crossed the wavy grey line; and at each point the same change occurred: first the faint grey line turned into a strong blue line, and then the colour extended to the enclosed space until the entire area of the stain stood out a conspicuous blue patch. 'You understand the meaning of this,' said Thorndyke. 'This is a bloodstain.'"

According to Mr. P. M. Stone, in his classic essay, "The Other Friendship: A Speculation," in *Profile by Gaslight, op. cit.,* pp. 97–103, Holmes and Thorndyke knew each other well. This is also the view of Mr. Francis M. Currier. See his "Holmes and Thorndyke: A Real Friendship," in *The Baker Street Journal,* Vol. III, No. 2, April, 1948, pp. 176–82.

of crime," he said. "You might start a journal on those lines. Call it *Police News of the Past*."

"Very interesting reading it would be, too," Holmes said, sticking a piece of plaster over the scratch on his finger. "I have to be careful," he continued, turning to Watson. "I dabble with poisons a good bit."

"We've come here on business," Stamford said, sitting down on a three-legged stool and pushing another one in Watson's direction with his foot. "My friend Dr. Watson wants to take diggings, and as you were complaining only yesterday that you could get no one to go halves with you, I thought that I had better bring the two of you together."

Holmes was delighted. "I have my eye on a suite in Baker Street," he said, "which would suit me down to the ground. You don't mind the smell of strong tobacco, I hope?"

"I always smoke 'ship's' myself," Watson answered.

"That's good enough. I generally have chemicals about, and occasionally do experiments. Would that annoy you?"

"Not at all."

"Let me see—what are my other shortcomings? I get in the dumps at times, and don't open my mouth for days. Don't think me sulky when I do that—just let me alone, and I'll soon be all right. Now, what do you have to confess?"

Watson laughed at this cross-examination. "Well," he said, "I object to rows because my nerves are shaken, and I get up at all sorts of ungodly hours, and I am extremely lazy. I have another set of vices when I'm well, but those are the principal ones at present."

"I think we may consider the matter settled—that is, if the rooms are agreeable to you," Holmes said.

"When shall we see them?"

"Call for me here at noon tomorrow, and we'll go together and settle everything."

"All right—noon exactly," Watson said, shaking Holmes's hand.

They left him working among his chemicals.

Holmes and Watson met at noon on the next day, as arranged, and inspected the rooms at No. 221B Baker Street. They consisted of a couple of comfortable bedrooms and a large, airy sitting room with two broad windows looking down on the west side of Baker Street.[3]

A bargain was struck on the spot. That very evening Watson moved his things from the hotel in the Strand where he had been living a comfortless and meaningless existence. Sherlock Holmes followed him the next morning with several large boxes and portmanteaus.

For a day or two they were busily engaged in unpacking and laying out their property to the best advantage. That done, they gradually settled down in their new surroundings.

During the first week or so they had no callers, and Watson had begun to think that Holmes was as friendless as himself. Presently, however, he found that Holmes had many acquaintances, and these in the most different classes of society. One little, rather pale, dark-eyed fellow—introduced to Watson as a Mr. Lestrade—came four times in a single week. One morning a young girl called, fashionably dressed, and stayed for half an hour. The same afternoon brought a gray-headed, seedy visitor, looking much like a peddler, who appeared to be very excited. He was followed by a slipshod elderly woman. On another occasion an old, white-haired gentleman had an interview with Holmes, and on another a railway porter in his velveteen uniform. When any of these individuals put in an appearance, Holmes would ask for the use of the sitting room, and Watson would retire to his bedroom. Holmes always apologized to Watson for putting him to this inconvenience. "I have to use this room as a place of

[3] The "B" in 221B of course indicates that the rooms were on the second (British *first*) floor of 221 Baker Street. Since, in Holmes's and Watson's day, the numbers on Baker Street proper *ended at 85*, no question has more troubled Sherlockian scholars than that of the true location of No. "221." The evidence of "The Adventure of the Empty House," *The Hound of the Baskervilles*, "The Red-Headed League," "The Adventure of the Blue Carbuncle," and "The Adventure of the Beryl Coronet" would seem to indicate that the home of Holmes and Watson for so many years was a house on the west (or left going north) side of Baker Street, *below* Dorset Street, and most probably *between* Blandford and Dorset streets. However a strong case for the present No. 31 (between Blandford and George streets) has recently been made by Mr. Bernard Davies in "The Back Yards of Baker Street" in *The Sherlock Holmes Journal*, Vol. IV, No. 3, Winter 1959, pp. 83–8.

business," he would say, "and these people are my clients."

On the morning of Friday, the fourth of March, as Watson noted in his journal, Holmes finally revealed to Watson that he was a consulting detective.

"I suppose I am the only one in the world," he said. "London of course has lots of official detectives and plenty of private ones. When these fellows are at fault they come to me, and I manage to put them on the right track. They lay all the evidence before me, and I am generally able, with the help of my knowledge of the history of crime, to set them straight. Lestrade, for example, is a very well-known detective, an inspector at Scotland Yard. He got himself into a fog recently over a forgery case, and that was what brought him here."

"And your other visitors?" Watson asked.

"They were sent mostly by private inquiry agencies. My clients are all people who are in trouble about something, and want a little enlightening. I listen to their story, they listen to my comments, and then I pocket my fee."

Watson had walked to the window and was looking out.

"I wonder what that fellow is looking for?" he said suddenly, pointing to a plainly dressed individual who was walking slowly down the east side of Baker Street, looking anxiously at the numbers. He had a large blue envelope in his hands.

"You mean the retired sergeant of marines," Holmes said, coming to the window.

"Brag and bounce!" Watson thought. "He knows that I cannot verify his guess."

The thought had hardly passed through his mind when the man they were watching caught sight of the number on their door and ran rapidly across the roadway. They heard a knock, the rumble of a deep voice, and heavy steps ascending the stairs.

"For Mr. Sherlock Holmes," the visitor said, stepping into the room and handing the letter to Holmes.

"May I ask," said Watson, "what your trade may be?"

"Commissionnaire, sir," the man said gruffly. "Uniform away for repairs."

"And you were?" Watson continued.

"A sergeant, sir. Royal Marine Light Infantry. No answer? Right, sir."

He clicked his heels together, saluted, and was gone.

Holmes handed the letter to Watson. It was signed, the doctor noticed, "Tobias Gregson."

"Gregson is the smartest of the Scotland Yarders," Holmes explained.

"He begs you to help him."

"Yes. I suppose we may as well go and have a look. What's that address again?"

"Three Lauriston Gardens, off the Brixton Road."

"Very well. Get your hat."

"You wish me to come?"

"If you have nothing better to do."

A minute later they were both in a hansom, driving for the Brixton Road.

It was a foggy morning, and a dun-colored veil hung over the housetops, looking like the reflection of the muddy streets beneath.

Holmes was in the best of spirits and prattled away about Cremona fiddles and the differences between a Stradivarius and an Amati.

When they arrived at last at No. 3 Lauriston Gardens they found an ill-looking house, dark and untenanted. Holmes walked up and down the pavement, gazing—vacantly, it seemed to Watson—at the ground, the sky, the houses opposite, the line of railings. At last he proceeded slowly down the fringe of grass which flanked the path, his eyes on the ground. Twice he stopped, and once Watson saw him smile and utter an exclamation.

At the door of the house they were met by a tall, flaxen-haired man with a notebook in his hand. He rushed forward and shook Holmes's hand.

"It's good of you to come!" he exclaimed. "I have left everything untouched. It's a queer case, and I know your taste for such things."

"You did not come here in a cab?" Holmes asked.

"No, sir."

"Nor Lestrade?"

"No, sir."

"Then let us look at the room," Holmes said, and strode into the house, followed by Watson and Gregson.

In the dining room, Watson's attention centered at once upon a grim, motionless figure which lay stretched upon the floor boards, with vacant, sightless eyes staring up at the discolored ceiling. It was that of a man about forty-three years old, middle-sized, broad-shouldered, with crisp, curling black hair and a short, stubbly beard. He was dressed in a heavy broadcloth frock coat and waistcoat, with light-colored trousers and immaculate collar and cuffs. A well-brushed top hat was placed on the floor beside him. His hands were clenched and his arms thrown wide, while his lower limbs were interlocked as though his death struggle had been a grievous one. On his rigid face there stood an expression of horror and, it seemed to Watson, of hatred such as he had never before seen on human features.

Lestrade, lean and ferret-like as ever, was standing by the doorway.

Sherlock Holmes approached the body and, kneeling down, examined it intently. "You are sure there is no wound?" he asked, pointing to the splashes of blood that lay all around.

"Positive," said both detectives.

"Then, of course, the blood belongs to a second individual —presumably the murderer, if murder has been committed. It reminds me of the circumstances attending the death of Van Jansen, in Utrecht, in the year 1834."

As Holmes spoke, his fingers were feeling, pressing, unbuttoning, examining.

Finally, he sniffed the dead man's lips, then glanced at the soles of his patent-leather boots.

"You can take him to the mortuary now," Holmes said at last. "There is nothing more to be learned."

Gregson had a stretcher and four men at hand. At his call they entered the room, and the dead man was lifted and carried out. As they raised the body, a ring tinkled down and rolled across the floor. Lestrade picked it up.

"There's been a woman here," he said. "This is a woman's wedding ring."

"What did you find in his pockets?" Holmes asked.

"We have it all here," Gregson replied. "A gold watch, gold Albert chain, gold ring with Masonic device. Russian-leather card case, with cards of Enoch J. Drebber of Cleveland, corresponding to the E. J. D. marked on his linen. No purse, but loose money to the extent of seven pounds thirteen. Pocket edition of Boccaccio's *Decameron,* with the name of Joseph Stangerson on the fly-leaf. Two letters—one addressed to E. J. Drebber, the other to Joseph Stangerson."

"At what address?"

"American Exchange, the Strand—to be left till called for. They are both from the Union Steamship Company, and refer to the sailing of their boats from Liverpool. It is clear that this unfortunate man was about to return to New York."

"Have you inquired about this man Stangerson?"

"I did so at once, sir," said Gregson. "I have had advertisements sent to all the newspapers, and one of my men has gone to the American Exchange, but he has not yet returned."

"Have you cabled to Cleveland?"

"We did so this morning."

Lestrade spoke suddenly. "Mr. Gregson," he said, "I have just made a very important discovery."

He struck a match on his boot and held it near the wall. In this corner of the room a large piece of paper had peeled from the wall, leaving a yellow square of plastering. Across this square was scrawled in blood-red letters a single word:

RACHE

"What do you think of that?" cried the detective. "The murderer has written it with his or her blood. See this smear where it has trickled down the wall! Why was this corner chosen to write it on? I will tell you. See that candle on the mantelpiece? It was lit at the time, and if it was lit this corner would be the brightest instead of the darkest part of the wall."

"And what does it mean, now that you have found it?" Gregson asked.

"Mean? Why it means that the writer was going to put the female name Rachel, but was disturbed before he or she had time to finish."

Holmes had whipped a tape measure and a large, round magnifying glass out of his pocket. With these he trotted about the room, sometimes stopping, occasionally kneeling, once lying flat on his face. Watson was reminded of a well-trained foxhound dashing backward and forward through a covert in search of a lost scent. Finally Holmes examined the word scrawled upon the wall, going over every letter with his magnifying glass.

"They say that genius is an infinite capacity for taking pains," he remarked with a smile.[4] "It's a very bad definition but it does apply to detective work."

"What do you think of it, sir?" Gregson asked.

"It would be robbing you of the credit if I presumed to help you," Holmes said with a smile. "You and Lestrade are doing so well now that it would be a pity for anyone to interfere. But if you will let me know how your investigations go, I shall be happy to give you any help I can. I'll tell you one thing which may help you in the case, though," he continued. "There has been murder done, and the murderer was a man. He was more than six feet tall, was in the prime of life, had small feet for his height, wore coarse, square-toed boots, and smoked a Trichinopoly cigar. He came here with his victim in a four-wheeled cab, which was drawn by a horse with three old shoes and one new one on his off fore-leg. In all probability the murderer had a florid face, and the fingernails of his right hand were remarkably long. These are only a few indications, but they may assist you."

Lestrade and Gregson glanced at each other with an incredulous smile.

"If this man was murdered, how was it done?" Lestrade asked.

"Poison," said Sherlock Holmes curtly, and strode off. "Oh, one thing more, Lestrade," he added, turning around at the door. "Don't waste your time looking for Miss Rachel. *Rache* is the German word for 'revenge.' "

The papers next day were full of what they called "The Brixton Mystery."

The deceased, said the *Standard,* was an American gentleman who had been residing for some weeks in London at the boardinghouse of Madame Charpentier, in Torquay Terrace, Camber-

4 Holmes is of course citing the most famous apothegm of the Scottish essayist and historian Thomas Carlyle (1795–1881). Earlier in *A Study in Scarlet,* Watson had written of Holmes: "Upon my quoting Thomas Carlyle, he inquired in the naïvest way who he might be and what he had done." An obvious twit, this. In those early days, Watson did not yet realize that Holmes had a well-developed sense of mischief.

well. He was accompanied in his travels by his private secretary, Mr. Joseph Stangerson. The two had said good-by to their land-lady on the Thursday evening, and departed to Euston Station with the avowed intention of catching the Liverpool express. They were afterward seen together on the platform. Nothing was known of them until Mr. Drebber's body was discovered in an empty house in the Brixton Road. Nothing was known of the whereabouts of Mr. Stangerson. "We are glad to learn that Mr. Lestrade and Mr. Gregson, of Scotland Yard, are both engaged upon the case, and it is confidently anticipated that these well-known officers will speedily throw light upon the matter."

Holmes and Watson read the notices over together at break-fast.

"I told you that whatever happened Lestrade and Gregson would be sure to score," Holmes said.

"That depends on how it turns out."

"Oh, bless you, it doesn't matter in the least. If the man is caught, it will be *on account* of their exertions. If he escapes, it will be *in spite of* their exertions. It's heads I win and tails you lose, as the Americans say. Whatever they do, they will have fol-lowers. *Un sot toujours un plus sot qui l'admire.*"[5]

At this moment there came the pattering of many steps in the hall and on the stairs, accompanied by loud expressions of disgust from Mrs. Hudson, the landlady.

"What on earth is that?" Watson exclaimed, rising from his chair.

"That is the Baker Street division of the detective police force," said Holmes gravely. As he spoke there rushed into the room half a dozen of the dirtiest and most ragged street Arabs that Watson had ever seen.

" 'Tention!" cried Holmes, in a sharp tone, and the six dirty little scoundrels stood in a line like so many disreputable statu-ettes. "In future you shall send Wiggins alone to report, and the rest of you must wait in the street. Have you found it, Wiggins?"

"No, sir, we hain't," said the tallest of the six youths.

"You must keep on until you do. Here are your wages." He handed each of them a shilling. "Now, off you go, and come back

[5] "A fool can always find a bigger fool to admire him"—the end line (232) of Canto I of *L'Art poétique* by Nicolas Boileau-Despréaux (1636–1711).

with a better report next time."

"Is it on this Brixton case that you have them working?" Watson asked when the youngsters had scampered away down the stairs like so many rats.

"Yes. There is a point about which I wish to be certain. It is merely a matter of time. Hullo! We are going to hear some news now. Here is Lestrade coming down the road. Bound for us, I imagine. Yes, he's stopping."

There was a violent peal at the bell, and in a few seconds the man from Scotland Yard burst into the sitting room.

"The secretary, Joseph Stangerson!" he cried. "He was murdered at Halliday's Private Hotel about six o'clock this morning!"

Despite the protestations of both Gregson and Lestrade, Holmes would take no further action on the Saturday.

"There will be no more murders," he said at last. "You can put that out of the question. You have asked me if I know the name of the murderer. I do. The mere knowing of his name is a small thing, however, compared with laying our hands on him. This I expect very shortly to do. But now it's time for lunch, and then I want to go to Halle's concert, to hear Norman-Neruda. Her attack and bowing are splendid. What's that little thing of Chopin's she plays so magnificently? Tra-la-la-lira-lira-lay."[6]

On the Sunday,[7] Holmes summoned Gregson and Lestrade to the Baker Street rooms.

[6] In Watson's account of *A Study in Scarlet* (written six years after the event) he states that Holmes attended the concert on Friday rather than the Saturday. This is clearly an error, as Mr. Paul S. Clarkson has shown in "'In the Beginning . . .'" in *The Baker Street Journal*, Vol. VIII, No. 4, New Series, October 1958, pp. 197–209. Mr. Clarkson points out that "Halle's concerts were always and only [given] on Monday nights and Saturday afternoons. . . ." Upon examining the actual records of the concert platform in London for the entire period, we shall find that the afternoon of *Saturday, March 5th, 1881*, is the only date that historically meets all of [the necessary] specifications. It was Mme. Norman-Neruda's last appearance of the season. On this occasion, however, she played no Chopin. Rather she executed Handel's *Sonata in D Major,* "'by desire.'" Let us hope that Holmes was not disappointed.

[7] In *The Chronological Holmes*, New York: Privately printed, 1955, I have demonstrated that "Watson, eager to make his first account of a Holmes case as dramatic as possible . . . *telescoped the events of two days into one*" (p. 6). It is only fair to state that this view has been hotly contested by my good friend and fellow chronologer, Dr. Ernest Bloomfield Zeisler.—W.S.B.-G.

Neither of the two Scotland Yarders had time to speak before there was a tap at the door, and the spokesman for the street Arabs, young Wiggins, introduced his unsavory person.

"Please, sir," he said to Holmes, touching his forelock, "I have the cab downstairs."

"Good boy," Holmes said blandly. "Why don't you introduce this pattern at Scotland Yard?" he asked the two detectives, displaying a pair of steel handcuffs he had taken from a drawer. "My friend Wilson Hargreave assures me that nothing else is ever used these days by the New York City police. See how beautifully the spring works. They fasten in an instant."

"The old pattern is quite good enough," Lestrade grumbled. "If we can find the man to put them on," he added.

"Very good, very good," said Holmes, smiling. "The cabman may as well help me with my boxes. Just ask him to step up, Wiggins."

Holmes was strapping up a small portmanteau when the cabman entered the room.

"Just give me a hand with this buckle, cabbie," Holmes said, kneeling over his task and never turning his head.

The cabman stepped forward with a somewhat sullen, defiant air, and put down his hands to assist. At that instant there was a sharp click, the jangling of metal, and Sherlock Holmes sprang to his feet again.

"Gentlemen," he cried, his eyes flashing, "let me introduce you to Mr. Jefferson Hope, the murderer of Enoch Drebber and of Joseph Stangerson!"

With a roar of fury, the prisoner wrenched himself free from Holmes's grasp and hurled himself through the window. Woodwork and glass gave way before him, but before he got through, Gregson, Lestrade, and Holmes sprang upon him like so many staghounds. Jefferson Hope was dragged back into the room.

"We have his cab," said Sherlock Holmes. "It will serve to take him to Scotland Yard. And now, gentlemen, we have reached the end of our little mystery. You perhaps have questions, and you are very welcome to put them to me now. There is no danger that I will refuse to answer them."[8]

8 The interested reader will of course find a full explanation of Holmes's methods in this case in Watson's account of the *Study in Scarlet.*

VII. THE FIRST MRS. WATSON: 1883–86

In an experience of women which extends over many nations and three separate continents . . .

JOHN H. WATSON, M.D.

It was early in April, in the year 1883, that Holmes and Watson journeyed to Stoke Moran, the home of that well-known Surrey family the Roylotts, to solve the singular case that Watson has chronicled under the title of "The Adventure of the Speckled Band."

Between the April of 1883 and the October of 1886, however, Dr. Watson has left us no record of the adventures of Mr. Sherlock Holmes.

There is good reason why. For most of this entire period, Dr. Watson was in the United States of America.

How well he remembered the day when the letter with the overseas postage had come to Baker Street. . . .

"Not bad news, I hope?" Sherlock Holmes had asked.

"It is my brother," Watson had replied. "He is penniless and very ill, in San Francisco."

"You must go to him."

Holmes had crossed to his desk, unlocked it, and removed from a drawer his bankbook.

"Business has been good of late," he remarked, thumbing the pages.[1] Then, tossing the bankbook to Watson, "You are welcome to any or all of it."

---

[1] It was undoubtedly during the period 1881–86 that Holmes handled the Arnsworth Castle business, the Darlington substitution scandal, the case of the woman at Margate and the delicate case of the King of Scandinavia. His success in the last led, in December 1890, to his service to the Royal Family of Scandinavia. Mr. T. S. Blakeney (see Appendix II) is mistaken in thinking that this is one and the same case.

Now, in the spring of 1884, when his brother seemed on the road to health again, Watson must plan how he could repay the money he had borrowed from Holmes. There was very little left of it, but enough, perhaps . . .

Dr. Watson, in nursing his brother, had discovered that he still possessed considerable skill as a medical man. If he could open a practice in San Francisco, he reasoned, he could soon earn enough to return to England and repay Holmes.

Dr. Watson was in luck. He found a practice he could just afford to buy, the practice flourished, and among the first patients who came to see him was Miss Constance Adams, twenty-seven years old.[2]

Though not beautiful, Constance Adams was of a type that appealed to the doctor: the round face, the wide mouth, the brown hair, the wide-spaced blue eyes, shading to sea green, which were her finest feature. Her gentleness, her complete unselfishness,[3] roused all his protective instincts. Constance was what they then called a home girl, loving needlework and an armchair by the fire. Watson met her in sorrow, and ended by falling deeply in love with her. Toward the end of April 1885, they were engaged, although there could be no hope of an immediate marriage.

Not until the late summer of 1886 did Dr. Watson feel that he could sell his San Francisco practice, return to England, repay Holmes, establish a practice in London, and settle down to married life with Constance.

Their marriage would be celebrated as soon as possible, the doctor assured the weeping girl as he held her in his arms on the deck of the ferry crossing over to the railroad depot in Oakland. He had promised Holmes in 1881 that the public should know the facts of the first case the two had ever shared together, he said. He would send for Constance as soon as he had completed his account of the *Study in Scarlet*[4]—as soon as ever he could

2 Watson, born in 1852, was himself thirty-two at this time.

3 "Folk who were in grief came to my wife like birds to a lighthouse," Watson was to write later ("The Man with the Twisted Lip").

4 It was to appear in *Beeton's Christmas Annual* in the December of 1887. In 1960 an exact replica of this collector's item was published jointly by the Sherlock Holmes Society of London and the Baker Street Irregulars, Inc. The replica itself is now a collector's item.

prepare Holmes for the loss of his companion.

Back in Baker Street, Watson found that the adventures came thick and fast in that October of 1886.

On Wednesday, the sixth, a close, rainy day, Holmes was called upon by Dr. Percy Trevelyan of 403 Brook Street.[5]

Dr. Trevelyan told of his cataleptic patient, the old Russian nobleman, and of his even queerer resident patient, the mysterious Mr. Blessington. On the very next day Blessington seemingly committed suicide, and it will be remembered how Holmes, by an examination of the footprints and the cigar ends found in his room, was able to prove that Blessington—in reality the criminal Sutton—had actually been murdered by members of his former gang for informing upon them after the great Worthingdon bank robbery.

The very next day—Friday, October 8[6]—came the adventure of the noble bachelor Lord Robert St. Simon, whose father, the Duke of Balmoral, was at one time Secretary for Foreign Affairs. A very painful event had occurred in connection with Lord Robert's wedding with Miss Hatty Doran, the fascinating daughter of a Californian millionaire: the lady had vanished immediately after the ceremony.

Lestrade could make neither head nor tail of the business, but Holmes had notes of several similar cases, one in Aberdeen, another in Munich. The affair was promptly concluded to the satisfaction of everyone except Lord Robert, who coldly refused a place at the quite epicurean little supper Holmes had ordered in celebration—a couple of brace of woodcock, a pheasant, a *pâté-de-foie-gras* pie, with a group of ancient and cobwebby bottles.

Only four days later—on Tuesday, October 12—came the most important international case that Holmes had up to then been called upon to handle. It was the loss of a letter from a foreign potentate—a document whose publication might lead to European complications of the utmost moment—that brought the illustrious Lord Bellinger, twice Premier of Britain, and the

---

[5] Watson at once recognized him as the author of a monograph upon obscure nervous lesions. It is apparent that Watson at this time was devoting himself to medical reading, in preparation for his forthcoming marriage and resumption of practice.

[6] Watson tells us that this was "a few weeks before my own marriage."

Right Honorable Trelawney Hope, Secretary for European Affairs and the most rising statesman in the country,[7] to the sitting room at Baker Street.

Again, Lestrade was baffled, but Holmes was quick to note the significance of the second stain on the flooring of the dingy old house in Godolphin Street.

"Mr. Holmes, you are a wizard, a sorcerer!" Lord Bellinger cried. "How came the letter back in the box?"

Holmes turned away smiling.

"We also have our diplomatic secrets," he said.

Fascinating as these cases proved to be, Watson was growing a little weary of the sitting room in Baker Street. His mind was far away, in San Francisco. He was dreaming of Constance Adams. On Monday, the first of November, 1886, at St. George's, Hanover Square, she became his wife.

[7] As many commentators have shown, there are only two periods during Holmes's active practice in which the Premier of Britain was holding that position for the *second* time. The first is 1880 to June 1885, when Mr. Gladstone was Premier for the second time. The second is 1886 to 1892, when Lord Salisbury was Premier for the second time. As the late Gavin Brend shrewdly observed (in *My Dear Holmes*), Watson's description of "Lord Bellinger"—"austere, high-nosed, eagle-eyed, dominant"—can hardly be described as a *disguise* of Gladstone. "Lord Bellinger" must therefore have been Lord Salisbury, and the year 1886, for only in that year were the office of Prime Minister and Foreign Secretary—Watson's "Secretary for European Affairs"—held by two different men. Salisbury's Foreign Secretary was Lord Iddesleigh, formerly Sir Stafford Northcote. Toward the close of the year 1886 occurred a series of startling ministerial changes in which Lord Iddesleigh was literally ousted from his post. Eight days later, England was shocked to learn that he had died suddenly in the anteroom of the Premier's official residence at No. 10 Downing Street.

VIII. *THE* WOMAN: NOVEMBER 1886 – MAY 1887

"She is . . . the daintiest thing under a bonnet on this planet."

SHERLOCK HOLMES

"To Sherlock Holmes," Watson wrote, "she is always *the* woman. I have seldom heard him mention her under any other name. In his eyes she eclipses and predominates the whole of her sex. . . . There was but one woman to him, and that woman was the late[1] Irene Adler, of dubious and questionable memory."

One remembers how that crowded year 1887 began: with Holmes summoned to Odessa in the case of the Trepoff murder, with the mission that Holmes accomplished so delicately and successfully for the reigning family of Holland, with his clearing up of the singular tragedy of the Atkinson brothers at Trincomalee,[2] and finally with the whole question of the Netherland-Sumatra Company and of the colossal schemes of Baron Maupertuis.

It was on the fourteenth of April that Watson received a telegram from Lyons, informing him that Holmes was lying ill in the Hotel Dulong. Within twenty-four hours he was in the sickroom, and was relieved to find that there was nothing formidable in Holmes's symptoms.

[1] Watson's "the late," at the time he wrote his account of the "Scandal in Bohemia," was an error, as we shall see in Chapter XII.

[2] It is highly unlikely that Holmes found it necessary to visit Ceylon to do this. Trincomalee was an important British naval base, and the tragedy was no doubt a high matter of state. It is probable that British diplomats at the Hague, during Holmes's mission in Holland, placed the facts before him, and he cleared up the matter long-distance, making this an "armchair" case.

"Wedlock suits you," Holmes remarked. "I think you have put on seven and a half pounds since I saw you."

"Seven," Watson answered.

"Indeed, I should have thought just a trifle more. And in practice again, I observe. You did not tell me that you intended to go into harness."

"Then how do you know?"

"I see it," Holmes said. "I deduce it. When a gentleman walks into my room with a black mark of nitrate of silver upon his right forefinger, and a huge bulge on the side of his top hat to show where he has secreted his stethoscope, I must be ill indeed if I do not pronounce him to be an active member of the medical profession."[3]

Three days later Holmes and Watson were back in London. It was evident to the doctor that his friend would be better for a change. Watson's old friend, Colonel Hayter, who had come under Watson's professional care in Afghanistan, had now taken a house near Reigate, in Surrey, and had frequently asked Dr. and Mrs. Watson to come down to him for a visit. "A little diplomacy was needed," Watson writes, "but when Holmes understood that the establishment was a bachelor one,[4] and that he would be allowed the fullest freedom, he fell in with my plans, and a week after our return from Lyons, we were under the Colonel's roof."

There Holmes was presented with a singular and complex problem, which gave him an opportunity for demonstrating his extraordinary skill at analyzing handwritings, still another weapon among the many with which he waged his lifelong battle against crime.

"I think our quiet rest in the country has been a distinct success, Watson," Holmes cried at the end of the adventure, "and I

---

[3] Students of the Sherlockian canon will recall that Watson reports this conversation as having taken place in May 1887 ("A Scandal in Bohemia") rather than in April 1887 ("The Reigate Squires"). It must be remembered that "A Scandal in Bohemia" was published *before* "The Reigate Squires." Watson, as writer, had to explain to readers of "A Scandal in Bohemia" that he was, at the time, both married and "in harness." He did so by inserting into his manuscript a conversation with Holmes that had actually taken place a month earlier.

[4] This statement explains why Watson did not bring Holmes into his own home; the detective would not want Mrs. Watson fussing over him when he was in good health, much less when he was ailing.

shall certainly return, much invigorated, to Baker Street tomorrow."

Now, on the night of Friday, May 20, 1887,[5] Watson was returning from a call on a patient, when his way led him through Baker Street. As he passed the well-remembered door of No. 221 he was seized with a keen desire to see Holmes. The detective's rooms were brilliantly lit, and even as Watson looked up, he saw Holmes's tall, spare figure pass in dark silhouette against the blind. He was pacing the room swiftly, eagerly, with his head sunk upon his chest, and his hands clasped behind him.

Watson was delighted, for Holmes was obviously at work again, hot on the scent of some new problem.

Holmes had been premature in saying that he would return to Baker Street from Reigate "much invigorated." His tremendous exertions in the spring of 1887 had left him a very sick man. For the past few weeks he had remained in his lodgings, buried among his old books. And, to Watson's deep distress, Holmes in his illness had turned for solace to cocaine.

Holmes tells us himself[6] that he found the influence of cocaine —and, later, of morphine—so transcendentally stimulating and clarifying to the mind as to make him careless of the ravages inevitable upon his body and soul. By September 1888, he was indulging in doses of seven-per-cent cocaine solution three times a day.[7]

It is pleasant to be able to record that Watson over the years was gradually able to cure Holmes completely of his drug mania. By the end of 1896,[8] Holmes under ordinary conditions no longer

---

[5] Watson's account of the case dates it as beginning "on the 20th of March, 1888." This is clearly an error. It can be demonstrated that the adventure must have begun on a Thursday or Friday; the twentieth of March 1888 was a *Tuesday*.

[6] *The Sign of the Four.*

[7] That Holmes indulged so frequently as three times a day—and that he took cocaine intravenously—in the jargon of the underworld, "main line"— is indeed sinister. But a seven-per-cent solution is *not* an extraordinarily heavy dosage of cocaine. In 1898, British pharmacology officially established the strength of *injectio cocainae hypodermica* at *ten* per cent.

[8] "The Adventure of the Missing Three-Quarter."

craved for this artificial stimulation.[9]

Holmes was glad to see Watson on that night in May 1887.

With hardly a word spoken, but with a kindly eye, he waved the doctor to an armchair, handed him a case of cigars, and indicated a spirit case and a gasogene[10] in the corner.

When the doctor had made himself comfortable, Holmes handed him a letter.

Written on a sheet of thick pink paper, undated, without signature or address, the note read:

"There will call upon you tonight, at a quarter of eight o'clock, a gentleman who desires to consult you upon a matter of the very deepest moment. Your recent services to one of the Royal Houses of Europe have shown that you are one who may safely be trusted with matters which are of an importance which can hardly be exaggerated. This account of you we have from all quarters received. Be in your chamber then at that hour, and do not take it amiss if your visitor wears a mask."

Watson carefully examined the writing, as he had seen Holmes do in the adventure of the Reigate Squires, as well as the paper upon which the note was written.

"The man who wrote this was presumably well-to-do," the doctor said at last. "Such paper could not be bought under half a crown a packet. It is peculiarly strong and stiff."

"Peculiar—that is the very word," said Holmes. "Hold it up to the light."

Watson did so, and saw a large *E* with a small *g*, a *P*, and a large *G* with a small *t* woven into the texture of the paper.

"The name of the maker, no doubt," he said. "Or his monogram, rather."

---

9 It is probable that Watson found satisfactory treatment for Holmes's addiction in a third drug, heroin, introduced from Germany as a "cure for the morphia habit," and not condemned as such until a *British Medical Journal* editorial in 1907.

10 It should perhaps be explained to the modern reader that the gasogene was a glass vessel shaped like the figure *8*—the upper part being crowned with a handle and a nozzle like the present-day soda siphon. The upper chamber of the gasogene was loaded with acid crystals and sodas to generate gas, which passed into the lower chamber, three parts filled with water. The gas generated in the upper chamber aerated the water in the lower chamber, producing soda water of a sort for swizzling into the whisky in the "spirit case," or tantalus.

"Not at all. The *G* with the small *t* stands for *Gesellschaft,* which is the German for 'Company.' It is a customary contraction like our 'Ltd.' or the U.S. 'Co.' *P,* of course, stands for *Papier.* Now for the *Eg.* Let us glance at our Continental Gazetteer." He took down a heavy brown volume from the shelf at the right of the fireplace. "Eglow, Eglonitz—here we are, Egria. It is a German-speaking country—in Bohemia, not far from Carlsbad. 'Remarkable as being the scene of the death of Wallenstein,[11] and for its factories and paper mills.' Well, my boy, what do you make of that?" Holmes's eyes sparkled, and he blew a great triumphant cloud of smoke from his cigarette.

"The paper was made in Bohemia," Watson said.

"Precisely. And the man who wrote the note is a German. Notice the peculiar construction of the sentence—'This account of you we have from all quarters received.' "

As he spoke there came the sharp sound of horses' hoofs and of wheels grating against the curb, followed by a sharp pull at the bell. Holmes whistled.

"A pair by the sound," he said. "Yes," he continued, glancing out of the window. "A nice little brougham and a pair of beauties. There's money in this case, Watson, if there is nothing else."

"I think I had better go, Holmes."

"Not a bit of it, Doctor. I am lost without my Boswell."[12]

A slow and heavy step, which had been heard upon the stairs and in the passage, paused immediately outside the door. Then there was a loud and authoritative knock.

"Come in!" said Holmes.

The man who entered was not less than six feet six inches in height, with the chest and limbs of a Hercules. His dress was rich with a richness that would, in England, be looked upon as akin to bad taste. Across the upper part of his face, extending down past the cheekbones, he wore a black vizard mask.

"You had a note?" he asked in a deep, harsh voice. "It told you that I would call."

---

[11] Properly, Albrecht Wenzel Eusebius von Waldstein (1583–1634) Duke of Friedland, Sagan, and Mecklenburg, Bohemian general in the Thirty Years' War, suspected of treason and assassinated. He is the subject of a tragedy by Schiller.

[12] Watson had by this time completed his account of the *Study in Scarlet,* although it would not be published for another seven months.

"Pray take a seat," Holmes said. "This is my friend and colleague, Dr. Watson. Whom have I the honor to address?" he asked slyly.

"You may address me as the Count von Kramm, a Bohemian nobleman. I understand that this gentleman, your friend, is a man of honor and discretion, whom I may trust with a matter of the most extreme importance. If not, I should much prefer to communicate with you alone."

Watson rose to go, but Holmes pushed him back into his chair. "It is both, or none," he said.

The count shrugged his broad shoulders. "Then I must begin," he said, "by asking you to excuse this mask. The august person who employs me wishes his agent to be unknown to you, and I may confess at once that the title by which I have just called myself is not exactly my own."

"I was aware of it," said Holmes dryly. He was now quite sure that he had been of service to this "Count von Kramm" nine years before—at a time when "the count" had called himself "Prince Florizel."

"The circumstances are of great delicacy," the visitor continued, "and every precaution must be taken to quench what might grow to be an immense scandal and seriously compromise one of the reigning families of Europe."

"I was also aware of that," murmured Holmes. "If Your Highness would condescend to state your case, I should be better able to advise you."

The man sprang from his chair, and paced up and down the room in uncontrollable agitation. "You are right," he cried to Holmes. Then, with a glance in Watson's direction, "You are addressing Wilhelm Gottsreich Sigismond von Ormstein, Grand Duke of Cassel-Falstein, and hereditary King of Bohemia."

"Indeed?" said Holmes, raising an eyebrow. He thought it best to allow his royal visitor to preserve the incognito he had presented for Watson's benefit; Holmes himself had no doubts as to the true identity of his client.[13]

13 Who, then, was this "Prince Florizel," this "hereditary King of Bohemia"? Sherlockian scholars do not all agree, but the late Edgar W. Smith, in "A Scandal in Identity" (*op. cit.*), in a piece of deductive reasoning worthy of Holmes, has proved beyond all reasonable doubt that Holmes's client was none other than the then Prince of Wales, Albert Edward, later King

"You can understand," said their visitor, sitting down once more and passing a hand over his high white forehead, "that I am not accustomed to doing such business in my own person. Yet the matter was so delicate that I could not confide it to an agent without putting myself in his power. I have come incognito for the purpose of consulting you."

"Then, pray, consult," Holmes said.

"The facts are briefly these: Some five years ago, during a lengthy visit to Warsaw, I made the acquaintance of the well-known adventuress, Irene Adler. The name is familiar to you?"

"Kindly look her up in my index, Doctor," Holmes murmured. For many years he had adopted a system of docketing all paragraphs concerning men and things, so that it was difficult to name a subject or a person on which he could not at once furnish information. In this case Watson found the biography Holmes had asked for sandwiched in between that of a rabbi and that of a staff commander who had written a monograph upon deep-sea fishes.

"Let me see," Holmes said. "Hum! Born in New Jersey in the year 1858. Contralto, La Scala. Prima donna, Imperial Opera of Warsaw. Retired from the operatic stage, living in London— quite so. Your Highness, as I understand, became entangled with this young person,[14] wrote her some compromising letters, and is now desirous of getting those letters back."

"Precisely. But how—"

"Was there a secret marriage?"

"None."

"No legal papers or certificates?"

"None."

"Then I fail to follow. If this young person should produce her letters, how is she to prove they are authentic?"

Edward VII (1841–1910). It shows remarkable attention to detail on his part that he should take the trouble to acquire genuine Bohemian writing paper before sending his anonymous letter to Holmes. But it is not surprising that he should have used a Germanic turn of phrase, for he spoke English with a guttural accent all his life, and both his parents were German. Holmes, as we shall see, was to be of service to the prince and later king on several other occasions.

14 When one considers that, at the time of this adventure, Irene was 29 years of age, and that Holmes himself was a mere 33, this superior attitude begins to look a little absurd.

"There is the writing."

"Pooh. A forgery."

"My private note-paper."

"Stolen."

"My own seal."

"Imitated."

"My photograph."

"Bought."

"We were both in the photograph."

"Oh, dear! That is bad. You have compromised yourself seriously."

"I was only Crown Prince then. I was young. I am but thirty now."[15]

"It must be recovered."

"She will not sell it, and five attempts have been made to steal it. Twice burglars in my pay ransacked her house. Once we diverted her luggage when she traveled. Twice she has been waylaid. There has been no sign of the photograph."

Holmes laughed. "It is quite a pretty little problem."

"But a very serious one to me."

"Very. Now as to money?"

"You have *carte blanche*."

"And for present expenses?"

The visitor took a heavy chamois leather bag from under his cloak and laid it on the table. "There are three hundred pounds in gold, and seven hundred more in notes," he said.

Holmes scribbled a receipt upon a sheet of his notebook, and handed it to him.

"Then good night, Your Highness, and I trust we shall soon have some good news for you. And good night to you, Watson," he added, as the wheels of the royal brougham rolled down Baker Street. "If you will be good enough to call tomorrow afternoon, I should like to chat this little matter over with you."

At three o'clock precisely Watson was at Baker Street, but Holmes had not yet returned. It was close upon four when the door opened, and a drunken-looking groom, ill-kempt and side-

---

[15] Crown Prince he was still. But thirty he was not. He was forty-six at the time.

whiskered, with an inflamed face and disreputable clothes, walked into the room.

With a nod, Sherlock Holmes vanished into his bedroom, emerging in five minutes tweed-suited and respectable.

In his character of a groom out of work, Holmes had made short work of finding Irene Adler's villa on Serpentine Avenue in St. John's Wood.

"It's called Briony Lodge," he told Watson, "and it has a garden to its back and a quite impregnable Chubb lock to its front door."

Holmes had then lounged down the street to the mews and helped Miss Adler's ostlers rub down her horses, for which he had received twopence, a glass of half-and-half, two fills of shag tobacco, and all the information he could desire.

"She has turned all the men's heads down in that part," he said. "But she has only one male visitor, although a good deal of him. He is a Mr. Godfrey Norton, a lawyer of the Inner Temple. Was Irene Adler, I asked myself, his client or his mistress?"

Holmes was still balancing the matter in his mind when a hansom cab drove up to Briony Lodge and a handsome gentleman sprang out, brushed past the maid who opened the door, and rushed into the house with the air of a man who was thoroughly at home there. This must be Godfrey Norton.

Half an hour later, he emerged, stepped to his cab and shouted to the driver: "Drive like the devil! First to Gross and Hankey's in Regent Street,[16] and then to the Church of St. Monica in the Edgware Road. Half a guinea if you do it in twenty minutes!"

Away they went, and Holmes was wondering whether he should not do well to follow them, when up the lane came a neat little landau. Miss Irene Adler shot out of the door of Briony Lodge and into it.

"The Church of St. Monica, John," the lady cried, "and half a sovereign if you reach it in twenty minutes."

("It was twenty-five minutes to twelve," Holmes said to Watson, "and of course it was clear what was in the wind.")

[16] Presumably a jeweler's shop, although it does not appear in the directories of the day. No doubt a bit of Watsonian misdirection.

Just then a hansom cab bumped through the street. "The Church of St. Monica," Holmes called to the driver, "and half a sovereign if you reach it in twenty minutes."

At the church, Holmes hurried in. Not a soul was there except the clergyman and the man and woman he had followed. The three turned to face him, and Norton called: "Thank God! You'll do! Come! Come! Only three minutes or it won't be legal."

"I was half dragged up to the altar," Holmes declared, "and before I knew where I was, I found myself mumbling responses which were whispered in my ear, and vouching for things of which I knew nothing, and generally assisting in the secure tying-up of Irene Adler, spinster, to Godfrey Norton, bachelor. It was all done in an instant, and there was the gentleman thanking me on the one side and the lady on the other, while the clergyman beamed on me in front. It was the most preposterous situation in which I ever found myself in my life. It seems that there had been some informality about the license, that the clergyman absolutely refused to marry them without a witness of some sort, and that my lucky appearance saved the bridegroom from having to sally out into the streets in search of a best man. The bride gave me a sovereign, and I mean to wear it on my watch-chain in memory of the occasion."[17]

"This is a very unexpected turn of events," Watson said. "What then?"

"Well, I found my plans very seriously menaced. It looked

[17] It is abundantly apparent that Holmes, on this occasion, was far from being his usual businesslike self. Both Holmes and Godfrey Norton, as a lawyer, should have known that marriages performed after noon were no longer illegal in England; two witnesses are always required, neither of whom makes, much less mumbles, any responses; marriage ceremonies in a Catholic church or a church of the Church of England (one of which St. Monica's, by its name, must have been) are not over with in an instant; no clergyman would marry a spinster and a bachelor if there were the slightest "informality" about the license. While the opportunities for speculation here are abundant, it seems clear that: 1) Godfrey Norton was *not* as versed in the law as he pretended to be, and that he was perhaps not even an Englishman; 2) the priest who performed the service was a very incompetent impostor and the marriage was therefore a false one; 3) Holmes's imcompetence must have been due to the fact that he had discovered, for the first time, that he was capable of an overpowering emotion: like "all the men . . . down in that part" he had found Irene Adler "the daintiest thing under a bonnet on this planet."

as if the pair might make an immediate departure. At the church door, however, they separated, he driving back to the Temple, she to her own house. 'I shall drive out in the Park at five as usual,' she said as she left him. I am likely to be busy this evening, Watson, and I shall want your co-operation."

"I shall be delighted."

"You don't mind breaking the law?"

Watson chuckled. "Not in the least," he said. "What is it you wish?"

"It is nearly five now. In two hours we must be on the scene of action. Miss Irene, or Madame, rather, returns from her drive at seven. We must be at Briony Lodge to meet her. I have already arranged what is to occur. There is only one point on which I must insist: you are not to interfere, come what may. There will probably be some little unpleasantness. Four or five minutes later the sitting-room window will open. You are to station yourself close to that open window. When I raise my hand—for I will be visible to you—you are to throw this into the room. At the same time you will raise a cry of fire."

Holmes handed Watson a long, cigar-shaped object. "It is nothing very formidable," he said. "Just a plumber's smoke rocket, fitted with a cap at either end to make it self-lighting. When you raise your cry of fire, it will be taken up by a number of people. You may then walk to the end of the street, and I will rejoin you in ten minutes."

Holmes disappeared into his bedroom and returned in a few minutes in the character of an amiable, rather simple-minded Nonconformist clergyman. "It was not merely that Holmes changed his costume," Watson wrote. "His expression, his manner, his very soul seemed to vary with every fresh part he assumed. The stage lost a fine actor when Sherlock Holmes became a specialist in crime."

It was a quarter-past six when Holmes and Watson left Baker Street, and it still wanted ten minutes to the hour when they found themselves on Serpentine Avenue.

Briony Lodge was just as Watson had pictured it from Holmes's description, but the locality appeared to be less private than he had expected. A group of shabbily dressed men smoked and laughed in a corner. A scissors grinder walked up and down the lane with his wheel. Two guardsmen flirted with a nursegirl, and several young men lounged up and down the street with cigars in their mouths.

Suddenly the gleam of the side lights of a carriage came around the curve of the avenue. As a smart little landau pulled up to the door of Briony Lodge, one of the men loafing at the corner dashed forward to open the door, but was elbowed aside by another loafer. A fierce quarrel broke out—increased by the two guardsmen, who took sides with one of the loungers, and by the scissors grinder, who was equally hot on the side of the other. A blow was struck, and in an instant the lady who had stepped from the carriage was the center of a little knot of flushed and struggling men who struck savagely at each other with their fists and sticks. Holmes, in his guise of a clergyman, dashed into the crowd to protect the lady, but just as he reached her, he gave a cry and dropped to the ground. Blood seemed to be running freely down his face. The loungers and the guardsmen fled, while a number of better-dressed people who had watched the scuffle without taking part in it crowded in to attend to the injured clergyman.

"Bring him into the sitting-room!" Irene Adler called.

Slowly and solemnly Holmes was carried into Briony Lodge, while Watson, from his post at the window, watched the proceedings. Now he took the smoke rocket from under his ulster. Holmes sat up on the couch, and Watson saw him motion like a man who needs air. A maid rushed across to open the window. At the same instant, Watson saw Holmes raise his hand, and at the signal he tossed the rocket into the room with a loud bellow of "Fire!"

The cry was no sooner out of his mouth than the whole crowd of spectators, well-dressed and ill, joined in a general shriek— "Fire!"

Thick clouds of smoke curled through the room and out at the open window. Watson made for the corner of the avenue. In ten minutes, Holmes joined him.

"You did it very nicely, Doctor," he remarked. "Nothing could have been better."

"Thank you, Holmes. You have the photograph?"

"No, but I know where it is."

"And how did you find out?"

"She showed me, as I knew she would."

"I am still in the dark."

"The matter was perfectly simple. You saw, of course, that everyone in the street was an accomplice. [18] And each reacted admirably to your cry of fire. Now, when a woman thinks her house on fire, her instinct is at once to rush to the thing she values most. A married woman grabs at her baby—an unmarried one reaches for her jewel-box. Irene Adler had nothing in her house more precious to her than the photograph. And she rushed to secure it.[19] The photograph is in a recess behind a sliding panel just above the right bellpull. When I cried to her that the fire was a false alarm, she replaced it, rushed from the room, and I have not seen her since. I made no attempt to secure the photograph, for the coachman had come into the room and was watching me narrowly. It seemed safer to wait.

"And now?" Watson asked.

"And now our quest is practically finished," Holmes said. "I shall call, with 'the King,' tomorrow, and with you, if you care to come with us. We will be shown into the sitting-room to wait for the lady, but it is probable that when she comes down she may find neither us nor the photograph."

They had reached Baker Street and had stopped at the door of No. 221. Holmes was searching his pocket for the key, when someone passing said: "Good night, Mr. Sherlock Holmes."

There were several people on the dimly lit pavement at the time, but the greeting appeared to come from a slim youth in an ulster who was hurrying by.

"I've heard that voice before," Holmes said. "Wiggins? No. I wonder who the deuce it could be?"

Watson slept at Baker Street that night, and he and Holmes were engaged upon their toast and coffee when the man who called himself the King of Bohemia burst into the room.

---

[18] Actors, all of them—recruited, of course, from among Holmes's fellow-players in the days when he was with "old" Sasanoff's company.

[19] Despite Holmes's earlier gibes at Dupin, he seems not above taking a leaf from the book of that "very inferior fellow." *Cf.* Edgar Allan Poe's "The Purloined Letter."

"You have got it?" he cried, grasping Sherlock Holmes by the shoulders.

"Not yet. But I have hopes."

"Then, come. My brougham is outside."

As they drew up on Serpentine Avenue, the door of Briony Lodge stood open, and an elderly woman stood on the step.

"Mr. Sherlock Holmes, I believe?" she said. "My mistress told me you were likely to call. She left this morning with her husband, by the 5:15 from Charing Cross for the Continent."

"What!" Holmes staggered back. Then he pushed past the servant and rushed into the drawing room, followed by the King and Watson. Holmes ran to the bellpull, tore back a small sliding shutter, and, plunging in his hand, pulled out—a photograph and a letter. The photograph was of Irene Adler in evening dress. The letter was addressed to "Mr. Sherlock Holmes. To be left till called for." Holmes tore it open and read:

"My dear Mr. Sherlock Holmes. You really did it very well. You took me in completely. Until after the alarm of fire, I had not a suspicion. But then, when I found how I had betrayed myself, I began to think. I had been warned about you months ago. I had been told that if the King employed an agent, it would certainly be you. And your address had been given me. Yet, with all this, you made me reveal what you wanted to know. Even after I became suspicious, I found it hard to think evil of such a dear, kind old clergyman. But, you know, I have been trained as an actress myself. Male costume is nothing new to me. I often take advantage of the freedom which it gives. I sent John, the coachman, to watch you, ran upstairs, got into my walking clothes, as I call them, and came down just as you departed.

"Well, I followed you to your door, and so made sure that I was really an object of interest to the celebrated Mr. Sherlock Holmes. Then I, rather imprudently, wished you good night, and started for the Temple to see my husband.

"We both thought the best resource was flight when pursued by so formidable an antagonist; so you will find the nest empty when you call tomorrow. As to the photograph, your client may rest in peace. I love and am loved by a better man than he. Your client may do what he will without hindrance from one he has cruelly wronged. I keep the photograph only to safeguard myself, and to preserve a weapon which will always secure me from any steps which he might take in the future. I leave a photograph which he might care to possess; and I remain, dear Mr. Sherlock Holmes, very truly yours,

"Irene Norton, *née* Adler."

"What a woman—oh, what a woman!" cried "the King of Bohemia. "I know that her word is inviolate. The photograph is now as safe as if it were in the fire."

"I am glad to hear Your Highness say so," said Holmes bitterly.

"I am immensely indebted to you. Pray tell me in what way I can reward you. This ring—" He slipped an emerald ring from his finger and held it out on the palm of his hand.

"Your Highness has something which I should value even more highly," Holmes said.

"You have but to name it."

"This photograph."

"Irene's photograph!" he cried. "Certainly, if you wish it."

"I thank Your Highness. Then there is nothing more to be done in the matter. I have the honor to wish you a very good morning."

Sherlock Holmes bowed, and, turning away without appearing to notice the hand which his client stretched out to him, he set off for his own chambers.

IX. ORANGE PIPS, RED-HEADED MEN, AND A BLUE CARBUNCLE: MAY–DECEMBER 1887

The year '87 furnished us with a long series of cases . . . of which I retain the records.

JOHN H. WATSON, M.D.

Certainly, for Sherlock Holmes, the Scandal in Bohemia was the most memorable of all the cases he handled in that memorable year 1887.

But for Watson there were many others. Among the headings that he found to set down under this one twelvemonth (in his introduction to "The Five Orange Pips") was an account of the adventure of the Paradol Chamber; of the Amateur Mendicant Society, which held a luxurious club in the lower vault of a furniture warehouse; of the facts connected with the loss of the British barque *Sophy Anderson;* of the singular adventures of the Grice Patersons in the island of Uffa;[1] of the Camberwell poisoning case, in which, it will be remembered, Sherlock Holmes was able, by winding up the dead man's watch, to prove that it had been wound up two hours ago, and that therefore the deceased had gone to bed within that time—a deduction which was of the greatest importance in clearing up the case.

---

[1] Holmesian scholars are not agreed on the location of Uffa. Mr. Rolfe Boswell identifies it with the great mound on which Norwich Castle stands. Professor Jay Finley Christ thinks it a combination of the names of the islands of Ulva and Staffa, off the western coast of Scotland. Dr. Julian Wolff has produced a U.S. Government map that shows an island of *Ufa* to exist in the broad expanses of the South Pacific.

In the June following the case of the Scandal in Bohemia, Watson, late one night, found himself in a vile opium den on Upper Swandam Lane. He had gone there in search of his patient, Isa Whitney, and he had found him. He had also found, in the guise of a wrinkled, bent-with-age old man, his friend Mr. Sherlock Holmes.

"I suppose, Watson," Holmes said, with a twinkle in his eye, "that you imagine that I have added opium-smoking to cocaine injections."

But such was not the case. Holmes was at work—on an investigation that was to uncover one of the most amazing double lives ever lived in fact or fiction.

Watson chronicled the adventure under the title of "The Man with the Twisted Lip."

It is, in many ways, a curious case, and it raises problems long argued by chronologists and other commentators.

We note, for example, that Mrs. Watson here calls her husband *James,* for the one and only time in the chronicles.[2]

The exact location of the vile opium den, the Bar of Gold, is still a matter of controversy.[3]

Holmes would appear to have added Irene Adler's coachman, John, to the list of his occasional assistants. "All right, John," Holmes says to the cabman who waited for him outside the Bar of Gold. "Here's half-a-crown. Look out for me tomorrow about eleven. . . ."

As for Mrs. Neville St. Clair, Holmes's client, she seemed strangely insistent that Holmes should stay at her house in Kent, a seven-mile drive from London, while he was investigating the loss of her husband. Holmes was careful to bring Watson with him to Kent, where Mrs. St. Clair, thinking the detective alone, "stood with her figure outlined against the flood of light" to greet him, "one hand upon the door, one half raised in eagerness, her body slightly bent, her head and face protruded, with eager

[2] Constance Watson disliked the name *John.* She preferred to call her husband, in private, by the English equivalent of his Scottish middle name, *Hamish.* See the late Dorothy L. Sayers' "Dr. Watson's Christian Name," in *Profile by Gaslight.*

[3] There is, of course, no "Upper Swandam Lane" in London. Lower Thames Street, which runs east from London Bridge to All Hallows by the Tower, is one distinct possibility.

eyes and parted lips, a standing question." Her attitude was hardly that of a bereaved wife, and Holmes that night got Watson to share his room with him. Even so, he sat up all night on a pile of cushions, smoking shag tobacco and ruminating.

That September, on a night when the rain beat against the windows and the wind cried and sobbed like a child in the chimney,[4] a ring at the bell brought young John Openshaw to visit Holmes on the matter of the Five Orange Pips.

"I question, sir," he said, whether in all your experience you have ever listened to a more mysterious and inexplicable chain of events than those which have happened in my own family."

It is melancholy to report that young John Openshaw has the distinction of being one of the only two clients to be murdered after consulting with Sherlock Holmes.[5]

Here, now, were three homicides—that of young John Openshaw himself, that of his uncle, that of his father. All, seemingly, the work of an American secret society, the Ku Klux Klan. All dismissed, in England, as "accident" or "suicide."

Holmes's gray eyes narrowed dangerously.

For months now, his agents in the London underworld had been bringing him word of a great, malignant, guiding brain, quietly organizing the worst elements of the Seven Dials and Whitechapel sections of London, itself never connected with the outrages that resulted.

And what did he look like, this Napoleon of Crime?

Few had seen him, and few who had would talk. Yet it was said that he was extremely tall, extremely thin. Clean-shaven, pale, ascetic-looking. He was thought by some to be a famous mathematician. And, yes,—he fascinated, as a snake in the zoo fascinates with its slithery power. For his head, its beady eyes protruding, was forever oscillating. . . .

Holmes raged when he heard of young Openshaw's death.

"This hurts my pride, Watson," he said. "It becomes a personal matter with me now. If God send me health, I shall set my hand upon . . ."

[4] Watson, his wife away on a visit, was for a few days at this time a dweller in Baker Street again.

[5] The other unfortunate was Hilton Cubitt, of "The Adventure of the Dancing Men."

He strode to the sideboard and plucked an orange from the bowl that stood beside the gasogene and tantalus. Tearing the fruit apart, he squeezed the pips onto the table. Carefully selecting five—"Their own 'black spot,' their own sign of death to come," he said, grimly—he thrust the pips into an envelope taken from his desk. On the inside of the flap he wrote: "S.H. for J.M." Then he sealed and addressed the envelope, to a name and street number that he carefully hid from Watson.

"Here I must be my own police," he said.

The death struggle above the Reichenbach Falls had begun.

On the eighteenth of October, a Tuesday, Miss Mary Sutherland called at 221 Baker Street, a Duchess-of-Devonshire hat tilted coquettishly over her ear.

For Holmes, her problem was a very simple one. "There was never any mystery in the matter," he said, "though some of the details are of interest."[6]

Later, in that same month of October 1887, Holmes was to solve one of the most extraordinary cases ever brought his way when the redheaded pawnbroker Jabez Wilson called upon him to explain why, for the past eight weeks, he had been paid four pounds a week to copy out the *Encyclopaedia Britannica* volume by volume.

"I had written about Abbots, and Archery, and Armor, and Architecture, and Attica, and hoped with diligence that I might get on to the B's before long," he said piteously, when—on that very Saturday morning—the League which had employed him had been precipitously dissolved![7]

---

[6] It at least gave him an opportunity to display, to Watson, the snuff-box of old gold, with an amethyst in the center of the lid, a belated souvenir from the "King of Bohemia" in return for Holmes's assistance in the case of the Irene Adler photograph. It also gave him the opportunity to refer to his knowledge of Hafiz (the popular name for Shams el-Din Mohammed, a Persian lyric poet who flourished in the fourteenth century) and Horace (Quintus Horatius Flaccus, 65–8 B.C.), the Roman lyric and satirical poet.

[7] The astute reader of Dr. Watson's chronicles will note that in his account of "The Red-Headed League," and in his account of at least three of the other 1887 cases—"A Scandal in Bohemia," "The Five Orange Pips," and "A Case of Identity"—Watson makes every attempt to imply that these cases took place *later* than they actually did. As we shall shortly see, Watson made many of the allusions and references found here *in a deliberate attempt to confuse and confound the contemporary reader.*

To Holmes, the whole fantastic affair reeked of—*Moriarty*. He did not expect, of course, to come to grips in this case with the Napoleon of Crime himself. Holmes was here content to settle his long-standing account with the fourth-most dangerous man in London, John Clay, murderer, thief, smasher, forger, old Etonian and graduate of Oxford, and grandson of a royal duke.[8]

It is enough to say that Holmes's quick perception completely destroyed John Clay's ingenious plot to rob the City and Suburban Bank of thirty thousand napoleons of gold borrowed from the Bank of France.

"You are a benefactor of the race," Watson cried in unfeigned admiration, as he sat enjoying a whisky-and-soda in the old sitting room at Baker Street.

Holmes shrugged.

"Well, perhaps, after all, I am of some little use," he remarked with a smile, " *'L'homme n'est rien, l'oeuvre tout,'* as Gustave Flaubert wrote to George Sand."[9]

In November came the case that Watson was to chronicle (a quarter of a century later) as "The Adventure of the Dying Detective."

Holmes was the detective who was dying, according to his landlady, Mrs. Hudson, when she came to Watson's rooms at the beginning of the second year of his married life.

Watson was convinced that Mrs. Hudson was right, when he saw Holmes's gaunt, wasted face staring at him from the bed and heard his babblings.

"Indeed, I cannot think," Holmes raved, "why the whole of the bed of the ocean is not one solid mass of oysters, so prolific the creatures seem."

---

[8] It is generally agreed that John Clay's grandfather was one of the seven sons of George III. As the erudite Dr. Julian Wolff has written (in *Practical Handbook of Sherlockian Heraldry*, p. 20): "Any one of them is a logical contender since the extra-curricular activities of all of them were quite notorious. . . . The truth is that there are too many suspects, none of them impossible—or even improbable."

[9] "The man is nothing, the work is everything." This will be found on page 348, Letter CCCI, of the English edition of *The George Sand-Gustave Flaubert Letters,* by Aimie L. McKenzie, New York: Boni & Liveright, 1921. Gustave Flaubert (1821–80) is of course the French novelist, author of *Madame Bovary*. George Sand is, of course, the pen name of Amantine Lucile Aurore Dupin Dudevant (1804–76), French novelist, author of *Indiana, Consuelo.*

But the deception Holmes found it necessary to practice on his devoted landlady and his old, dear friend was but a part of his subtle trap to catch a monster murderer, the unspeakable Culverton Smith—and the case ended with a healthy—but very hungry—Holmes and his companion Dr. Watson enjoying "something nutritious" at Simpson's.[10]

Then, in December, an affair that appeared at first to be a mere whim soon developed into a serious investigation.

Watson had called upon Holmes "upon the second morning after Christmas, with the intentions of wishing him the compliments of the season,"[11] and found his friend studying a very seedy and disreputable hard felt hat that hung from the back of a wooden chair.

The hat was to lead to a good fat goose—and in its crop, the Countess of Morcar's missing blue carbuncle, valued at more than twenty thousand pounds!

It is true that Holmes let the miserable culprit go, but, as he said to Watson: "It is the season of forgiveness. Chance has put in our way a most singular and whimsical problem, and its solution is its own reward. If you will have the goodness to touch the bell, Doctor, we will begin another investigation, in which also a bird will be the chief feature."

---

[10] There were several eating houses called Simpson's in the London of Holmes and Watson—for example, Simpson's Restaurant at 38½ Cornhill. But Holmes surely intended his "something nutritious" to be served at Simpson's in the Strand, where, years later, "at a small table in the front window, and looking down at the rushing stream of life in the Strand," he met Watson by appointment, in the unpleasant case of Baron Adelbert Gruner and Miss Violet de Merville ("The Adventure of the Illustrious Client").

The description above, as Mr. Michael Harrison notes (*In the Footsteps of Sherlock Holmes*, p. 22) no longer applies—"there are no front windows at Simpson's now . . .

Simpson's in Holmes's day was famous not only as a restaurant but as a meeting place for amateur chess players, and Mr. Harrison surmises that Holmes once received "an unforgettable drubbing over a chessboard at Simpson's"—a defeat that explains his belief that skill at chess was "one mark, Watson, of a scheming mind" ("The Adventure of the Retired Colourman").

[11] And to present him, no doubt, with a suitably inscribed copy of Beeton's just-published *Christmas Annual*, featuring *A Study in Scarlet* on its red, yellow, and black cover.

A happy note on which to close a crowded year.

But, for Watson, dark personal tragedy lay just ahead as '87 ended and '88 began.

X. BACK TO BAKER STREET: JANUARY 1888

"That's genius, Watson. But if I am spared by lesser men our day will surely come."

SHERLOCK HOLMES.

Within three days of Dr. Watson's holiday call on his friend Mr. Sherlock Holmes, Constance Watson, always a delicate woman, was dead, the victim of a sudden and virulent attack of diphtheria.

"Come back to Baker Street, Watson," Holmes had urged. And he added, as he would have to add again, a little over six years later, "Work is the best antidote to sorrow."[1]

In that winter of 1887–88, Holmes did his best to cheer the lonely, brokenhearted doctor. He dropped his usual secretiveness, and told Watson for the first time of his early cases, the adventure of the *Gloria Scott* and the adventure of the Musgrave Ritual, and how they had started him on the road to becoming the world's only consulting detective.

Yet Watson, who had found complete happiness in those home-centered interests which rise up about the man who first finds himself master of his own establishment, now found some cause to complain.

"An anomaly which often struck me in the character of my friend Sherlock Holmes," Watson wrote,[2] "was that, although in his methods of thought he was the neatest and most methodical of mankind, and although also he affected a certain quiet prim-

---

[1] "The Adventure of the Empty House."
[2] In his introduction to the adventure of "The Musgrave Ritual."

ness of dress, he was none the less in his personal habits one of the most untidy men that ever drove a fellow lodger to distraction. Not that I am in the least conventional in that respect myself. The rough-and-tumble work in Afghanistan, coming on the top of a natural Bohemianism of disposition, has made me rather more lax than befits a medical man. But with me there is a limit, and when I find a man who keeps his cigars in the coal-scuttle, his tobacco in the toe-end of a Persian slipper, and his unanswered correspondence transfixed by a jack-knife into the very centre of his wooden mantelpiece, then I begin to give myself virtuous airs. I have always held, too, that pistol practice should distinctly be an open-air pastime; and when Holmes in one of his queer humours would sit in an arm-chair, with his hair-trigger[3] and a hundred Boxer cartridges,[4] and proceed to adorn the opposite wall with a patriotic V.R. [Victoria Regina] done in bullet-pocks . . . I felt strongly that neither the atmosphere nor the appearance of our rooms was improved by it.

"Our chambers were always full of chemicals and of criminal relics, which had a way of wandering into unlikely positions, and of turning up in the butter-dish, or in even less desirable places. But his papers were my great crux. He had a horror of destroying documents, especially those which were connected with his past cases, and yet it was only once in every year or two that he would muster energy to docket and arrange them, for as I have mentioned somewhere in these incoherent memoirs, the outbursts of passionate energy when he performed the remarkable feats with which his name is associated were followed by reactions of lethargy, during which he would lie about with his violin and books, hardly moving, save from the sofa to the table. Thus month after month his papers accumulated, until every corner of the room was stacked with bundles of manuscript which were on no ac-

---

3 Mr. Robert Keith Leavitt, in his essay, "Annie Oakley in Baker Street," in *Profile by Gaslight,* suggests that Holmes's hair-trigger was almost certainly a single-shot "salon" pistol of Continental make. Captain Hugh B. C. Pollard, the British authority, in *The Book of the Pistol* (New York: Robert McBride & Co., 1917), calls these "wonderfully complicated . . . [but] so delicate . . . as to [be] practically worthless for ordinary use. . . . For trick work, like shooting the pips off the ace of clubs, they are invaluable."

4 A center-fire cartridge—a form of ammunition perfected by Colonel Boxer, R.A., in 1867.

count to be burned, and which could not be put away save by their owner."

Fortunately, Holmes and Watson were to be plunged almost at once into one of Holmes's most significant cases—the adventure Watson was to publish[5] under the title of *The Valley of Fear.*

We can believe that there must have been some small celebration of Holmes's thirty-fourth birthday on the night of Friday, January 6, 1888, for he sat the next morning leaning his head on his hand, his breakfast in front of him, untasted.

"I am inclined to think—" Watson began.

"I should certainly do so," Holmes snapped.

"Really, Holmes," Watson replied severely, "you can be a little trying at times."

Happily, at that moment, there was a brisk rap at the door, a brusque "Come!" from Holmes, and the page boy—newly hired by Mrs. Hudson—entered and handed the detective a letter.

Holmes tore open the envelope and read the slip of paper it contained. Then he held the envelope to the light and very carefully studied both the exterior and the flap.

"It is Porlock's writing," he said thoughtfully. "I can hardly doubt that it is Porlock's writing, though I have seen it only twice before. The Greek *e* with the top flourish is distinctive."

"Who, then, is Porlock?" Watson asked, his vexation disappearing in the interest Holmes's words had awakened in him.

"Porlock, Watson, is a *nom de plume,* a mere identification mark,[6] but behind it lies a shifty and evasive personality. Porlock is important, not for himself, but for the great man with whom he is in touch. Picture to yourself the pilot-fish with the shark, the jackal with the lion—anything that is insignificant in companionship with that which is formidable. Not only formidable, Watson, but sinister— in the highest degree sinister. You have probably never heard of Professor Moriarty?"

[5] More than a quarter of a century later, in *The Strand Magazine,* September 1914–May 1915.

[6] Literary scholars will recall that Coleridge was unable to complete his famous poem, *Kubla Khan,* because he was called from his table "by a person on business from Porlock" and detained by him above an hour. When he returned to his manuscript the closing lines had faded from his mind. See Vincent Starrett's fine essay "Persons from Porlock," in *Bookman's Holiday: The Private Satisfactions of an Incurable Collector;* New York: Random House, 1942.

"Never."

"Aye, that's the wonder of the thing!" Holmes cried. "The man pervades London, and no one has heard of him. That's what puts him on a pinnacle in the records of crime. I tell you, Watson, in all seriousness, that if I could beat that man, if I could free society of him, I should feel that my own career had reached its summit."

"What has he done, then?" Watson asked.

"His career has been an extraordinary one. He is a man of good birth and excellent education, endowed by nature with a phenomenal mathematical faculty. But the man had hereditary tendencies of the most diabolical kind. A criminal strain ran in his blood which was increased and rendered infinitely more dangerous by his extraordinary mental powers. Dark rumors gathered round him at the university where he held the Mathematical Chair, and eventually he was compelled to resign and come to London, where he set up as an Army coach."

Holmes paused reminiscently.

"Some of this I knew a very long time ago," he said, "but much that I am telling you now I discovered only recently. As you are well aware, Watson, there is no one who knows the criminal world of London so well as I do. For years past I have continually been conscious of some power behind the malefactor, some deep organizing power which forever stands in the way of the law, and throws a shield over the wrongdoer. Again and again in cases of the most varying sorts—forgery cases, robberies, murders—I have felt the presence of this force, and I have deduced its action in many crimes discovered and undiscovered, in some of which I myself have been personally concerned. You did not know it at the time, Watson, but ex-Professor Moriarty played some part in the unfortunate affair of John Openshaw, as well as in the more successful matter of the League of the Red-Headed Men.

"He is the Napoleon of Crime, Watson. He is the organizer of half that is evil and nearly all that is undetected in this great city. He sits motionless, like a spider in the center of its web, but that web has a thousand radiations, and he knows every quiver in each of them. He does little himself. He only plans. But his agents are numerous and splendidly organized. If there is a crime to be done, a paper to be abstracted, we will say, a house to be rifled, a man to be removed—the word is passed to the Professor, the matter is organized and carried out. The agent may be caught. In that case money is found for his bail or his defense. But the central power which uses the agent is never caught— never so much as suspected.[7] That's genius, Watson. But if I am spared by lesser men our day will surely come."[8]

"May I be there to see it!" Watson exclaimed devoutly. "But you were speaking of this man Porlock."

"Ah, yes—the so-called Porlock is a link in the chain some little way from its great attachment. Porlock is not quite a sound link, between ourselves. He is the only flaw in the chain that I have so far been able to discover."

"But no chain is stronger than its weakest link."

"Well said, my dear Watson. Hence the extreme importance of Porlock. Encouraged by an occasional ten-pound note sent to him by devious methods, he has once or twice given me advance information which has been of the highest value.[9] I cannot doubt if we had the cipher we should find that this communication is of the same nature."

Holmes flattened out the paper upon his unused plate. Watson rose and, leaning over him, stared down at a curious inscription:

534 C2 13 127 36 31 4 17 21 41
DOUGLAS 109 293 5 37 BIRLSTONE
26 BIRLSTONE 9 127 171

"What do you make of it, Holmes?"

"It is clearly a reference to the words on a page of some book. 'Douglas' and 'Birlstone' are in clear because those words are not contained on that page."

"Then why has he not indicated the book?"

---

[7] Ex-Professor Moriarty's organization had a peculiarly similar modern-day counterpart in the late unlamented Murder, Inc.

[8] Sherlockian scholars may object that much of the above conversation was recorded by Watson, not in *The Valley of Fear*, but in "The Final Problem." It must be remembered that "The Final Problem" was published twenty-one years before *The Valley of Fear*. Watson, as writer, wished to introduce the Napoleon of Crime to his readers as dramatically as possible. He therefore stated (in "The Final Problem") that he had "never heard" of Moriarty, in order to insert an explanation from Holmes which had actually been made to him three years earlier.

[9] It was undoubtedly information from Porlock that led Holmes to suspect that Moriarty was implicated in the death of John Openshaw, his father, and his uncle ("The Five Orange Pips").

"Your native shrewdness, Watson, that innate cunning which is the delight of your friends, would surely prevent you from enclosing cipher and message in the same envelope. Should it miscarry, you are undone. As it is, both have to go wrong before any harm comes of it. Our second post is now overdue, and I shall be surprised if it does not bring us either a further letter of explanation or, as is more probable, the very volume to which these figures refer."

In a very few minutes the page appeared with another letter.

"The same writing," Holmes remarked, tearing open the envelope, "and actually signed!" But his brow clouded as he read the message:

"Dear Mr. Holmes. I will go no further in this matter. It is too dangerous. He suspects me. I can see that he suspects me. He came to me quite unexpectedly after I had actually addressed this envelope with the intention of sending you the key to the cipher. I was able to cover it up. If he had seen your name upon it, it would have gone hard with me. But I read suspicion in his eyes. Please burn the cipher message, which can now be of no use to you.

Fred Porlock."

"It is maddening," Watson said. "To think that an important secret may lie here on this slip of paper, and that it is beyond human power to penetrate it."

"I wonder," Holmes said. He leaned back in his armchair and stared at the ceiling. "The message begins with 534, does it not? We may take it as a working hypothesis that 534 is the page to which the cipher refers. So our book is a *large* book. The next symbol is C2. If that does not indicate 'Column 2,' then I am very much mistaken. So now we begin to visualize a large book printed in double columns. Had the volume been an unusual one, Porlock would have sent it to me. Instead of that he had intended, before his plans were nipped, to send me a clue to it in this envelope. This would seem to indicate that the book is one which he thought I would have no difficulty in finding for myself. In short, Watson, it is a very common book."

"The Bible!" Watson cried triumphantly.

"Good, Watson, good! But not quite good enough, if I may say so. The editions of Holy Writ are so numerous that Porlock could hardly suppose that two copies would have the same page numbers. This is clearly a book which is standardized."

"Bradshaw!"[10]

"There are difficulties, Watson. The vocabulary of Bradshaw is terse but limited. The selection of words would hardly lend itself to the sending of general messages. The dictionary, is, I fear, inadmissible for the same reason. What, then, is left? Let us consider the claims of Whitaker's Almanack. It is in common use. It has the requisite number of pages. It is printed in double columns. Though reserved in its earlier vocabulary, it becomes quite garrulous towards the end."

He picked up the volume from his desk.

"Here is page 534," he continued. "Column two is a substantial block of print dealing with the trade and resources of British India. Jot down the words, Watson. Number thirteen is *Mahratta*. Not, I fear, a very auspicious beginning. Number one hundred and twenty-seven is *Government*, which at least makes sense. What does the Maharatta Government do? Alas! The next word is *pigs'-bristles*. We are undone, my good Watson! It is finished. But wait! Perhaps we pay the price for being too up-to-date. This being the seventh of January, we have very properly laid in the new almanack. It is more than likely that Porlock took his message from the old one."

Holmes dashed to a cupboard, from which he emerged with a second yellow-covered volume in his hand.

"Now let us see what page 534 has in store for us," he said. "Number thirteen is *There*, which is much more promising. Number one hundred and twenty-seven is *is*. Aha! Number thirty-six—*danger*. Capital! *There is danger may come very soon one Douglas. Rich. Country. Now at Birlstone House, Birlstone. Confidence is pressing.* There is our result, and a very workmanlike little bit of analysis it was."

Holmes was still chuckling over his success when the page swung open the door and Inspector MacDonald of Scotland Yard was ushered into the room.

"You're an early bird, Mr. Mac," Holmes said. "I fear this means there is some mischief afoot."

---

[10] While no British reader need be told what a Bradshaw is, all American readers may not know that "Bradshaw" was the guide to British railways first compiled by an English map engraver, George Bradshaw (1801–53).

"If you said 'hope' instead of 'fear' it would be nearer the truth, I'm thinking, Mr. Holmes," the inspector answered with a knowing grin. "And you're right. A Mr. Douglas of Birlstone Manor House was horribly murdered last night."

It was at eleven forty-five on the night of January 6 that the first alarm had been sounded. Mr. Cecil Barker, of Hales Lodge, a frequent and always welcome visitor at Birlstone Manor House, had rushed up to the door of the small local police station and pealed furiously upon the bell. A tragedy had occurred at the manor house, he told Sergeant Wilson of the Sussex Constabulary. Mr. John Douglas had been murdered.

On reaching the manor house, Sergeant Wilson had found the drawbridge down, the windows all lighted, and the entire household in a state of wild confusion. The sergeant, Mr. Barker and Dr. Wood, a brisk and capable general practitioner from the village, had entered the fatal room—the study—together. The dead man lay upon his back, sprawling with outstretched limbs in the center of the room. He was clad only in a pink dressing gown which covered his night clothes. There were carpet slippers upon his bare feet. The man had been horribly injured. Lying across his chest was a curious weapon, a shotgun with the barrel sawed off a foot in front of the triggers, the triggers wired together to make a simultaneous discharge more destructive. It was clear that this had been fired at close range, and that Douglas had received the whole charge in the face, blowing his head almost to pieces. The long, diamond-paned window of the room was open to its full extent, and a smudge of blood like the mark of a boot sole showed upon its wooden sill. On the floor beside the dead man lay a card. The initials *V.V.* and, under it, the number *341* were rudely scrawled upon it in ink. Upon the rug in front of the fireplace lay a substantial, workmanlike hammer. "Mr. Douglas was changing the pictures around yesterday," Cecil Barker explained.

The sergeant had raised his lamp and was walking slowly around the room.

"Hello!" he cried excitedly, drawing the window curtain to one side. "Someone has been hiding here, sure enough. The marks of muddy boots are clearly visible."

The doctor had taken the lamp and was scrutinizing the body. "What's this mark?" he asked.

The dead man's right arm was thrust out from the sleeve of his dressing gown and exposed as high as the elbow. About halfway up the forearm was a curious brown design, a triangle inside a circle.

"It's not tattooed," the doctor said. "This man has been burned at some time—branded, as men brand cattle."

Ames, the Birlstone butler, had given an exclamation of astonishment, and was pointing at the dead man's outstretched hand.

"They've taken his wedding ring!" he gasped. "Master always wore a plain gold wedding ring on the little finger of his left hand. That ring with the rough gold nugget was above it, and the twisted snake ring he wore on his third finger. There's the nugget and there's the snake, but the wedding ring is gone!"

"Do you mean to tell me," the sergeant said, "that the wedding ring was *below* the other?"

"Always."

"Then the murderer first took off this ring you call the nugget ring, then the wedding ring, and afterwards put the nugget ring back."

"That is so."

The country policeman shook his head.

"Seems to me the sooner we get London to work on this case the better," he said.

Holmes, Watson, and Inspector MacDonald were met at the train by White Mason, the chief Sussex detective. In ten minutes they found quarters in the village inn, the Westville Arms. In ten more minutes they were seated in the parlor of the inn and treated to a rapid sketch of the events. Mason had found no stain upon the hammer. He had examined the gun and found the letters *PEN* inscribed on the barrel.

"A big *P* with a flourish above it—the *E* and *N* smaller?" Holmes asked.

"Exactly."

"It is the mark of the Pennsylvania Small Arms Company— a well-known American firm," Holmes said.

"Mr. Douglas was an American, or had lived long in America. So had Mr. Barker."

"May I ask," Holmes said, "whether you examined the farther side of the moat, to see if there were any signs of a man having climbed out of the water?"

"There were no signs, Mr. Holmes. But it is a stone ledge, and one could hardly expect them."

"Ha! Would there be any objection to our going down to the manor house at once? There may possibly be some small points which might be suggestive."

At Birlstone Manor House, Holmes walked to the edge of the moat and looked across it. Then he examined the stone ledge and the grass border beyond it. In the murder room, he knelt beside the body.

"There is a small piece of plaster on the angle of Mr. Douglas' jaw," he observed to the butler. "Did you see that in life?"

"Yes, sir. Mr. Douglas cut himself shaving yesterday morning."

"Suggestive," said Holmes. "Well, we will pass to the card. It is rough cardboard. Have you any of this sort in the house?"

"I don't think so, sir."

Holmes walked across to the desk and dabbed a little ink from each bottle onto the blotting paper. "The card was not printed in this room," he said. "This is black ink, and the other is purple. The writing on the card was done by a thick pen, and the pens here are all fine. Hm. Now, what's this under the table?"

"Mr. Douglas' dumbbells," said the butler.

"*Dumbbell*—there's only one. Where's the other?"

"I don't know, Mr. Holmes."

"One dumbbell—" Holmes said seriously, but his remarks were interrupted by a sharp knock at the door. Cecil Barker looked in.

"Sorry to interrupt your consultation," he said, "but they've found a bicycle. The murderer left his bicycle behind him, within a hundred yards of the hall door."

"What in the name of all that is wonderful made the fellow leave it behind?" Inspector MacDonald said. "We don't seem to get a gleam of light in this case, Mr. Holmes."

"Don't we?" Holmes answered thoughtfully. "I wonder."

While Watson returned to the village inn, Holmes spent the whole afternoon at the manor house in consultation with his two colleagues. He returned about five in a most cheerful humor and with a ravenous appetite for the high tea Watson had ordered for him.

"My dear Watson," he said, "when I have exterminated that fourth egg I will be ready to put you in touch with the whole situation. I don't say we have fathomed it—far from it—but when we have traced the missing dumbbell—"

"The dumbbell!"

"Dear me, Watson, is it possible that you have not penetrated the fact that the case hangs upon the missing dumbbell?" Holmes lit his pipe and settled back in the inglenook. "A lie, Watson— that's what meets us on the threshold. The whole story told by Barker is a lie. But Barker's story is corroborated by Mrs. Douglas. Therefore she is lying also. Why are they lying? What is the truth which they are trying so hard to conceal? I am able to show that the blood mark on the windowsill was deliberately placed there by Barker. I have no doubt that a quarter of eleven was the real instant of the murder. But what could Mr. Barker and Mrs. Douglas be doing from then until a quarter-past eleven when they summoned the servants? I think, Watson, that an evening alone in that study would help me very much. I propose to go there presently. I have arranged it with the butler. By the way, you have that big umbrella of yours, have you not? I'll borrow it, if I may."

"Certainly—but the weather is clear, and an umbrella makes a wretched weapon. If there is danger—"

"Nothing serious, my dear Watson, or I should certainly ask for your assistance. But I'll take the umbrella. At present I am only awaiting the return of Mr. Mason and Inspector MacDonald from Tunbridge Wells, where they are engaged in trying to find a likely owner to that bicycle."

It was nightfall before Inspector MacDonald and White Mason came back from their expedition, exultant.

"We took the bicycle to Tunbridge Wells and showed it at the hotels," MacDonald explained. "It was identified at once by the manager of the Eagle Commercial as belonging to a man named

Hargrave who had taken a room there two days before. He was a man about five foot nine in height, fifty or so years of age, his hair slightly grizzled, a grayish mustache, a curved nose, and a face which all of them described as fierce and forbidding."

"Bar the expression, that might almost be a description of Douglas himself," Holmes said. "Well, I propose to make a little investigation of my own tonight, and it is just possible that it may contribute something to the common cause."

"Can we help you, Mr. Holmes?"

"No, no. Darkness and Dr. Watson's umbrella. My wants are simple. All my lines of thought lead me invariably to one basic question. Why should an athletic man develop his frame upon so unnatural an object as a single dumbbell?"

Next morning after breakfast Holmes and Watson found Inspector MacDonald and Mr. White Mason seated in close consultation in the small parlor of the local police sergeant.

"I want you to write a note to Mr. Barker," Holmes said. "I'll dictate, if you like. 'Dear Sir. It has struck me that it is our duty to drain the moat, in the hope that we may find some—"

"It's impossible!" said the inspector.

"Tut, tut. '—in the hope that we may find something which may bear upon our investigation. I have made arrangements, and the workmen will be at work early tomorrow morning diverting the stream—"

"Impossible!"

"'—diverting the stream, so I thought it best to explain matters beforehand.' Now sign that, and send it by hand about four o'clock. At that hour we shall meet again in this room."

Evening was drawing in when they reassembled. Holmes was very serious, Watson very curious, the detectives critical and annoyed.

"Well, gentlemen," said Holmes gravely, "I am asking you now to put everything to the test with me, and you will judge for yourselves whether the observations which I have made justify the conclusions to which I have come. It is a chill evening, and I do not know how long our expedition may last, so I beg that you will wear your warmest coats. It is of the first importance that we should be in our places before it grows dark, and so, with your permission, we will get started at once."

In the gathering gloom they followed Holmes to the shrubbery which lay nearly opposite to the main door and the drawbridge of Birlstone Manor House.

Their vigil was a long and bitter one.

Slowly the shadows darkened over the long, somber face of the old house. A cold, damp reek from the moat chilled them to their bones and set their teeth to chattering. There was a single lamp over the gateway and a steady glow of light in the fatal study, but everything else was dark and still.

At last the bright yellow light in the study was obscured by somebody passing to and fro before it. The window was thrown open, and they could see the dark outline of a man's head and shoulders looking out into the night. For some minutes he peered forth in a furtive, stealthy fashion, as one who wishes to be sure that he is unobserved. Then he leaned forward, and in the intense silence the watchers were aware of the soft lapping sound of agitated water. The man in the study seemed to be stirring up the moat with something which he held in his hand. Then suddenly he hauled something in as a fisherman lands a fish. . . .

"Now!" cried Holmes. "Now!"

Holmes ran swiftly across the bridge and rang violently at the bell. There was the rasping of bolts from the other side, and the amazed Ames, the Birlstone butler, stood at the entrance. Holmes brushed him aside without a word, and, followed by the others, rushed to the study. The light of an oil lamp shone upon the strong, resolute face of Cecil Barker.

"What the devil is the meaning of this?" he cried.

Holmes glanced swiftly around and then pounced upon a sodden bundle tied together with cord which lay where it had been thrust under the writing table.

"That is what we are after," he said. "This bundle, weighted with a dumbbell, which you, Mr. Barker, have just raised from the bottom of the moat."

"How in thunder do you know anything about it?" Cecil Barker asked.

"Simply that I put it there," Holmes replied. "Or perhaps I should say 'replaced it there.' When water is near and a weight is missing, look for something that has been sunk in the water. Last night, with the help of Ames and the crook of Dr. Watson's umbrella, I was able to fish up and inspect this bundle. It was of the first importance, however, that we should be able to prove who placed it there. This we accomplished by the very obvious device of announcing that the moat was to be drained."

Holmes put the sopping bundle on the table beside the lamp and untied the cords which bound it. From within he drew out a dumbbell and a pair of boots—"American, you perceive," he remarked. Then he laid upon the table a long, deadly knife. Finally he unraveled a bundle of clothing, made up of a set of underclothes, socks, a gray tweed suit, and a short yellow overcoat. "You will perceive," he said, "that the inner pocket of the overcoat has been lengthened into the lining to give ample space for the sawed-off shotgun. The tailor's tab is on the neck—'Neale, Outfitter, Vermissa, Pennsylvania.' Vermissa is a flourishing little town at the head of one of the best-known coal and iron valleys in the United States. I have some recollection, Mr. Barker, that in one of our conversations you associated coal districts with Mr. Douglas's first wife. It would surely not be too farfetched to infer that the V. V. upon the card by the dead body might stand for Vermissa Valley.[11] And now, Mr. Barker, I seem to be standing in the way of your explanation."

"If there is any secret here it is not my secret, and I am not the man to give it away."

The deadlock was broken by the entrance of Mrs. Douglas.

"You have done enough for us, Cecil," she said. "Whatever comes of it in the future, you have done enough."

"There is much that is still unexplained," said Holmes. "I strongly recommend that you ask *Mr. Douglas* to tell us his own story."

Suddenly, from the dark in a corner of the room, a man appeared, blinking with the dazed look of one who has just stepped into the light.

"I've been cooped up for two days now in that rattrap of a priest's hole," the newcomer said. "Can I smoke as I talk? You'll

---

[11] "Vermissa Valley"—Watsonese for Shenandoah Valley. The town of "Vermissa," where Neale had his men's toggery, was most probably Pottsville, near the Schuylkill anthracite region.

guess, Mr. Holmes, what it is like to be sitting for two whole days with tobacco in your pocket and afraid that the smell of smoking it will give you away! Well," he continued, lighting the cigar that Holmes had quickly handed to him, "it all comes down to this: that there are some men that have good cause to hate me and would give their last dollar to know they had got me. The day before these happenings I was over in Tunbridge Wells, and I got a glimpse of a man in the street. He was the worst enemy that I had among them all. I was on my guard all the next day and never went out into the park. After the drawbridge was up that night, I put the thing clear out of my mind. I never figured on his getting into the house and waiting for me. But when I made my round in my dressing gown, as my habit was, I had no sooner entered this room than I scented danger. Next instant I spotted a boot under the window curtain. I put down my candle and jumped for a hammer that I'd left on the mantel when I was changing around some pictures in this room. At the moment that man sprang at me, I sprang at him. I saw the glint of a wicked knife in his hand, and I lashed out at him with the hammer. I got him somewhere, for the knife tinkled down on the floor. He dodged round the table as quick as an eel, and a moment later he'd got his gun from under his coat. I heard him cock it, but I had got hold of it before he could fire. He never lost his grip, but he got it butt downwards for a moment too long. Maybe I pulled the trigger. Maybe we just jolted it off between us.

"Anyway, he got both barrels full in the face, and there I was, staring down at all that was left of Ted Baldwin. I was hanging on to the side of the table when Barker came hurrying down. The servants had heard nothing. It was at that instant that the idea came to me. The man's sleeve had slipped up, and there was the branded mark of the lodge that I wear on my own forearm. There was his height and his hair and his figure—about the same as my own. No one could swear to his face, poor devil! I brought down this suit of clothes, and in a quarter of an hour Barker and I had put my dressing gown on him and he lay as you found him. We tied all his things in a bundle, and I weighted them with the only weight I could find and slung them through the window. The card he had meant to lay upon my body was lying beside his own. My rings were put on his fingers, but when it came to my wedding ring, I found I could not get it off. On the other hand, I brought a bit of plaster down and put it where I am wearing one myself at this instant.

"Well, that was the situation. If I could lie low for a while and then get away from here, someplace where I could be joined by my wife, we would have a chance at last of living at peace for the rest of our lives. I knew all about this hiding place. So I retired into it, and it was up to Barker to do the rest. He opened the window and made the mark on the sill to give an idea of how the murderer must have escaped. Then he rang the bell for all he was worth. What happened afterwards, you know."

There was a silence, broken by Sherlock Holmes.

"I would ask," he said, "how this man knew that you lived here, or how to get into your house, or where to hide to get you."

"I know nothing of this."

Holmes's face was very white and grave.

"The story is not over yet, I fear," he said. "I see trouble before you, Mr. Douglas. You'll take my advice and still be on your guard."

At the assizes, John Douglas was acquitted as having acted in self-defense.

"Get him out of England at any cost," Holmes wrote to his wife. "There are forces here which may be far more dangerous than those he has escaped."

Two months passed. Then one morning an enigmatic note, without superscription or signature, was slipped into the letter-box at 221 Baker Street.

It was a very short and very simple note.

"Dear me, Mr. Holmes! Dear me!" it read.

Holmes crushed it in his hand and threw it into the fireplace.

"Devilry, Watson, devilry!" he said.

Late that night Cecil Barker called on Holmes.

"I've terrible news, Mr. Holmes," he said.

"I feared as much."

"You have not had a cable?"

"I have had a note from someone who has."

"Jack and Mrs. Douglas started for South Africa in the *Palmyra* three weeks ago. The ship reached Capetown last night.

I received a cable from Mrs. Douglas this morning. 'Jack has been lost overboard in gale off St. Helena. No one knows how accident occurred.' "

"Ha! It came like that, did it?" said Holmes. "Well, I've no doubt it was well stage-managed."

"You mean this was no accident?"

"None in the world."

"Jack was murdered?"

"Exactly. There is a master hand at work here, Mr. Barker. You can tell an old master by the sweep of his brush, and I can tell a Moriarty when I see one."

"How came this man—this Moriarty—to have anything to do with it?"

"I can only say that the first word that ever came to us of this business was from one of his lieutenants. Having an English job to do, these Americans took into partnership the world's greatest consultant in crime. From that moment their man was doomed. At first he would content himself by using his machinery to find their victim. Then he would indicate how the matter might be treated. Finally, when he read of the failure of his agent, he would step in himself."

Barker beat his head with his clenched fist in impotent anger.

"Can no one ever get level with this king-devil!" he cried.

Holmes's gray eyes seemed to be looking into the future.

"I don't say that," he said at last. "I don't say that at all. But you must give me time—you must give me time!"

INTERRUPTION. THREE STORIES FROM THE LONDON TIMES: AUGUST 10, SEPTEMBER 1, SEPTEMBER 10, 1888

In the early hours of the morning of Easter Tuesday, April the 3rd, 1888, a London tram driver making his way home from work came upon a mutilated and dying woman in front of a warehouse on Osborn Street. She was soon identified as Emma Elizabeth Smith, a widow of forty who had lately taken to walking the streets.

Crime in the Whitechapel district of London was hardly rare in the closing years of the nineteenth century—indeed, crime was so common there that The Times *of London carried no report at all of the murder of Emma Elizabeth Smith, streetwalker.*

From the London *Times,* Friday, August 19, 1888:

"Yesterday afternoon Mr. G. Collier, Deputy Coroner for the South-Eastern Division of Middlesex, opened an inquiry respecting the death of the woman[1] who was found on Tuesday last with thirty-nine stabs on her body at Grove-Yard Buildings, Whitechapel.

"Dr. T. R. Killeen said that he was called to the deceased and found her dead. She had thirty-nine stabs on the body. She had been dead some three hours. The left lung was penetrated in five places, and the right lung was penetrated in two places. The heart, which was rather fatty, was penetrated in one place. The liver was healthy but was penetrated in five places, the spleen was penetrated in two places, and the stomach—which was perfectly

[1] Martha Tabram, also a streetwalker.

healthy—was penetrated in six places. The witness did not think all the wounds were inflicted with the same instrument.

"It was one of the most dreadful murders anyone could imagine. The man must have been a perfect savage to inflict such a number of wounds on a defenceless woman in such a way."

From the London *Times,* Saturday, September 1, 1888:

"Another murder of the foulest kind was committed in the neighborhood of Whitechapel in the early hours of yesterday morning, but by whom and with what motive is at present a complete mystery. At a quarter to four o'clock Police Constable Neill when in Bucks Row, Whitechapel, came upon the body of a woman[2] lying on a part of the footway, and on stooping to raise her up in the belief that she was drunk, he discovered that her throat was cut almost from ear to ear. She was dead but still warm. He procured assistance and at once sent to the station and for a doctor. Dr. Llewellyn, whose surgery is not above a hundred yards from the spot, was aroused at a solicitation from a constable, dressed and went at once to the scene. He made a hasty examination and then discovered that besides the gash across the throat the woman had terrible wounds in the abdomen.

"The police have no theory with respect to the matter except that a gang of ruffians exists in the neighborhood which, blackmailing women of the 'unfortunate' class, takes vengeance on those who do not find money for them. They base that surmise on the fact that within twelve months two other women have been murdered in the district by almost similar means—one as recently as the 6th of August last [sic]—and left in the gutter of the street in the early hours of the morning."

From the London *Times,* Monday, September 10, 1888:

"Whitechapel and the whole of the East of London have again been thrown into a state of intense excitement by the discovery early on Saturday morning of a woman[3] who had been murdered in a similar way to Mary Ann Nichols at Bucks Row on Friday week. In fact the similarity in the two cases is startling, as the

---

[2] Mary Ann Nichols, also a streetwalker.
[3] Annie Chapman, also a streetwalker.

victim of the outrage had her head almost severed from her body and was completely disembowelled. This latest crime, however, even surpasses the others in ferocity.

"The scene of the murder, which makes the fourth in the same neighborhood within the past few weeks, is at the back of the house at 29 Hanbury Street, Spitalfields. This street runs from Commercial Street to Bakers Row, the end of which is close to Bucks Row. The house, which is rented by a Mrs. Emilia Richardson, is let out to various lodgers, of the poorer class. In consequence, the front door is open both day and night, so that no difficulty would be experienced by anyone in gaining admission to the back portions of the premises.

"Shortly before six o'clock on Saturday morning John Davis, who lives with his wife at the top portion of No. 29, went down into the backyard, where a horrible sight presented itself to him. Lying close up against the wall, was the body of a woman. Davis could see that her throat was severed in a terrible manner and that she had other wounds of a nature too shocking to be described. The deceased was lying on her back with her clothes disarranged.

"Without nearer approaching the body but telling his wife what he had seen, Davis ran to the Commercial Street Police Station and gave information to Inspector Chandler, who was in charge of the station at the time. That officer, having dispatched a constable for Dr. Phillips, repaired to the house accompanied by several policemen. The body was still in the same position and there were large clots of blood all around it. It was evident that the murderer thought he had completely cut the head off, as a handkerchief was found wrapped round the neck as though to hold it together. There were spots and stains of blood on the wall. One or more rings seem to have been torn from the middle finger of the left hand. . . .

"The police believe that the murder has been committed by the same person who perpetrated the three previous ones in the district and that only one person is concerned in it. This person might be, is doubtless labouring under some terrible form of insanity, as each of the crimes has been of a most fiendish character, and it is feared that unless he can speedily be captured more outrages of a similar class will be committed."

We may be sure that these stories from the London *Times* found a place in the scrapbooks of people and things of interest kept so assiduously by Mr. Sherlock Holmes.

Perhaps, as Holmes made the cuttings from the *Times* with his jackknife—temporarily displaced from its accustomed job of holding down the unanswered correspondence on the mantel—Watson, deep in his armchair with a volume of Clark Russell's sea stories—watched him, worried, wondered, and waited.

XI. TO MEET MR. MYCROFT HOLMES: WEDNESDAY, SEPTEMBER 12, 1888

. . . it is only natural that I should dwell rather upon his successes than upon his failures.
                                        JOHN H. WATSON, M. D.

It was after tea on the evening of Wednesday, September 12, 1888, and the conversation, which, Watson tells us,[1] had roamed in a desultory, spasmodic fashion from golf clubs to the causes of the change in the obliquity of the ecliptic, came around at last to the question of atavism and hereditary aptitudes.

"In your case," Watson said to Holmes, "it seems obvious that your faculty of observation and your peculiar facility for deduction are due to your own systematic training."

"To some extent," Holmes answered thoughtfully. "But, nonetheless, my turn that way is in my veins."

"And how do you know that it is hereditary?"

"Because my brother Mycroft possesses it in an even larger degree than I do."

This was indeed news to Watson. If there were another man with such singular powers in England, how was it that neither police nor public had heard of him?

"Oh, he is very well known in his own circle," Holmes said.

"Where, then?"

"Well, in the Diogenes Club, for example. It is the queerest club in London, Watson, and Mycroft one of the queerest men. He is always there from a quarter to five till twenty to eight. It's

---

[1] "The Greek Interpreter."

six now, so if you care for a stroll this beautiful evening I shall be very happy to introduce you to two curiosities."

Five minutes later they were in the street, walking toward Regent Circus.

"You wonder," Holmes said, "why Mycroft does not use his powers for detective work. He is incapable of it."

"But you said—"

"I said that he was my superior in observation and deduction. If the art of the detective began and ended in reasoning from an armchair, my brother Mycroft would be the greatest criminal agent the world has ever seen. But he has no ambition and no energy. He would not even go out of his way to verify his own solutions, and would rather be considered wrong than to take the trouble to prove himself right. Time and again I have taken a problem to him and received an explanation which has afterwards proved to be the right one. And yet he is absolutely incapable of working out those practical points which must be gone into before a case can be laid before a judge and jury."

"Detective work is not his profession, then?"

"By no means. He has an extraordinary faculty for figures, and audits the books in a Government department. Mycroft lodges in Pall Mall, and he walks round the corner into Whitehall every morning and back every evening. From year's end to year's end he takes no other exercise, and is seen nowhere else, except only at the Diogenes Club, which is just opposite to his rooms."

They had reached Pall Mall as they talked, and were walking down it from the St. James's end. Holmes stopped at a door some little distance from the Carlton and led the way into a hall. Through a glass paneling Watson caught a glimpse of a large and luxurious room in which a considerable number of men were sitting about and reading papers, each in his own little nook. Holmes showed him into a small chamber which looked out on to Pall Mall.

"The Strangers' Room," Holmes said. "It is the only place in the Diogenes Club where talking is permitted. Pray excuse me for a moment."

He soon came back with a companion, who Watson knew, could only be his brother.

Mycroft Holmes was a much larger and stouter man than Sherlock. His body was absolutely corpulent, but his face, though massive, had preserved something of the sharpness of expression which was so remarkable in that of his brother. His eyes, which were of a peculiarly light, watery gray, seemed to retain always that faraway, introspective look which Watson had observed in Sherlock's eyes only when he was exerting his full powers.

"I am glad to meet you, sir," said Mycroft Holmes, putting out a broad, flat hand like a seal's flipper. "I hear of Sherlock everywhere since you became his chronicler. By the way, Sherlock, I expected to see you round last week to consult me over that manor house case. It was Adams, of course?"

"Yes, it was Adams."

"I was sure of it from the first." The two brothers sat down together in the bow window of the club. "To anyone who wishes to study mankind this is the spot," Mycroft said. "Look at those two men coming towards us, for example."

"The billiard marker and the other?"

"Precisely. What do you make of the other?"

"An old soldier, I perceive," said Sherlock.

"And very recently discharged," said Mycroft.

"Served in India, I see."

"And a non-commissioned officer."

"Royal Artillery, I fancy."

"And a widower."

"But with a child."

"Pfui, my dear boy. Children."

Mycroft, smiling, took snuff from a tortoise-shell box and brushed away the wandering grains from his coat with a large silk handkerchief. "By the way, Sherlock," he said, "I have had something quite after your own heart—a most singular problem —submitted to my judgment. I really had not the energy to follow it up, but it gave me a basis for some very pleasing speculations. If you would care to hear the facts—"

"My dear Mycroft, I should be delighted."

Mycroft Holmes scribbled a note upon the leaf of his pocket-book, and, ringing the bell, he handed it to the waiter.

"I have asked Mr. Melas to step across," he said. "He lodges on the floor above me. Mr. Melas is a Greek, and earns his living partly as an interpreter in the law courts, partly as a guide to wealthy Orientals. But I think I will leave him to tell his own remarkable experience in his own fashion."

A few minutes later they were joined by a short, stout man with olive face and coal-black hair. He shook hands eagerly with Sherlock Holmes, and his dark eyes sparkled with pleasure when he understood that the detective was anxious to hear his story.

"This is Wednesday evening," Mr. Melas began. "Well, then, it was on Monday night—only two days ago—that a Mr. Latimer came to my rooms and asked me to accompany him in a cab.

"For nearly two hours we drove without my having the least clue as to where we were going; it was a quarter-past seven when we left Pall Mall, and my watch showed me that it was ten minutes to nine when we at last came to a standstill. I caught a glimpse of a low, arched doorway with a lamp burning above it. As I was hurried from the carriage, it was opened by a small, mean-looking, middle-aged man with rounded shoulders. He showed the way into a room which appeared to me to be very richly furnished. Mr. Latimer had left us, but he suddenly returned, leading with him a gentleman clad in some sort of loose dressing gown. He was deadly pale and terribly emaciated. But what shocked me most was that his face was grotesquely criss-crossed with sticking plaster, and that one large strip of it was fastened over his mouth.

" 'Have you the slate, Harold?' the middle-aged man cried to Mr. Latimer. 'Are his hands loose? Then give him a pencil. Now, Mr. Melas, you are to ask the questions and this man will write the answers. Ask him first whether he is prepared to sign the papers.'

" 'Never,' the emaciated man wrote on the slate in Greek.

" 'On no conditions?' I asked at the bidding of the middle-aged man.

" 'Only if I see her married in my presence by a Greek priest whom I know.'

"Soon," Mr. Melas continued, "a happy thought came to me. I took to adding little sentences of my own to each question. Our conversation then ran something like this:

" 'You can do no good by this obstinacy. *Who are you?*'

" 'I care not. *I am a stranger in London.*'

" 'Your fate will be on your own head. *How long have you been here?*'

" 'Let it be so. *Three weeks.*'

" 'The property can never be yours. *What ails you?*'

" 'It shall not go to villains. *They are starving me.*'

" 'You shall go free if you sign. *What house is this?*'

" 'I will never sign. *I do not know.*'

" 'You are not doing her any service. *What is your name?*'

" 'Let me hear her say so. *Karatides.*'

" 'You shall see her if you sign. *Where are you from?*'

" 'Then I shall never see her. *Athens.*'

"At that instant a door opened and a woman stepped into the room. 'Harold!' she cried, speaking English with a broken accent. 'I could not stay away any longer. It is so lonely up there—oh, my God, it is Paul!' These last words were in Greek, and at the same instant the man, with a convulsive effort, tore the plaster from his lips and screamed out, 'Sophy! Sophy!'

"The younger man seized the woman and pushed her out of the room, while the elder easily overpowered his emaciated victim, and dragged him away through the other door. Soon the older man returned.

" 'Here are five sovereigns,' he said to me, 'which I hope will be a sufficient fee. But if you speak to a single human soul about this —well, may God have mercy upon your own soul!'

"I was hurried through the hall and into the carriage, Mr. Latimer following closely at my heels. In silence we drove for an interminable distance, with the windows raised, until at last, just after midnight, the carriage pulled up. I was pushed out, and the carriage rattled away. I was on Wandsworth Common. By walking a mile or so to Clapham Junction, I caught a train to town. So that was the end of my adventure, Mr. Holmes. I told the whole story to Mr. Mycroft the next morning, and, subsequently, to the police."

Sherlock Holmes looked across at his brother. "Any steps?" he asked.

Mycroft Holmes picked up the *Daily News*, which was lying on a side table.

" 'Anybody supplying any information as to the whereabouts

of a Greek gentleman named Paul Karatides, from Athens, who is unable to speak English, will be rewarded,' " he read. " 'A similar reward paid to anyone giving information about a Greek lady whose first name is Sophy. X2473.' I placed that in all the dailies. No answer. Will you take up the case, Sherlock?"

"Certainly," Sherlock Holmes said, rising from his chair. "Be on your guard, Mr. Melas. They must of course know through these advertisements that you have betrayed them."

Back at Baker Street, Holmes ascended the stairs first, and as he opened the sitting-room door, he gave a start of surprise. Looking over his shoulder, Watson was equally astonished. Mycroft Holmes was sitting smoking in an armchair.

"Come in, Sherlock! Come in, sir!" he cried blandly. "You don't expect such energy of me, do you, Sherlock? But somehow this case attracts me."

"How did you get here?"

"While you walked, I passed you in a hansom."

"There has been some new development?"

"You had hardly left when I had an answer to my advertisement."

"And to what effect?"

"See for yourself. Here it is. It is written with a J pen on royal cream paper—"

"—by a middle-aged man—"

"—with a weak constitution. 'Sir,' he says, 'in answer to your advertisement, I beg to inform you that I know the young lady in question well. If you should care to call upon me, I could give you some particulars as to her painful history. She is living at the present time at The Myrtles, Beckenham. Yours faithfully, J. Davenport.' He writes from Lower Brixton. Do you not think that we might drive to him now, Sherlock, and learn these particulars?"

"My dear Mycroft, the brother's life is more valuable than the sister's story. I think we should call at Scotland Yard for Inspector Gregson, and go straight out to Beckenham."

"We had better pick up Mr. Melas on our way," Watson suggested. "We may need an interpreter."

"Excellent, Watson!" said Sherlock Holmes. "Send the page

boy for a four-wheeler, and we shall be off at once." He opened the table drawer as he spoke, and Watson noticed that he took from it, not the hair-trigger which he used for target practice, but his Webley.[2] "Yes," he said in answer to Watson's glance. "I should say from what we have heard that we are dealing with a particularly dangerous gang."

It was almost dark before they found themselves in Pall Mall, at the rooms of Mr. Melas. A gentleman had just called for him, and he was gone.

"Can you tell me where?" Mycroft Holmes asked the landlady.

"I don't know, sir. I only know that he drove away with the gentleman in a carriage."

"Quickly, Mycroft!" Sherlock Holmes cried. "Along with you! This grows serious!"

But it was more than an hour later before they could get Inspector Gregson to comply with the formalities which would enable them, legally, to enter the house. It was a quarter to ten before they had reached London Bridge Station, and half-past before the four of them alighted on Beckenham platform. With Sherlock Holmes still fuming at the regularities which had delayed them, they drove for half an hour to The Myrtles—a large, dark house, standing well back from the road in its own grounds.

"Our birds are flown and the nest is empty!" Sherlock Holmes growled to Gregson.

"Why do you say so?" the Inspector asked.

"Look at the drive, Gregson! A carriage, heavily loaded, has passed out during the last hour."

"I see the wheel tracks in the light of the gate lamp," Gregson agreed, "but where does the luggage come in?"

"You fail to observe the same wheel tracks going the other way," Mycroft Holmes explained. "The outward-bound ones are very much deeper—so much so that Sherlock can say with certainty that there was a very considerable weight on the carriage."

"You get a trifle beyond me there," Gregson said, shrugging his shoulders. He pounded loudly at the knocker and pulled at the

[2] Holmes's revolver was the Metropolitan Police Model with its short 2½" barrel.

bell, with no success. Sherlock Holmes had slipped away, but he came back in a very few minutes.

"I have a window open," he said.

"It is a mercy that you are on the side of the force, and not against it, Mr. Holmes," Gregson said, as he noticed the clever way in which the detective had slipped back the catch. "Well, I think that, under the circumstances, we may enter."

One after the other they made their way into a large apartment, the heavy Mycroft Holmes not without some difficulty. A low, moaning sound was coming from somewhere above their heads. Sherlock Holmes rushed to the door and out into the hall. He dashed up the stairs, Gregson and Watson at his heels, while his brother Mycroft followed as quickly as his vast bulk would permit.

Three doors faced them upon the floor above, and it was from the central of these that the sinister sounds were issuing. The door was locked, but the key was on the outside. Sherlock Holmes flung open the door and rushed in, but he was out again in an instant with his hand to his throat.

"It's charcoal!" he cried. "Give it time! It will clear."

Peering in, they could see two figures crouched against the wall. With a rush they got the poisoned men and dragged them to the landing. One was the Greek interpreter, the other was a tall young man in the last stage of emaciation. A glance showed Watson that, for the tall man, help had come too late. Mr. Melas, however, still lived, and in less than an hour, with the aid of ammonia and brandy, Watson had the satisfaction of seeing him open his eyes.

By communicating with the gentleman who had answered Mycroft Holmes's advertisement, Sherlock Holmes soon learned that the unfortunate young lady came of a wealthy Grecian family. While on a visit to friends in England, she had met a young man named Harold Latimer, who eventually persuaded her to fly with him. Her friends, shocked at the event, at once informed her brother in Athens. Imprudently, on his arrival in England, the brother had placed himself in the power of Latimer and of his associate, whose name was Wilson Kemp—a man of the foulest antecedents. These two had kept him a prisoner, and had tried, by cruelty and starvation, to make him sign away his own and his sister's property. They had kept him in the house without the girl's knowledge, and with plaster over his face to make recognition difficult should she ever catch a glimpse of him. . . .

Months later, a curious newspaper cutting reached Holmes from Budapest. It told how two Englishmen who had been traveling with a woman had met with a tragic end. They had been stabbed, it seemed, and the Hungarian police were of the opinion that they had quarreled and had inflicted mortal injuries upon each other.

Sherlock Holmes, however, was of a different way of thinking.

"If one could find the Grecian girl," he said to Watson, "one might learn how the wrongs of herself and her brother came to be avenged. And how did Wilson Kemp come to associate himself with Latimer? I sense behind these crimes another hand at work."

"Professor James Moriarty?" Watson asked softly.

"The Napoleon of Crime himself, Watson," Holmes nodded. "But I have said before and I will say again: Our day will surely come."

XII. THE SIGN OF THE FOUR: TUESDAY, SEPTEMBER 18– FRIDAY, SEPTEMBER 21, 1888

"There is something devilish in this, Watson."
SHERLOCK HOLMES.

"Which is it today?" Watson asked. "Morphine or cocaine?"

Holmes raised his eyes languidly from the old black-letter volume. "It is cocaine," he said. "A seven-per-cent solution."

"But consider!" Watson said earnestly. "Count the cost! Why should you, for a mere passing pleasure, risk the loss of those great powers with which you have been endowed? Remember that I speak not only as one friend to another, but as a medical man."

Holmes did not seem to be offended. On the contrary, he put his finger tips together and leaned his elbows on the arms of his chair, like one who has a relish for conversation.

"My mind," he said, "rebels at stagnation. Give me a problem to work on, give me the most abstruse cryptogram or the most intricate analysis, and I am in my proper atmosphere. I can dispense then with artificial stimulants. But I abhor the dull routine of existence. I crave for mental exaltation. That is why I have chosen my own particular profession—or, rather, created it, for I am the only unofficial consulting detective in the world."

Watson, shaking his head, rose from his armchair and limped[1]

[1] Watson's account of the *Study in Scarlet* makes it clear that he was struck at the battle of Maiwand by a jezail bullet that wounded his *left shoulder*. Yet, in his account of *The Sign of the Four*, he tells us that he sat nursing his wounded *leg*. "I had had a jezail bullet through it some time before, and though it did not prevent me from walking it ached wearily at every change in the weather."

While Sherlockian commentators have suggested dozens of explanations for to the window. "It is a pity," he said, "that you have no professional inquiry on foot at present."

Holmes nodded his agreement. "Yes," he said, "I cannot live without brainwork. What else is there to live for? What is the use of having powers, Watson, when one has no field upon which to exert them? Oh, crime is commonplace and existence is commonplace, and no qualities save those which are commonplace have any function upon this earth!"

Watson had opened his mouth to reply to this tirade when, with a crisp knock, Mrs. Hudson entered, bearing a card upon a brass salver.

"A young lady to see you, sir," the landlady said, presenting the salver to Holmes."

" 'Miss Mary Morstan,' " the detective read. "I have no recollection of the name. Ask the young lady to step up, Mrs. Hudson. No, don't go, Watson. I prefer that you remain."

Miss Morstan was a blonde young lady, small, dainty, well gloved, and dressed in the most perfect taste. Her dress was a quiet grayish beige, untrimmed and unbraided, and she wore a small turban of the same dull color, relieved only by a suspicion of white feather on the side.

"Her face had neither regularity of feature nor beauty of complexion," Watson wrote, "but her expression was sweet and amiable, and her large blue eyes were singularly spiritual and sympathetic. . . ."

"I have come to you, Mr. Holmes," Miss Morstan said, "because you once enabled my employer, Mrs. Cecil Forrester, to unravel a little domestic complication. She was much impressed by your kindness and skill."

Watson's seeming confusion, many students of the canon now believe that Watson sustained a *second* wound—in the leg—late in April or early in May 1888. Almost certainly Watson suffered this second wound while assisting Holmes on a case. It is of course curious that the doctor should have been wounded twice by a jezail bullet—that is, by a bullet fired from a long and heavy musket of the type used in Afghanistan. An explanation of Watson's second wound which is quite new to this writer has recently been submitted by one who wishes to remain anonymous. "May it not have been of *psychosomatic* origin?" this correspondent asks. "For some . . . reason [Watson may have been] inhibited from running after Holmes at this time and by a *phenemenon of transference* [have] put the blame on the old jezail bullet. . . . Unimaginative men like Watson are often more susceptible to nervous disorders than is generally recognized."

"Mrs. Cecil Forrester," Holmes replied thoughtfully. "I believe that I was of some slight service to her. But the case, as I remember it, was a very simple one."

"At least you cannot say the same of mine. I can hardly imagine anything more strange, more utterly inexplicable, than the situation in which I find myself."

Holmes rubbed his hands, and his gray eyes glistened. He leaned forward in his chair with an expression of extraordinary concentration upon his clear-cut, hawklike features. "State your case," he said, in brisk, businesslike tones.

The facts were these:

In December of the year 1878, the motherless Mary Morstan, at a boarding establishment in Edinburgh, had received a telegram from her father, an officer in the 34th Bombay Infantry. Captain Morstan had arrived home on leave, and he desired his daughter to join him at once at the Langham Hotel in London.[2] On reaching the Langham, Mary was told that her father had gone out on the night before and had not yet returned; no word was ever heard of him again. Four years later—upon the fourth of May 1882—an advertisement appeared in the *Times* asking for the address of Miss Mary Morstan. Mary, on the advice of Mrs. Forrester, had published her address in the "agony" column. The same day there arrived in her mail a cardboard box containing a large and lustrous pearl.

"Since then," she concluded, "every year upon the same date there has always appeared a similar box, containing a similar pearl, without any clue to the sender."

"Your statement is most interesting," Holmes said.

"I should also show you this," Miss Morstan continued. "It was found in my father's desk."

She handed Holmes a curious paper.

"It is of native Indian manufacture," Holmes remarked. "It has at some time been pinned to a board. The diagram upon it appears to be part of a plan of a large building with numerous

[2] Captain Morstan chose well. The Langham Hotel, today used as offices, was magnificent in 1878. A building seven stories high, covering an acre of ground, at the southern end of Portland Place, it contained more than six hundred rooms and apartments. There was an entrance hall fifty feet square, a dining room one hundred feet long and forty feet wide, a spacious winter garden. Completed in 1865, The Langham was thirteen years old at the time of Captain Morstan's visit.

halls, corridors, and passages. At one point is a small cross done in red ink, and above it is '3–37 from left,' in faded pencil writing. In the left-hand corner is a curious hieroglyphic like four crosses in a line with their arms touching. Beside it is written, in very rough and coarse characters, 'The sign of the four—Jonathan Small, Mahomet Singh, Abdullah Khan, Dost Akbar.'[3] It is evidently a document of importance. It has been kept carefully in a pocketbook, for the one side is as clean as the other. Preserve it carefully, then, Miss Morstan, for it may prove to be of use to us. Now, has anything else occurred?"

"Yes, and no later than today. That is why I am here. This morning, I received this letter."

" 'Be at the third pillar from the left outside the Lyceum Theatre tonight at seven o'clock,' " Holmes read aloud. " 'If you are distrustful, bring two friends. You are a wronged woman, and shall have justice . . .' "

"Well! The three of us shall most certainly go. Dr. Watson and I shall look for you here at six."

At the Lyceum Theatre the crowds were thick at the side entrances. In front a continuous stream of hansoms and four-wheelers came and went, discharging their passengers.[4]

Holmes, Watson, and Mary Morstan had hardly reached the third pillar when a small, dark, brisk man in the dress of a coachman asked their names. On being assured that neither Holmes nor Watson was a police officer, he led them to a four-wheeler, ushered them in, and himself mounted to the box. They plunged at a furious pace through the foggy streets. Watson soon lost his bearings, but Holmes muttered the names of the streets as the cab rattled through squares and in and out of tortuous byways.

---

[3] Watson later tells us—repeatedly—that Abdullah Khan, Dost Akbar and Mahomet Singh were *Sikhs.* As one who had served in the second Afghan war, Watson of course knew very well that the first and second of these names are Mohammedan, the third a bizarre Mohammedan-Sikh combination. Once again, in reporting this case, the doctor decided to be discreet.

[4] Holmes the ex-actor would surely have noticed that Sir Henry Irving and his co-star, Miss Ellen Terry, were playing Shakespeare there that night. And Holmes the detective and his good friend the doctor would surely be found in seats in the Lyceum Theatre on the night of September 2, 1901. For it was there and then that the play *Sherlock Holmes,* written by William Gillette and starred in by him, was first performed in London.

"Rochester Row," Holmes said. "Now Vincent Square. Now we come out on the Vauxhall Bridge Road. We are making for the Surrey side apparently. Yes, I thought so. Now we are on the bridge. You can catch glimpses of the water."

The labyrinth of streets through which they were now driving was familiar country to Holmes. Here he had lived and gone to school as a boy of ten.

"Wordsworth Road," he continued.[5] "Priory Road. Lark Hall Lane. Stockwell Place. Robert Street.[6] Cold Harbor Lane. Our quest does not appear to take us to very fashionable regions."

At last the cab drew up—at the third house in a new terrace. They knocked at the door, which was at once thrown open by a Hindu servant clad in a yellow turban, white, loose-fitting clothes, and a yellow sash.

"The sahib awaits you," he said, and even as he spoke there came a high, piping voice from some inner room. "Show them in to me, *khitmutgar*,"[7] it cried. "Show them straight in to me."

They followed the servant down a passage, ill lit and worse furnished, until they came to a door upon the right. There stood a small man with a very high forehead, a bristle of red hair, and a bald, shining scalp. He writhed his hands together as he stood, and his features were now smiling, now scowling, but never for an instant in repose.

"Your servant, Miss Morstan," he kept repeating in a thin, high voice. "Your servant, gentlemen. Mr. Thaddeus Sholto, that is my name."

[5] So reads Watson's account. But Wordsworth Road is miles away in another direction. What Holmes of course really muttered was *Wandsworth Road;* Watson, who had no personal knowledge of the area, misunderstood him.

[6] One of the earliest of Sherlockian commentators was the late Harold Wilmerding Bell (1885–1947). Certainly he was also one of the most perspicacious. In his "Three Identifications" (in *Profile by Gaslight*) he wrote (p. 286, Note 3): "The mention of this street is not without interest. On 30 April, 1880, it was combined with Park Street to form Robsart Street, of which it forms the eastern end. For Holmes to have recognized it by night and in a fog, and to have called it by a name which it had not borne in . . . years . . . indicates that at some period, before meeting Watson, he must have had an intimate knowledge of the district."

[7] In Hindu and Persian, a male servant.

"This is Mr. Sherlock Holmes, and this Dr. Watson."

"A doctor, eh!" he cried, much excited. "Have you your stethoscope? Might I ask you—would you have the kindness? I have grave doubts as to my mitral valve. The aortic I may rely on, but I should value your opinion upon my mitral."

Watson listened to his heart as requested. "It seems to be normal," he said. "You have no cause for uneasiness."

"You will excuse my anxiety, Miss Morstan," he remarked. "Had your father refrained from throwing a strain upon his heart, he might have been alive now."

Miss Morstan sat down, and her face grew white to the lips. "I knew in my heart that he was dead," she said.

"I can give you every information," Thaddeus Sholto said. "And what is more, I can do you justice. I will, too, whatever brother Bartholomew may say. We shall certainly have to go to Norwood and see him."

"If we are to go to Norwood, it would perhaps be as well to start at once."

"Oh, that would hardly do!" Thaddeus Sholto cried. "I must prepare you first by showing you how we all stand to each other."

Thaddeus Sholto, he explained to them, was the son of Major John Sholto, once of the Indian Army. The major had retired some eleven years before, and gone to live at Pondicherry Lodge, in Upper Norwood. Major Sholto had been a friend of Captain Morstan—Thaddeus and his twin brother, Bartholomew, knew this, and were shocked when they read in the papers of the disappearance of Captain Morstan.

"Never did we suspect," he said, "that my father had the whole secret hidden in his breast—that of all men he alone knew the fate of Arthur Morstan."

They did know, however, that some danger overhung their father. He was very fearful of going out alone. He employed two prize fighters to act as porters at his lodge. He also had a most marked aversion to men with wooden legs. Then, early in 1882, Major Sholto received a letter from India which was a great shock to him. He sickened, and towards the end of April his sons were told that the major, beyond all hope, wished to make a last communication to them.

"I have one thing," the father said, "that weighs heavily upon my mind. It is my treatment of poor Morstan's orphan. Half at least of the great Agra treasure should have been hers. But send her nothing until I am gone. Now I will tell you how poor Morstan died. He had suffered for years with a weak heart, but I alone knew it. When in India, he and I, through a remarkable chain of circumstances, came into possession of a considerable treasure. I brought it to England, and on the night of Morstan's arrival he came straight here to claim his share. Morstan and I had a difference of opinion as to the division of the treasure, and we came to heated words. Morstan sprang out of his chair in a paroxysm of anger, when he suddenly pressed his hand to his side, his face turned a dusky hue, and he fell backward. When I stooped over him I found, to my horror, that he was dead. An official inquiry could not be made without bringing out some facts about the treasure which I was particularly anxious to keep secret. My servant and I disposed of the body in the night, and within a few days the papers were full of the mysterious disappearance. Now I wish to make some retribution. The treasure is hidden in—"

At this moment a horrible change came over his expression. His eyes stared wildly, his jaw dropped, and he screamed: "Keep him out! For Christ's sake, boys, keep him out!"

Thaddeus and Bartholomew stared round at the window behind them. Looking in at them out of the darkness was a bearded face with wild, cruel eyes and an expression of concentrated malevolence. They rushed toward the window, but the man was gone. When they returned to their father his pulse had ceased to beat.

They searched the garden that night, but found no sign of the intruder, save just under the window a single footmark. Soon, however, they had another proof that secret agencies were at work. In the morning the window of their father's room was found open, his cupboards and boxes rifled, and upon his chest a piece of paper with the words "The sign of the four" scrawled across it.

For weeks and months after this, the brothers dug in every part of the garden without discovering the treasure. But their father before his death had shown them a chaplet of pearls, and one of these pearls Thaddeus Sholto had sent to Mary Morstan every fourth of May since 1882.

"Yesterday," Thaddeus Sholto concluded, "I learned that an event of extreme importance has occurred. The treasure has been discovered. I hastily communicated with Miss Morstan, and it only remains for us to drive to Norwood and demand our share."

Pondicherry Lodge stood in its own grounds, surrounded by a high stone wall topped by broken glass. A single narrow iron-clamped door was the only means of entrance. On this Thaddeus Sholto knocked.

The door swung heavily back, and a short, deep-chested man stood in the doorway.

"Mr. Thaddeus?" said the man in a gruff voice. "But who are the others? I had no orders about them."

"No, McMurdo? You surprise me. I told my brother last night that I should bring visitors with me."

"He hain't been out of his rooms today, and I have no orders. I can let you in, Mr. Thaddeus, but your friends must stop where they are. I don't know none of them."

"Oh, yes, you do, McMurdo," said Sherlock Holmes. "I don't think you can have forgotten me. Don't you remember the amateur who fought three rounds with you at Alison's rooms on the night of your benefit?"

"Not Mr. Sherlock Holmes!" roared the prize fighter. "God's truth! If instead o' standin' there so quiet you had just stepped up and given me that cross-hit of yours under the jaw, I'd ha' known you without a question. Ah, you're the one that has wasted your gifts, you have! You might have aimed high, had you joined the fancy."

Holmes smiled. "You won't keep us out in the cold now, I'm sure," he said.

"In you come, sir, in you come," McMurdo answered.

"That is Bartholomew's window up there where the moonlight strikes," said Thaddeus Sholto. "There is no light from within, I think. But hush! What is that?"

From the great black house there sounded through the silent night the shrill, broken whimpering of a frightened woman.

"It is Mrs. Bernstone, the housekeeper," Thaddeus Sholto

said. He hurried for the door and knocked. They could see a tall old woman admit him. In a moment the door of the house burst open, and Thaddeus Sholto came running out, his hands thrown forward and terror in his eyes.

"There is something amiss with Bartholomew!" he cried.

"Come into the house," Holmes said in his crisp, firm, quiet way. He took the lamp and led the way up the stairs. The third flight ended in a straight passage, with three doors on the left. The third—that of Bartholomew Sholto's room—was locked on the inside. Holmes bent down to the keyhole, then instantly rose with a sharp intake of his breath.

"What do you make of it, Watson?" he said.

Watson stooped to the keyhole, and recoiled in horror. Moonlight was streaming into the room, and by it Watson could see a face with the same high, shining forehead, the same bristle of red hair, the same bloodless countenance of their companion, Thaddeus Sholto. Watson had forgotten, for the moment, that the two brothers were twins.

"This is terrible!" Watson said, as he stared at the features of the man in the room—features fixed in a horrid, unnatural grin. "What is to be done?"

"The door must come down," Holmes answered, and he put all his weight against it.

Bartholomew Sholto had been dead for many hours. By his hand upon the table there lay a peculiar instrument—a brown, close-grained stick, with a stone head like a hammer, rudely lashed on with coarse twine. Beside it was a sheet of note paper with some words scrawled upon it. Holmes glanced at it, then handed it to Watson.

"'The sign of the four,'" Watson said. "In God's name, Holmes, what does it all mean?"

"It means murder," Holmes said. He pointed to what looked like a long, dark thorn stuck in the skin just above the ear.

They had almost forgotten Thaddeus Sholto's presence. Suddenly, however, he broke into a sharp cry.

"The treasure is gone!" he screamed. "There is the hole in the ceiling through which we lowered it from the secret garret!"

"You must report this matter to the police at once," Holmes said. "Dr. Watson and I shall wait here until you return."

"Now, Watson," Holmes said, rubbing his hands together briskly, "we have half an hour to ourselves. Let us make good use of it. Just sit in the corner there, that your footprints may not complicate matters. Now, in the first place, how did these folks come and how did they go? The door has not been opened since Bartholomew Sholto locked it last night. What of the window? Snibbed on the inner side. No side hinges. Let us open it. No water pipe near. Roof quite out of reach. Yet a man has mounted by the window. It rained a little last night, and here is the print of a foot in mold upon the sill. And here is a circular muddy mark, and here again upon the floor, and here again by the table."

Watson looked at the round, well-defined, muddy discs. "This is not a footmark," he said.

"No, it is the impression of a wooden leg. But there has been someone else here, too. Could you scale that wall, doctor?"

"It is absolutely impossible," Watson said.

"Without aid it is so. But suppose you had a friend up here who lowered you this good, stout rope which I see in the corner, securing one end of it to this great hook in the wall? Then, I think, if you were an active man, you might swarm up, wooden leg and all. You would depart in the same fashion, and your ally would draw up the rope, untie it from the hook, shut the window, snib it on the inside, and get away as he had originally come."

"This is all very well," Watson said. "But how came the ally into the room? By the chimney?"

"The grate is much too small," Holmes answered. "You will not apply my precept. How often have I said to you that when you have eliminated the impossible, whatever remains, *however improbable,* must be the truth?"

"He came through the hole in the ceiling!" Watson cried.

"Of course he did. Now, if you will have the kindness to hold the lamp for me, we shall extend our researches to the secret room above in which the treasure was found."

He mounted the stepladder which stood in a corner of the room, and, seizing a rafter with either hand, he swung himself up into the garret. Then, lying on his face, he reached down for the lamp and held it while Watson followed him.

"Here you are, you see," said Sherlock Holmes. "A trapdoor

which leads out onto the roof. I press it back, and here is the roof itself." He held the lamp to the floor beneath the trapdoor, and they saw that it was covered thickly with the prints of a naked foot—clear, well defined, perfectly formed—but scarcely half the size of those of an ordinary man.

"Holmes," Watson said in a whisper, "a child has done this horrid thing."

"I think that there is nothing else of importance here, but I will look," Holmes said, when they had regained the lower room, which Bartholomew Sholto had fitted up as a chemical laboratory. Suddenly be broke into a loud crow of delight.

"We are in luck," he said. "You see this carboy? It has been cracked, and some of the creosote it contained has leaked out. The mysterious ally had the misfortune to tread in it."

"What then?" Watson asked.

"Why, we've got him, that's all," Holmes said. "I know a dog that would follow the scent of creosote to the end of the world. But hello! These must be the representatives of the law."

Heavy steps and the clamor of loud voices were heard from below, and the hall door shut with a loud crash. A moment later a large man in a gray suit strode heavily into the room. He was red-faced and burly, with a pair of very small eyes which looked out from between swollen and puffy pouches.

"I think you must remember me, Mr. Athelney Jones," Holmes said quietly.

"Why, of course I do!" the newcomer cried in a muffled, husky voice. "It's Mr. Sherlock Holmes, the theorist. Remember you! I'll never forget how you lectured us all at the Yard on causes and inferences and effects in the Bishopsgate jewel case. It's true that you set us on the right track, but you'll own now that it was more by good luck than good guidance."

"It was a piece of very simple reasoning."

"Oh, come now. Never be ashamed to own up. But what is all this? Bad business! Bad business! Stern facts here—no room for theories." With great agility, considering his bulk, he sprang up the stepladder and squeezed himself into the garret. Imme-diately afterward they heard his voice proclaiming that he had found the trap door to the roof.

"He can find something, at any rate," Holmes admitted,

shrugging his lean shoulders. "*Il n'y a pas des sots si incommodes que ceux qui ont de l'esprit!*"[8]

"You see," said Athelney Jones, reappearing down the steps again, "facts are better than mere theories after all. My view of the case is confirmed. Mr. Sholto, it is my duty to inform you that anything which you may say may be taken down and used in evidence. I arrest you in the Queen's name as being concerned in the death of your brother."

"Don't trouble yourself about it, Mr. Sholto," said Holmes quickly. "I think I can clear you of the charge."

"Don't promise too much, Mr. Theorist, don't promise too much!" sneered the man from Scotland Yard.

"Not only will I clear him, Mr. Jones," Holmes returned, "but I will make you a free present of the name and description of one of the two people who were in this room last night. His name, I have every reason to believe, is Jonathan Small. He is a poorly educated man, small, active, with his right leg off, and wearing a wooden stump which is worn away upon the inner side. His left boot has a coarse, square-toed sole, with an iron band around the heel. He is a middle-aged man, much sunburned, and has been a convict. These few indications may be of some assistance to you, coupled with the fact that there is a good deal of skin missing from the palm of his hand. The other man—"

"Ah, the other man—" asked Athelney Jones.

"—is a rather curious person," Sherlock Holmes finished, turning upon his heel. "I hope before so very long to be able to introduce you to the pair of them. A word with you, Watson."

At the head of the stair, Holmes said: "You must escort Miss Morstan home. It is not right that she should remain here. When you have dropped her in Lower Camberwell, I want you to go on to No. 3 Pinchin Lane, down near the water's edge at Lambeth. The third house on the right-hand side is both the home and workshop of a very old friend of mine—a bird stuffer, Sherman by name. You will see a weasel holding a young rabbit mounted in his bow window. Knock old Sherman up, and tell him, with

8 This is number 451 of *Les Maximes* of François Duc de La Rochefoucauld (1613–80). Holmes made one minor change which does not affect the meaning; the original has *point* insteal of *pas*. The usual translation is, "There are no fools so troublesome as those who have some wit."

my compliments, that Mr. Sherlock wants to borrow Toby at once. You will bring Toby back in the cab with you."

"A dog, I suppose."

"Yes—a queer mongrel, with a most amazing power of scent. I would rather have Toby's help in this case than that of the whole detective force of London."

"I shall bring him, then," Watson said. "It is one now. I ought to be back before three, if I can get a fresh horse."

"And I," said Sherlock Holmes, "I shall study the great Jones and his methods and listen to his not too delicate sarcasms. '*Wir sind gewohnt dass die Menschen verhöhnen was sie nicht verstehen.*' Goethe is always pithy."[9]

It had just struck three when Watson found himself back at Pondicherry Lodge. Holmes was standing on the doorstep with his hands in his pockets, smoking his pipe.

"Ah, you have him there!" he cried. "Good dog, Toby! Athelney Jones has gone. He has arrested not only friend Thaddeus, but the gatekeeper, the housekeeper, and the Indian servant. Now, are you game for a six-mile trudge, Watson?"

"Certainly," Watson answered.

"Your leg will stand it?"

"Oh yes."

"Then here you are, Toby! Smell it, boy, smell it!" Holmes pushed a handkerchief soaked in creosote under the dog's nose. Then he fastened a stout cord to the mongrel's collar and led him to the foot of a water barrel which stood against the side of the house. "With this, and the waterpipe," Holmes said, "the mysterious ally ascended to the roof." The dog had caught again the scent of creosote in which the ally had stepped, and with his nose to the ground and his tail in the air he pattered off upon the trail at a pace which strained at his leash. On reaching the boundary wall, Toby ran along, whining eagerly, underneath its shadow, and stopped finally in a corner screened by a young beech. Holmes clambered up the wall, and, taking the dog from Watson, he dropped it over upon the other side.

[9] The quotation is taken from *Faust*, Part I, and is found in the monologue by Faust when he addresses the Poodle in the Study-Room. Bayard Taylor's translation is, "We are used to see that Man despises what he never comprehends."

"There's the print of wooden-leg's hand," he remarked as Watson mounted beside him.

Across the wall, Toby never hesitated or swerved, but waddled on in his peculiar rolling fashion. They were beginning to come now among streets where laborers and dockmen were already astir, and slatternly women were taking down shutters and brushing doorsteps. At the square-topped corner public houses business was just beginning, and rough-looking men were emerging, rubbing their sleeves across their beards after the morning's first drink. Strange dogs sauntered up and stared wonderingly as they passed, but Toby looked neither to the right nor left. With his nose to the ground and an occasional eager whine, which spoke of a hot scent, he trotted on—across Streatham, Brixton, Camberwell, and then into Kennington Lane. They turned now through Belmont Place and Prince's Street, but at the end of Broad Street the trail ran right down to the water's edge, where there was a small wooden wharf. Toby took them to the very edge of this, and there the dog stood, whining.

"We are out of luck," said Holmes. "Here they took to a boat."

Close to the wharf was a small brick house, with a wooden placard slung through a window. "Mordecai Smith" was printed across it in large letters, and, underneath, "Boats to hire by the hour or day." At this moment the door of the house opened, and a little, curly-haired lad of six came running out.

"Dear little chap!" Holmes said strategically. "Is there anything you would like to have?"

"I'd like a shillin'," the boy said.

"Nothing better?"

The boy thought a moment. "I'd like two shillin' better," he said at last.

"Here you are, then! Catch!" said Holmes. "A fine child, Mrs. Smith," he continued, turning to a stoutish, red-faced woman who had appeared in the doorway.

"Lor' bless you, sir, he is that. Almost too much to manage, when my man is away for days at a time."

"Away now, is he?" Holmes asked.

"Since yesterday morning."

Holmes glanced at a great pile of coke upon the jetty. "I

wanted to hire his steam launch," he said.

"Why, bless you, sir, it's in the steam launch he has gone. And that puzzles me, for there weren't more coals in her than would take her to Woolwich and back. Besides, I don't like that wooden-legged chap, wi' his ugly face and his outlandish talk."

"A wooden-legged man?" said Holmes blandly.

"Yes, sir, a brown, monkey-faced chap that's called more'n once on my old man. It was him that roused him up yesternight. He tapped at the winder—about three it would be. 'Show a leg, matey,' says he, 'time to turn out the guard.' My old man woke up Jim—that's my eldest—and away they went."

"I am sorry, Mrs. Smith, for I wanted a steam launch, and I have had good reports of the—let me see, what is her name?"

"The *Aurora*, sir."

"Ah, yes—the *Aurora*. She's the green launch, with a yellow line, very broad in the beam."

"Oh, no, indeed, sir. She's a trim little thing, fresh-painted black with two red streaks."

"Oh, of course," said Holmes. "Well, a very good morning, Mrs. Smith."

A bath at Baker Street and a complete change freshened both Holmes and Watson wonderfully.

When Watson came into the sitting room, he found the breakfast laid and Holmes already pouring out coffee. At this moment there was a loud ring at the bell, and they heard the voice of Mrs. Hudson, the landlady, wailing in dismay.

"Good heavens, Holmes," said Watson, half rising.

"It is only my unofficial force," Holmes said. "The Baker Street Irregulars again. I wired Wiggins to be with us after breakfast."

As he spoke there came a swift pattering of naked feet upon the stairs, a clatter of high voices, and in rushed a dozen dirty and ragged little street Arabs.

"Got your message, sir," said the lad called Wiggins, taller and older than the others.

"Right," said Holmes. "Now, here's what I want. There's a steam launch called the *Aurora*, owner Mordecai Smith, black she is, with two red streaks, down the river somewhere. You must find her. The old scale of pay, plus a guinea to the boy who spies her first. All clear?" He handed them each a shilling, and away they buzzed down the stairs.

"If the launch is above water, they will find her," Holmes said. And he took up his violin from the corner.

Not a word came from Wiggins on the Wednesday afternoon nor all day Thursday.

At breakfast on the Thursday morning, Holmes looked worn and haggard, with a little fleck of feverish color upon each cheek. Up to the early hours of the next morning, Watson could hear the clinking of test tubes, as the detective busied himself with some abstruse chemical analysis. In the early dawn, the doctor woke with a start and found Holmes standing by his bedside, wearing a rude sailor dress, with a pea jacket, and a coarse red scarf around his neck.

"I am off down the river, Watson," he said. "I have been turning it over in my mind, and I can see only one way out of it."

It was a long day.

Late in the afternoon there was a loud peal at the bell, an authoritative voice in the hall, and a few moments later Athelney Jones was shown up.

"I have a telegram from Holmes," he said. "Dated from Poplar at twelve o'clock. 'Go to Baker Street at once. Wait for me. I am close on the track. You can come with us tonight if you want to be in at the finish.' I don't hold with Holmes's methods," the inspector concluded, shaking his head, "but I must admit I never saw a case yet that he could not throw a light upon."

"Your own case has not prospered?" Watson asked.

"It has all come to nothing! I have had to release two of my prisoners, and there is no evidence against the other two."

Holmes returned a short time later.

"Well," he said, when he had heard the inspector's story, "perhaps I shall give you two prisoners in place of the two you have lost. But you must put yourself under my orders. Is that entirely agreed?"

"Entirely, if you will help me to the men."

"Well, then, in the first place I shall want a fast police boat—
a steam launch—to be at the Westminster Stairs at seven o'clock."

"That is easily managed."

"Then I shall want two staunch men, in case of resistance."

"There will be two or three in the boat. What else?"

"Only that I insist upon your dining with us. I have oysters
and a little brace of grouse, with something a little choice in
white wine. Watson, you have never yet recognized my merits
as a housekeeper."

The meal was a merry one. Holmes spoke on a quick succession of subjects—on miracle plays, on medieval pottery, on
Stradivarius violins, on the Buddhism of Ceylon, on the warships
of the future—handling each as though he had made a special
study of it.

When the cloth was cleared, Holmes glanced at his watch,
and filled up three glasses of port. "A bumper," he said, "to the
success of our little expedition. And now it is high time we were
off. Have you a pistol, Watson?"

"I have my old service revolver in my desk."[10]

"You had best take it, then."

It was a little past seven when they reached the Westminster
wharf and found their launch awaiting them.

"Where to?" asked Jones.

"To the Tower," Holmes replied. "Tell them to stop opposite
Jacobson's Yard."

Their craft was a fast one. They shot past the long lines of
loaded barges as though they were stationary. Holmes smiled
with satisfaction.

"I have found the *Aurora*," Holmes said, "and I have learned
that she plans to sail from Jacobson's Yard at eight tonight. One
of my boys is stationed as sentry over her, and will signal us
when she starts."

It was twilight when they reached Jacobson's Yard, a bristle of
masts and rigging on the Surrey side of the Thames.

[10] This would be, as Robert Keith Leavitt has pointed out in "Annie
Oakley in Baker Street," the Adams six-shot caliber .450 breechloader, with
a good, honest six-inch barrel, standard in the British Army in the second
Afghan war. *Cf.* J. N. George, *English Pistols and Revolvers*, Small Arms
Technical Publishing Co., Marines, N.C., 1938.

"Cruise gently up and down under cover of this string of lighters," Holmes said, as he took a pair of night glasses from his pocket.

"There is your boy!" Watson cried suddenly. "I can see him plainly in the gaslight. He is waving a handkerchief."

"And there is the *Aurora!*" Holmes cried. "And going like the devil! Full speed ahead, engineers! Heap it on, stokers!"

The furnaces roared, and the powerful engines whizzed and clanked like a great metallic heart. The sharp, steep prow of the police launch cut through the still river water and sent two great waves rolling to right and left. They flashed past barges, steamers, merchant vessels—through the Pool, past the West India Docks, down the long Deptford Reach, around the Isle of Dogs. The dull blur in front of them resolved itself into the dainty *Aurora*. One man sat by the stern, with something black between his knees. Beside him lay a dark mass which looked to Watson like a Newfoundland dog. The boy Jim Smith held the tiller, while against the red glare of the furnace they could see old Smith, stripped to the waist and shoveling coal for dear life.

Now there were only four boat lengths between the two craft. Jones yelled to the *Aurora* to stop. At his hail the man in the stern sprang up from the deck. Watson could see that he was a good-sized, powerful man, and that from the thigh downward on his right side there was but a wooden stump. Then there was movement in the huddled bundle upon the deck. It straightened itself into a little black man with a great misshapen head, a shock of tangled, disheveled hair, eyes that glowed and burned with a somber light, and thick lips that writhed back from his teeth.

"Fire if he raises his hand," Holmes said quietly.

Even as he spoke, the little black man plucked from under his covering a short, round piece of wood and clapped it to his lips. Holmes and Watson fired together. The little black man whirled around, threw up his arms, and, with a kind of choking cough, fell sideways into the stream. At the same time the wooden-legged man threw himself upon the rudder and put it hard down. The *Aurora* with a dull thud ran upon a mudbank. The one-legged man sprang out, but his stump sank its length into the sodden soil. It was only by throwing a rope over his shoulders that they were able to haul him out and drag him over the side into the police launch, writhing like some evil fish.

Watson has told the strange story of Jonathan Small, and how the one-legged man and the Andaman Islander, Tonga, recovered the great Agra treasure, only to send it to the bottom of the Thames when it seemed certain that the police launch would catch the *Aurora*.

Whoever had lost a treasure, Watson had gained one.

"Miss Morstan has done me the honor to accept me as a husband in prospective," he told Holmes as the two sat smoking in the old room at Baker Street.

Holmes raised an eyebrow.

"But, my dear Watson," he said, "it is only nine months since—"

"We will not, of course, be married until spring," Watson said rather stiffly.

"Well, I really cannot congratulate you," Holmes said. "Miss Morstan is one of the most charming young ladies I have ever met, but love is an emotional thing, and whatever is emotional is opposed to that true, cold reason which I place above all things."

It was Watson's turn to raise an eyebrow. He was about to speak, but then he laughed instead.

"Well, I trust that my judgment may survive the ordeal," he said. "But the division seems rather unfair. You have done all the work in this business. I get a wife out of it. Jones gets all the credit—I understand that his position at the Yard is now a very important one. And what remains for you?"

"For me," said Sherlock Holmes, "there still remains this."

And he stretched out his long white hand for the cocaine bottle.

XIII. DR. JAMES MORTIMER AND SIR HENRY BASKERVILLE: TUESDAY, SEPTEMBER 25– SATURDAY, SEPTEMBER 29, 1888

"What do you make of it, Watson?"
SHERLOCK HOLMES.

"I have in my pocket a manuscript," said Dr. James Mortimer.

"I observed it as you entered the room," said Mr. Sherlock Holmes of Baker Street.

Dr. James Mortimer was a very tall, very thin man, with a nose like a beak, which shot out between two keen gray eyes, set closely together and sparkling brightly from behind a pair of gold-rimmed glasses. He was dressed in a professional but rather slovenly manner, for his frock coat was dingy and his trousers frayed. Though young, his long back was already bowed, and he walked with a forward thrust of his head and a general air of peering benevolence. Now he stared at Sherlock Holmes and Dr. Watson from his seat in the basket chair, as he drew a document from his breast pocket with long, quivering fingers.

"It is a family paper," Dr. Mortimer continued, "committed to my care by Sir Charles Baskerville, whose sudden and tragic death some three months ago created so much excitement in Devonshire. I may say that I was his personal friend, as well as his medical adviser."

"It appears to be a statement of some sort," Dr. Watson said.

"Yes," said Dr. Mortimer, "it is a statement of a certain legend which runs in the Baskerville family. At the time of the Great Rebellion, the manor of Baskerville was held by one Hugo, a most wild, profane and godless man. One Michaelmas this Hugo, with five or six idle and wicked companions, carried off a maiden, the daughter of a yeoman, whom they locked in an upper chamber of the hall, while they caroused below. The maiden escaped by climbing down a growth of ivy which covered (and still covers) the south wall of the hall. When Hugo found her gone, he ran from the house, crying to his grooms that they should saddle his mare and unkennel his pack. Giving the hounds a kerchief of the maiden's, he swung them to the line, and so off full cry in the moonlight over the moor.

"The revelers took horse and started in pursuit. They had gone a mile or two when they passed a shepherd, and they cried to him to know if he had seen the hunt. The man was so crazed with fear that he could hardly speak, but at last he said that he had indeed seen the unhappy maiden, with the hounds upon her track. 'But I have seen more than that,' said he, 'for Hugo Baskerville passed me upon his big black mare, and there ran silent behind him such a hound of hell as God forbid should ever be at my heels.'

"The drunken squires cursed the shepherd and rode on. Soon there came a sound of galloping, and the black mare, dabbled with froth, went by them with trailing bridle and empty saddle. Then they came upon the hounds, whimpering in a cluster at the head of a dip. The company came to a halt, and three of the boldest rode forward into the dip. There lay the unhappy maid, dead of fear or fatigue. But it was not the sight of her body, nor even that of Hugo Baskerville, which lay near her, that raised the hair upon the heads of those drunken roisterers. It was this: standing over the body of Hugo Baskerville, and plucking at his throat, there stood a great black beast, shaped like a hound, yet larger than any hound that mortal eye had ever rested upon. And even as they looked, the thing tore the throat out of Hugo Baskerville, and then turned its blazing eyes and dripping jaws upon them. The roisterers shrieked out with fear and rode for dear life. One died that very night of what he had seen, and the others were broken men for the rest of their days.

"And that," said Dr. Mortimer, pushing his spectacles up on his forehead, "is the story of the coming of the Hound. Do you not find it interesting?"

"To a collector of fairy tales," Holmes yawned.

Dr. Mortimer drew a folded newspaper out of his pocket.

"Then, Mr. Holmes, we will give you something a little more recent. This is the Devon County *Chronicle*. It gives a short account of the death of Sir Charles Baskerville in June of this year. Sir Charles was in the habit of walking down the famous Yew Alley of Baskerville Hall every night before going to bed. On the 4th of June he went out as usual for his nocturnal walk. He never returned. At twelve o'clock his butler, Barrymore, became alarmed, and, lighting a lantern, he went in search of his master. He found Sir Charles's body at the far end of the Yew Alley, by a gate which leads to the moor. No signs of violence were discovered upon Sir Charles's person."

Dr. Mortimer refolded the paper and replaced it in his pocket.

"Those are all the public facts?" Holmes asked.

"They are."

"Then let us hear the private ones."

"Very well," said Dr. Mortimer. "On the night of Sir Charles's death, Barrymore sent for me. I followed Sir Charles's footprints down the Yew Alley, and I examined the body carefully. Sir Charles lay on his face, his arms out, his fingers dug into the ground, and his features twisted with some strong emotion. There was no physical injury of any kind. Barrymore said at the inquest that there were no traces upon the ground around the body. He did not observe any. But I did—some little distance off, but fresh and clear.

"Footprints?"

"Footprints."

"A man's or a woman's?"

"Mr. Holmes," said Dr. Mortimer, "they were the footprints of a gigantic hound."

Holmes leaned forward, his eyes glittering.

"If I had only been there!" he cried. "To think, Dr. Mortimer, that you did not call me in then. How can I assist you now?"

"By advising me what I should do with Sir Henry Baskerville, who arrives at Waterloo Station in exactly one hour and a quarter."

"He being the heir?"

"Exactly. On the death of Sir Charles we inquired for this young gentleman, and found that he had been farming in Canada."

"Why should he not go to the home of his fathers?"

"It seems natural, does it not? And yet, consider that every Baskerville who goes there meets with an evil fate."

Holmes considered for a time.

"Well," he said at last, "I recommend that you take a cab and proceed to Waterloo Station to meet Sir Henry Baskerville."

"And then?"

"And then you will say nothing to him at all until I have made up my mind about this matter."

"And how long will it take you to make up your mind?"

"Twenty-four hours. At ten o'clock tomorrow, Dr. Mortimer, I will be much obliged if you will call upon me here, and it will be of help to me in my plans for the future if you will bring Sir Henry with you."

Sir Henry Baskerville proved to be a small, alert, dark-eyed man about thirty years of age, very sturdily built, with thick black eyebrows, and a strong, pugnacious face.

"If my friend Dr. Mortimer had not proposed coming round to you this morning," he said to Holmes, "I should have come on my own. I've had a little puzzle this morning which wants more thinking out than I am able to give it."

"Pray take a seat, Sir Henry," Holmes said. "What is this remarkable experience?"

"It was this letter, if you can call it a letter, which reached me at the Northumberland Hotel this morning."

Out of the envelope which Sir Henry handed to him Holmes took a half sheet of foolscap folded into four. " 'As you value your life or your reason keep away from the moor,' " he read. "The sentence has been formed by the expedient of pasting printed words together. Only the word 'moor' is written in ink. These printed words could only have been taken from a *Times* leader and nothing else. The detection of types is one of the most elementary branches of knowledge to the expert in crime, though I confess that once when I was very young I confused the Leeds *Mercury* with the *Western Morning News*. And now, Sir Henry, has anything else of interest happened to you since you have been in London?"

Sir Henry smiled. "I don't know much about British life yet, for I have spent nearly all of my time in the States and Canada. But I hope that to lose one of your boots is not part of the ordinary routine of life over here."

"You have lost one of your boots?"

"Well, mislaid it, anyhow. I bought a new pair of brown boots last night in the Strand. I put them outside my door last night to be varnished, and this morning there was only one."

"Hm," said Holmes. "I suspect that it will not be long before the missing boot is found. And now, Dr. Mortimer, I think you could not do better than to tell your story as you told it to us yesterday."

Sir Henry Baskerville listened with the deepest attention, and with an occasional exclamation of surprise.

"Well," he said, when Dr. Mortimer had finished his narrative, "I seem to have come into an inheritance with a vengeance. But I tell you this, Mr. Holmes. There is no devil in hell, and there is no man upon the earth, who can prevent me from going to the home of my own people. Now I am going back to my hotel. Suppose you and Dr. Watson come round and lunch with us at two?"

They heard the steps of their visitors descend the stair and the bang of the front door. In an instant Holmes changed from the languid dreamer to the man of action.

"Your hat and boots, Watson, quick! There is not a moment to lose!"

They hurried together down the stairs and into the street. Dr. Mortimer and Sir Henry Baskerville were still visible, walking about two hundred yards ahead of them in the direction of Oxford Street. Holmes quickened his pace until he had decreased the distance by half, then, keeping a hundred yards behind, he and Watson followed into Oxford Street and so down Regent Street. Soon Holmes gave a little cry of satisfaction, and, following the direction of his eyes, Watson saw a hansom cab with a man inside.

"There's our man, Watson! Come along! We'll have a good look at him, if we can do no more."

At that instant Watson was aware of a bushy black beard and a pair of piercing eyes turned upon them through the side window of the cab. Instantly the trap door at the top flew up, something was screamed to the driver, and the cab flew madly off down Regent Street. No empty cab was in sight in which Holmes and Watson could follow.

"There now!" said Holmes bitterly. "Was ever such bad luck and such bad management, too? I fear, Watson, that if you are an honest man you will record this also and set it against my successes."

"What a pity that we did not get the number of the cab."

"My dear Watson, clumsy as I have been, you surely do not seriously imagine that I neglected to get the number? 2704 is our man. But that is of no use to us at the moment. Let us drop into one of the Bond Street picture galleries and fill in the time with art until we are due at the hotel."

For two hours Holmes was absorbed in the paintings of the modern Belgian masters, and he would talk of nothing but art as he and Watson walked to the Northumberland Hotel.

As they came around the top of the stairs they encountered Sir Henry Baskerville. His face was flushed with anger, and he held an old and dusty boot in one hand.

"Still looking for your boot?" Holmes asked.

"Yes, sir, and mean to find it."

"But surely you said that it was a new brown boot?"

"So it was, sir. And now it's an old black one."

"What! You don't mean to say—"

"I had only three pairs in the world—the new brown, the old black, and the patent leathers which I am wearing. Last night they took one of the new brown ones, and today they have sneaked one of the old black. Well, Mr. Holmes, you'll excuse me for troubling you about such a trifle—"

"I think it's well worth troubling about," Holmes said thoughtfully.

They had a pleasant luncheon in which little was said of the business which had brought them together, and repaired afterward to a private sitting room.

"What are your intentions, Sir Henry?" Holmes asked.

"To go to Baskerville Hall at the end of the week."

"On the whole, I think your decision is wise. Did you know that you were followed this morning?"

Dr. Mortimer started violently. "Followed! By whom?"

"By a man with a full, black beard. Do you have among your neighbors or acquaintances on Dartmoor such a man?"

"Barrymore, Sir Charles's butler, is a man with a full, black beard."

"Then we had best ascertain if Barrymore is really at Baskerville Hall, and not in London. Give me a telegraph form."

Holmes wrote and dispatched the telegram. Then he turned to Sir Henry again. "Well," he said, "I am agreed that you should go to Devonshire without delay. There is only one provision I must make. You certainly must not go alone."

"Dr. Mortimer returns with me."

"But Dr. Mortimer has his practice to attend to, and his house is miles away from yours. No, Sir Henry, you must take with you a trusty man who will be always at your side."

"Whom would you recommend, then?"

Holmes laid his hand upon Watson's arm.

"If my friend would undertake it, there is no man who is better worth having at your side when you are in a tight place. No one can say that more confidently than I."

"Well," said Sir Henry, "if Dr. Watson will come down to Baskerville Hall and see me through this business I'll never forget it."

"I will come with pleasure," Watson said.

"And you will report very carefully to me," Holmes said. "I must, as you know, remain in London for the present. One of the most revered names in England is being besmirched by a blackmailer, and only I can stop a disastrous scandal."

He and Watson had risen to go, when Sir Henry gave a cry of triumph and, diving into one of the corners of the room, he drew a brown boot from under a cabinet.

"My missing boot!" he cried.

"What a very singular thing," Dr. Mortimer remarked. "I searched this room most carefully, every inch of it, just before lunch."

Holmes sat in silence in the cab as he and Watson drove back to Baker Street. All afternoon and late into the evening he sat lost in tobacco and thought. Just before dinner a telegram was handed in to him by the page boy: "Have just heard that Barrymore is at the Hall. Baskerville."

"We still have the cabman who drove the spy," Watson said.

"Exactly. I have wired to get his name and address from the Official Registry. I should not be surprised if this were an answer to my question."

The door opened and a cabman looked in.

"John Clayton, 3 Turpey Street, the Borough," he said. "Cab No. 2704."

"Ah, Clayton," Holmes said, "tell me all about that fare who came and watched this house at ten o'clock this morning and afterwards followed two gentlemen down Regent Street."

The cabman looked surprised and a little embarrassed.

"Well," he said, "he hailed me at half-past nine in Trafalgar Square. He said he was a detective, and he offered me two guineas if I would do exactly what he wanted all day and ask no questions. First we drove down to the Northumberland Hotel, and waited there until two gentlemen came out and took a cab that we followed until it pulled up somewhere near here. We waited an hour and a half. Then the two gentlemen passed us walking and we followed down Baker Street until we got three-quarters down Regent Street. Then my gentleman threw up the trap and cried that I should drive to Waterloo Station as hard as I could go. I whipped up the mare, and we were there under ten minutes. Then he paid up his two guineas, like a good one, and away he went into the station. Only just as he was leaving he turned around and mentioned his name."

Holmes cast a swift glance of triumph at Watson.

"And what was the name he mentioned?" he cried eagerly.

"His name," said the cabman, "was Mr. Sherlock Holmes."

"The cunning rascal!" Holmes cried. "It's an ugly business, Watson, an ugly, dangerous business, and the more I see of it the less I like it. Yes, my dear fellow, you may laugh, but I give you my word that I shall be very glad to see you back safe and sound in Baker Street once more."

INTERRUPTION. TWO STORIES FROM THE LONDON TIMES: OCTOBER 1 AND 2, 1888

From the London *Times,* Monday, October 1, 1888:

"In the early hours of yesterday morning two more horrible murders were committed in the East End of London, the victim in both cases belonging, it is believed, to the same unfortunate class.[1] No doubt seems to be entertained by the police that these terrible crimes were the work of the same fiendish hands which committed the outrages which had already made Whitechapel so painfully notorious. The scenes of the two murders just brought to light are within a quarter of an hour's walk of each other, the earlier-discovered crime having been committed in a yard in Berner Street, a low thoroughfare out of the Commercial Road, while the second outrage was perpetrated within the city boundary in Mitre Square, Aldgate . . . ."

From the London *Times,* Tuesday, October 2, 1888:

"Two communications of an extraordinary nature, both signed 'Jack the Ripper,' have been received by the Central News Agency, the one on Thursday last and the other yesterday morning. The first was a letter bearing the E.C. postmark in which reference was made to the atrocious murders previously committed in the East End, which the writer confessed in a brutally jocular vein to have committed, stating that in the 'next job' he did he would 'clip the lady's ears off' and send them to the police, and also asking that the letter might be kept back until he had done 'a bit more work.'

---

[1] The victims: Elizabeth Stride and Catherine Eddowes, both streetwalkers.

"The second communication was a postcard and, as above stated, it was received yesterday morning. It bore the date 'London, E. October 1' and was as follows: 'I was not coddling, dear old Boss, when I gave you the tip. You'll hear about Saucy Jacky's work tomorrow. Double event this time. Number One squealed a bit; couldn't finish straight off. Had not time to get ears for police. Thanks for keeping last letter back till I got to work again.' The postcard was sent to Scotland Yard. No doubt is entertained that the writer of both communications, whoever he may be, is the same person. . . ."

XIV. THE HORROR HOUND: SUNDAY, SEPTEMBER 30– SATURDAY, OCTOBER 20, 1888

"I am not sure that of all the five hundred cases of capital importance which I have handled there is one which cuts so deep."

SHERLOCK HOLMES.

From Baskerville Hall in Devonshire, Watson reported faithfully to Holmes in London:

Selden, the Notting Hill murderer, had escaped from Princetown Prison, and was being hunted on the moor.

On his first night in Baskerville Hall, Watson had heard the sobbing of a woman. He noticed, next morning, that the eyes of Mrs. Barrymore, the housekeeper, wife of the Baskerville butler, were red, and that she glanced at him with swollen lids.

Walking on the moor, Watson had met Sir Henry Baskerville's neighbors, John Stapleton, the naturalist, and his charming sister Beryl, of Merripit House.

"Events are now crowding thick and fast upon us," Watson wrote to Holmes on October 15. Watson and Sir Henry had discovered that Selden, the escaped convict, was Mrs. Barrymore's brother. Hunting Selden on the moor, the two men had heard the cry of a hound—strident, wild, and menacing—and Watson had glimpsed the figure of a man "outlined as black as an ebony statue" against the moon. It was not the convict, whom Watson had also sighted, but a much taller, a much thinner man.

Within the next few days, Watson established two other

facts of great importance: "The one," as he recorded in his diary, "that Mrs. Laura Lyons of Coombe Tracey had written to Sir Charles Baskerville and made an appointment with him at the very place and hour that he met his death, the other that the lurking man on the moor was to be found among the stone huts" —those relics of neolithic man which could still be found dotting the moors of Devonshire.

Watson resolved to visit Mrs. Lyons of Coombe Tracey—a great beauty she was, Watson found—and she acknowledged that she had made an appointment with Sir Charles at the hour and place at which he met his death—to ask for financial aid, she said, but she denied that she had kept the appointment.

Why not, Watson thought as he made his way back to Baskerville Hall, why not on the way visit the stone hut where the stranger lurked?

He found the place empty, but there were ample signs that he had not come upon a false scent. Some blankets were rolled in a waterproof which lay upon a stone slab. The ashes of a fire were heaped in a rude grate, before which lay some cooking utensils and a bucket half full of water. A litter of empty tins showed that the place had been occupied for some time. A pannikin and a half-full bottle of spirits stood in a corner.

Could this, Watson wondered, be the temporary home of the same mysterious stranger who had followed Sir Henry Baskerville and Dr. Mortimer in London? With tingling nerves, but a fixed purpose, he sat in the dark recess of the hut and waited with somber patience for the coming of its tenant.

And then at last Watson heard him. From far away came the sharp clink of a boot striking upon a stone. Watson cocked the pistol in his pocket. There was a long pause, then once more the footsteps approached and a shadow fell across the opening of the hut.

"It is a lovely evening, my dear Watson," said a well-known voice. "I really think that you will be more comfortable outside the hut than in."

"You have been invaluable to me in this, as in so many other cases," said Sherlock Holmes, "and I beg you to forgive me if I have seemed to play a trick upon you. Had I come to Devonshire with you and Sir Henry, my presence would have warned our very formidable opponents to be on their guard. As it is, I remain an unknown factor in the business, ready to throw in all my weight at a critical moment.

"Another day—two at the most—and I have my case complete, but until then—hark!"

A terrible scream—a prolonged yell of horror and anguish—burst out of the silence of the moor. Again the agonized cry swept through the silence, louder and nearer than before. And now a new sound mingled with it—a deep muttered rumble, rising and falling like the low, constant murmur of the sea.

"The hound!" cried Holmes. "Come, Watson, come!"

Blindly they ran through the gloom, blundering against boulders, forcing their way through gorse bushes, panting up hills and rushing down slopes, heading always in the direction from which the sounds had come.

A low moan fell upon their ears. On their left, at the foot of a sheer cliff, a man lay prostrate on the ground. Not a whisper rose now from the dark figure over which they stooped. Holmes lit a match. There was no chance of either of them forgetting the peculiar, ruddy tweed suit the prostrate body wore. It was the suit that Sir Henry Baskerville had worn on the first morning they had seen him.

Holmes groaned—but then he uttered a cry as he bent over the body.

"A beard!" he exclaimed. "This man has a beard. This is not Sir Henry—it is the convict, Selden!"

Then Watson remembered: Sir Henry had handed his old wardrobe to Barrymore, the butler, and Barrymore had passed it on to his brother-in-law, Selden.

"Then the clothes have been the poor fellow's death," Holmes said. "It is clear enough that the hound has been set on the trail by some article of Sir Henry's—the boot which was abstracted at the Northumberland Hotel. Let us carry the body into one of the huts until we can communicate with the police. And now I see no reason for further concealment. Let us both walk together to Baskerville Hall."

"I understand that you are engaged to dine with the Stapletons at Merripit House tonight," Holmes said to Sir Henry Baskerville the next day.

"I hope that you and Dr. Watson will come also."

"I fear that we must go to London."

Sir Henry's face lengthened. "I had hoped that you were going to see me through this business," he said. "The hall and the moor are not very pleasant places when one is alone."

"My dear fellow, you must trust me implicitly and do exactly as I say. I wish you to drive to Merripit House. Send back your trap, however, and let the Stapletons know that you intend to walk home."

"To walk across the moor?"

"It is essential that you should do so."

"Then I will do it."

"Very good. And as you value your life, do not go across the moor in any direction save along the straight path which leads from Merripit House to the Grimpen Road, and is your natural way home."

A few hours afterward Holmes and Watson were at the station of Coombe Tracey. At the station office Holmes asked for a telegram, and handed it to Watson. "Wire received," it read. "Coming down with unsigned warrant. Arrive five-forty. Lestrade."

At that moment the London express came roaring into the station, and the small, wiry detective sprang from a first-class carriage.

"Anything good?" he asked Holmes eagerly.

"The biggest thing for years. We have two hours before we need think of starting. I think we might employ it in getting some dinner. And then, friend Lestrade, we will take the London fog out of your throat by giving you a breath of the pure night air of Dartmoor."

Above them hung a dense white fog. The moon shone on it, and it looked like a great shimmering ice field, with the heads of the tors like rocks borne upon its surface. Holmes's face was turned toward it, and he muttered impatiently as he watched its sluggish drift.

A sound of quick steps broke the silence of the moor. Through the fog, as through a curtain, stepped Sir Henry Baskerville. As he walked he glanced continually over either shoulder, like a man who is ill at ease.

"Hist!" whispered Holmes, and Watson and Lestrade heard the sharp click of a cocking pistol. "Look sharp—it's coming!"

There was a thin, crisp, continuous patter from somewhere in the heart of the crawling fog-bank. Watson glanced at Holmes. The detective's hawklike face was pale but exultant, and his eyes shone brightly in the moonlight. But suddenly Holmes's eyes started forward in a rigid, fixed stare, and Holmes's lips parted in amazement. At the same instant Lestrade gave a yell of terror and threw himself face downwards upon the ground. Watson sprang to his feet, his hand grasping his pistol, but his mind paralyzed by the dreadful shape which had sprung out of the fog and the shadows.

It was a hound, an enormous coal-black hound, but such a hound as mortal eyes had never before seen. Fire burst from its open mouth, its eyes glowed with a smoldering glare, its muzzle and hackles and dewlap were outlined in flickering flame. With great bounds the creature was leaping down the track, hard upon the footsteps of Sir Henry Baskerville.

Holmes and Watson fired together, and the creature gave a hideous howl. It did not pause, however, but bounded onward. Far away on the path they saw Sir Henry looking back, his face white in the moonlight, his hands raised in horror, glaring helplessly at the frightful thing which was hunting him down.

"Never," Watson wrote, "have I seen a man run as Holmes ran that night. I am reckoned fleet of foot, but he outpaced me as much as I outpaced the little professional"—Scotland Yard's Inspector Lestrade.

In front of them as they flew up the track they heard scream after scream from Sir Henry and the deep, constant baying of the horrid hound.

Watson was in time to see the beast spring upon its victim, hurl him to the ground and worry at his throat. But the next instant Holmes had emptied five barrels of his revolver into the creature. With a last howl of agony and a vicious snap in the air, it rolled upon its back, four feet pawing furiously, and then fell limp upon its side. Watson stooped and put his pistol to the dreadful, shimmering head. It was useless to press the trigger. The Hound of the Baskervilles was dead.

"My God!" Sir Henry whispered. "What in heaven's name, or hell's, was that animal?"

"It's dead, whatever it is," Holmes said. "Sir Henry, we've laid your family's ghost."

Watson placed his hand upon the glowing muzzle. As he held it up his own fingers smoldered and gleamed in the darkness.

Dr. Watson chuckled. *"Phosphorus,"* he said.

It was a raw and foggy November night, and Holmes and Watson sat on either side of a blazing fire in the sitting room at Baker Street.

"The whole course of events," said Sherlock Holmes, "revolved around the man who called himself Stapleton. This fellow was a Baskerville—the son of Sir Charles's younger brother. Stapleton —we will continue to call him that—married Beryl Garcia, one of the beauties of Costa Rica. In Devonshire, she posed as his sister.

"Stapleton learned that only two lives intervened between him and a valuable estate. His first act was to establish himself as near to the ancestral home as possible, and his second was to cultivate a friendship with Sir Charles Baskerville and with the other neighbors.

"Sir Charles himself told Stapleton about the family hound, and so prepared the way for his own death. Stapleton knew that the old man's heart was weak, and that a shock would kill him— so much he learned from Dr. Mortimer. Stapleton's ingenious mind instantly suggested a way in which the baronet could be done to death.

"The dog he bought in London. It was the strongest and most savage he could get. He kenneled it on an island in the Grimpen Mire. But his chance was a long time coming. Sir Charles could not be decoyed out of his grounds at night.

"Stapleton found a way out of his difficulties through that unfortunate woman, Mrs. Laura Lyons. By representing himself as a single man, Stapleton acquired complete influence over her, and gave her to understand that in the event of her obtaining a divorce from her husband he would marry her. He put pressure upon Mrs. Lyons to write a letter, imploring Sir Charles to give her an interview. Stapleton then prevented her from going. He got his hound, treated it with his infernal paint, and brought the beast round to the gate at which he had reason to expect that he would find Sir Charles waiting. The dog, incited by his master, sprang over the wicket gate and pursued the unfortunate baronet, who fell dead at the end of the Yew Alley from heart disease and terror.

"When Sir Henry Baskerville arrived in England, Stapleton's first idea was that he might be done to death in London. Disguised in a beard, Stapleton followed Sir Henry and Dr. Mortimer to Baker Street, and afterwards to the Northumberland Hotel. His wife had some inkling of his plans. She dared not warn Sir Henry with a letter, so she adopted the expedient of cutting out printed words that would form a message. It reached Sir Henry, as we know, and gave him his first warning of danger.

"It was very essential for Stapleton to get some article of Sir Henry's attire, so that, in case he was driven to use the dog, he might have a means of setting the animal upon the track. By chance, however, the first boot he stole was a new one, and so useless for his purpose. He had it returned and obtained another.

"By the time that you discovered me upon the moor I had a complete knowledge of the whole business, but I had not a case which could go to a jury. Even Stapleton's attempt upon Sir Henry, which ended in the death of the unfortunate convict, did not help us much in proving murder against our man. There seemed to be no alternative but to catch him red-handed, and to do so we had to use Sir Henry as bait. And now, my dear Watson, I do not know that anything essential has been left unexplained. We have had some weeks of severe work, and for one evening, I think, we may turn our thoughts into more pleasant channels. I have a box for *Les Huguenots*. Have you heard the De Reszkes?"[1]

"I have not heard the De Reszkes," Watson replied, "but I have read in the papers that Mme. Godfrey Norton, *née* Irene Adler, has recently returned to the operatic stage. The role of the

[1] Jean de Reszke (1850–1925), Polish operatic tenor and teacher, was known for both lyric and Wagnerian roles. He was the leading tenor of the Metropolitan Opera, New York, from 1891 to 1901. His brother Edouard de Reszke (1855–1917), was a leading bass at the Metropolitan from 1891 to 1903.

page Urbain in *Les Huguenots* is a rich one, if I recall correctly, and it is a role that is often played by a contralto. 'Male costume is nothing new to me.' "

Holmes took a cigar from the coal scuttle. "I believe I have often remarked to you, Watson," he said, "that you know my methods and should endeavor to apply them. It is a remark that seems to be sinking in."

XV. JACK THE HARLOT KILLER: FRIDAY, NOVEMBER 9– SUNDAY, NOVEMBER 11, 1888

"I never saw a case yet that he could not throw a light upon."

INSPECTOR ATHELNEY JONES.

"You must help us, Mr. Holmes, you really must!" the man from Scotland Yard cried. "There is a reign of terror over the whole East End of London. At the Yard we are at a complete dead end. We must have your assistance, and I have been instructed to get it."

"Instructed?" asked Sherlock Holmes.

"Instructed," said Inspector Athelney Jones. "Instructed by Sir Melville himself.[1] I think, Mr. Holmes, that of all your cases you will find none more fantastic than this one."

Holmes smiled. "Not even the Sign of the Four?" he asked.

"Not even the Sign of the Four," Inspector Jones replied.

Holmes leaned back in his armchair and placed the tips of his fingers together. His keen gray eyes gazed at the inspector quizzically.

"You refer, of course, to the Ripper killings," he said. "They have hardly escaped my attention. But these have been busy weeks for both Dr. Watson and myself. The little matter of the Greek interpreter, the case of the Sign of the Four, in which you

---

[1] Sir Melville Macnaughten, then a high official at Scotland Yard.

yourself played a part, the sinister business of the Hound of the Baskervilles—"

Watson turned from the bow window.

"Do not forget," he said, "that since our return from Devonshire you have been engaged in two affairs of the utmost importance."[2]

Holmes shrugged.

"One cannot be everywhere," he said. "About the Ripper murders I know only what I have read in the *Times*. Six drabs have been outraged."

Inspector Athelney Jones looked up from his cigar, his little eyes peering at Holmes over pouches more swollen and puffy than ever.

"*Seven* drabs, Mr. Holmes," he said. "And the seventh outrage the worst of the lot."

Holmes leaned forward, his eyes glittering.

"A seventh Ripper killing?" he asked. "It happened when? This morning?"

"Early this very morning," the inspector replied. "At No. 26 Dorset Street."

Watson could see that Holmes was mentally reviewing his vast knowledge of the lanes and byways of London.

"No. 26 Dorset Street," Holmes said at last. "It is, if I recall correctly, only a few hundred yards from the spot where the Ripper's third victim, Mary Ann Nichols, was found."

"That is quite correct," said Athelney Jones. "But in this murder there is a difference. For the first time the crime was committed indoors."

"You have no doubt that the murderer in this instance is the same person who committed the previous crimes?"

Jones shook his head. "Not a doubt in the world, Mr. Holmes," he said. "The character of the mutilations—exactly the same."

2 Watson of course referred to the two cases to which he alluded in the closing chapter of *The Hound of the Baskervilles*. In the first of these, Holmes had exposed the atrocious conduct of Colonel Upwood in connection with the famous card scandal at the Nonpareil Club. In the second he had defended the unfortunate Mme. Montpensier from the charge of murder which hung over her in connection with the death of her stepdaughter, Mlle. Carère, the young lady who, as it will be remembered, was found six months later alive and married in New York City. See Appendix I: The Chronological Holmes.

"Give me all the facts," said Holmes. "But first—a whisky-and-soda?"

"Well, half a glass," the inspector said. "I have had a good deal to worry and try me."

Watson reached for the tantalus and the gasogene. When Jones had settled back in the basket chair with his drink, the Inspector continued:

"Like all the others, Mary Jane Kelly was an immoral woman. Although she lived at 26 Dorset Street, as I told you, the entrance to her room is up a narrow court—Miller's Court, it's called—in which there are some half a dozen houses. The room she occupied is entirely separated from the other portion of the house, and has an entrance all its own, leading into Miller's Court. The room is known as No. 13. Nearly the whole of the houses in this street are common lodging houses, and the one opposite where this murder took place has accommodations for some three hundred men."

"It is fully occupied every night?" Holmes asked. "It was fully occupied last night?"

The inspector nodded agreement.

"About a year ago," he continued, "this Mary Jane Kelly, about twenty-four years of age at that time, came to the owner of the house—a man named M'Carthy—with a man she called Joseph Kelly. She said Kelly was her husband, a porter, employed at the Spitalfields Market. They rented this room on the ground floor—the same in which the poor woman was murdered—at a price of four shillings a week.

"About a fortnight ago, the woman had a quarrel with Kelly. Some blows were exchanged. Kelly left the room and did not return. Since then, the woman has been walking the streets for her living.

"Now we come to last night—Thursday evening.

"None of those living in Miller's Court, none of those living at No. 26 Dorset Street, saw anything of Mary Jane Kelly after eight o'clock last night. But she was seen in Commercial Road just before the closing of the public house there. She looked the worse for drink.

"Now, Mary Jane Kelly was 35 shillings behind with her rent. At a quarter to eleven o'clock this Friday morning, the owner of the house—that's M'Carthy, as you'll remember—said to a man who works for him, John Bowyer his name is, 'Go to No. 13 and try to get some rent money.'

"Well, Bowyer did as he was told. First he knocked on the door, but he got no answer. Then he tried the handle of the door and found it locked. Then he looked through the keyhole, and found the key missing. Now, the left-hand side of the room faces the court—Miller's Court—and in it are two large windows. Bowyer knew that when the man Kelly and the dead woman had their quarrel a pane of glass in one of the windows was broken. It had not yet been repaired. So Bowyer went round to the side, put his hand through the hole in the window, and pulled aside the muslin curtain inside.

"Mr. Holmes and Dr. Watson, a shocking sight met his eyes.

"He could see the woman lying on her back on the bed, entirely naked, covered with blood. He ran to his employer. M'Carthy went at once to look for himself. One glance through the broken window and he sent Bowyer off to the Commercial Road Police Station, where I myself was in charge.

"I went to No. 13 with Bowyer, Dr. Phillips, the divisional surgeon, and Superintendent Arnold. Mr. Arnold ordered one of the windows to be entirely removed. A more horrible or sickening sight could hardly be imagined. The woman—her throat was cut from ear to ear, right down to the spinal column. Her ears and nose had been cut clean off. The breasts— And the missing parts—"

The inspector buried his head in his hands.

"And to think, Mr. Holmes, that only ten hours before she had been so young, so rosy, so happy that she was singing—"

Holmes rose and walked to the window. Hands behind his back, he stood looking down into Baker Street.

"The man who calls himself Jack the Ripper is one of a long line," he said at last, still staring down into the yellow fog that swirled through the street. "Joseph Phillipe, the French ripper, operated in Paris during the 1860's, robbing his victims besides slaying them. They called him 'The Terror of Paris.' He did away with eight women, all of them streetwalkers. William Palmer, that prince of poisoners. Within ten years he murdered seven of his children, four legitimate, three illegitimate, as well as his wife, his mother, an aunt, an uncle, his mother-in-law and three close friends. He tried to kill three others, but failed. America, too. Jesse Pomeroy, still in his teens, slew and mutilated twenty-seven boys and girls between the ages of seven and ten. Pomeroy lived in South Boston. His crimes took place in the year that we met, Watson."

"I am no theorist, Mr. Holmes, as you well know," said Inspector Athelney Jones, "but Sir Melville has insisted that we follow up even the most farfetched clues. There is a popular belief that when a person dies the last scene that person has witnessed is indelibly printed on the pupils of the eyes—"

"Twaddle," said Holmes.

"Nevertheless," Jones went on, "we have photographed the eyes of three of the Ripper's victims, in the hope that an enlarged print would give some sort of picture of the murderer."

"Utterly unscientific," said Holmes. "Have no more rational attempts been made to determine this killer's identity?"

"I can tell you only one thing more," the inspector said. "Dr. Phillips, the divisional surgeon I mentioned to you earlier, as well as doctors who testified at inquests held on the Ripper's other victims, all these are of the opinion that the Ripper is himself a surgeon, or at least has had some months of medical training. A certain knowledge of anatomy, it seems, would be needed to account for some of the mutilations—"

"Even if this wretch is caught," Watson broke in, "he will probably be found to be mad, and so cheat the gallows."

"Mad he is, indeed," Holmes said. "But I cannot believe that he is a harlot slayer, and slays *only* harlots, for no good reason. Imagine a son, infected with a loathsome disease by an East End prostitute. Imagine a doting father, set out to avenge his son's ravages. As the father searches through Whitechapel he questions the drabs about the one he seeks. Girls of this profession often change their names—the father is not immediately successful in finding the offender. But so insistent are his questions that he must kill each girl he questions, lest she identifies him with the killings when at last he finds the guilty one."

"This has reasoning, but insufficient proof," Watson replied. "Why should a son be required to suffer the disease? Why not the Ripper himself? This disease might well affect the brain and cause him to declare his insane war on the special class from which he is choosing his victims. The mutilations are but the result of his blood lust and a desire to wreak his hatred even on the lifeless bodies of these unfortunates. Also I should say that this Ripper has a secret lair or hiding place in the district at which he is able to remove all signs of his fearful deeds. I add one thing more: that there are those in London who more than suspect his proclivities, but who have some reason not to denounce him."

Holmes turned from the window.

"I never get your limits, Watson," he said. "There are unexplained possibilities about you."

"You will agree to take the case?" asked Inspector Athelney Jones.

"I think I shall," said Holmes. "But my methods in solving it may be—irregular."

"You have *carte blanche,* Mr. Holmes," said Inspector Athelney Jones.

The papers next day were full of the seventh Whitechapel murder, and on that Saturday morning Dr. Watson spent a long hour with his *Times.*

Holmes had been up long before the doctor, but the detective was not in a communicative humor. He sat in his armchair by the fire, staring into the flames, his violin across his knees. Now and again he would raise the bow and bring forth chords both sonorous and melancholy.

In the middle part of the morning Watson rose from his chair and donned his greatcoat and his top hat. An hour later he returned to Baker Street.

Holmes was still sitting, staring into the fire.

"You have been to the Wigmore Street Post-office," he said as Watson entered. "You went there to dispatch a telegram."

"*Telegrams,*" Watson corrected him. "But I confess I don't see how you arrived at even one. It was a sudden impulse upon my part."

"It is simplicity itself," Holmes remarked. "It is so absurdly simple that an explanation is superfluous. And yet it may serve to define the limits of observation and deduction. Observation tells me that you have a little reddish mold adhering to your instep. Just opposite the Wigmore Street Post-office they have taken up the pavement and thrown up some earth, which lies in such a way that it is difficult to avoid treading in it on entering. The earth is of that peculiar reddish color which is found nowhere else in the neighborhood. So much is observation. The rest is deduction."

"How, then, did you deduce a telegram?"

"Why, of course, I knew that you had not written a letter, since I have been sitting opposite you all morning. I see also that in your open desk you have a sheet of stamps and a thick bundle of postcards. What could you go into the post office for, then, but to send a wire? Eliminate all other factors, and the one which remains must be the truth."

"In this case it certainly is so," Watson replied, after a little thought. "The thing, however, is, as you say, of the simplest. Have you decided on the course you will take in solving these Whitechapel murders?"

"Yes, a plan of action has occurred to me. I put it into effect late tonight."

"I am prepared to accompany you."

Holmes sprang from his chair. "It is most essential that you do not!" he cried.

"But there may be danger."

"There will most certainly be danger."

"Have I ever failed you?"

Holmes dropped his hand on Watson's shoulder. "I have said before and I will say again that there is no one I would rather have at my side in a moment of crisis. But my plan here calls for action on my part alone. You must on no account follow me when I leave Baker Street tonight."

"You insist?"

"I must insist."

"Very well," said Watson, "I will on no account follow you."

"I hold you to your word," Holmes said, picking up his violin. "And now, Doctor, for some of your favorites. What shall it be? Mendelssohn or Gilbert and Sullivan on this foggy, foggy morning?"

"Sixpence," the woman begged. "Sixpence only."

The keeper of the public house was not in the habit of lending money to a customer, particularly a customer he had never set eyes on before. That she was a streetwalker was obvious. It was also obvious that even in Whitechapel she would find it hard to make a living. Her hair was her best feature. Blonde. Dyed, of course. Without rouge, her cheeks would be pale. The lips were thin, but they had been painted into a sensuous Cupid's bow. Her nose was hawklike. She was too tall, too thin. And, to cap it all, she limped—only slightly, but enough so that she found it necessary to carry a stick to aid her.

"You'll get no sixpence from me," the publican growled. "Nor no more gin, neither. It's closing time. Closing time!" he repeated, in a louder voice.

The drab limped to the door, throwing a curse over her shoulder at the publican as she went out into the foggy, squalid streets.

There was only one other customer in the public house at this late hour. In a dark corner of the room, a man rose from a table. He was not a tall man, but his body, wrapped in a black cloak, was broad and burly. Little could be seen of his face. His hat with its broad brim was pulled far down on his head, and a thick woolen muffler was wound many times around his throat and the lower part of his face. His little eyes looked keenly out from between swollen and puffy pouches.

The man tossed money for his drinks on the scarred top of his table. Reaching down, he picked up from the floor at his feet a small black bag. Bulky, plethoric, unaturally silent, he followed the drab into the fog that filled the Commercial Road.

The drab had limped to the corner of the street. Undecided what she should do, she stood hesitating under the gas lamp. Quickly, despite his bulk, the man in the black cloak caught up with her.

"Sixpence, you wanted," he said in a deep, husky voice, his hand resting lightly on her arm. "I'll give you more than sixpence. For services rendered."

The drab smirked.

"I live off Cable Street," she said.

Swiftly, in spite of her limp, she turned and started down

the road to the left. The man in the cloak, bag in hand, followed her. Soon they stood, shivering in the cold and damp, at the entrance to a dirty court. The fog had increased, and it was very dark. A wind swirled in the corners of the court.

Pulling the folds of his muffler closer around his face, the man in the black cloak looked quickly up and down the court. He and the drab were quite alone there, and no light shone from the windows in the buildings above them. Not even the top of the wall of the court was visible in the thickening darkness.

"This is where you live?" the man whispered.

The woman nodded agreement, and put out a hand to her door.

"A moment," the man said softly. He placed the little black bag on the ground, snapped it open. From it he withdrew a razor-keen, nine-inch-long butcher's knife. The man straightened, the knife in his hand.

The drab pressed back against her door.

"Jack?" she breathed.

"Jack the Ripper, Jack the Harlot Killer," the man snarled, and lunged at her with his knife.

The woman's right hand went to the stick she carried in her left. With a single movement, incredibly swift and deft, she twisted the head of the stick. Now in her right hand a long and sharp and burnished sword blade glittered in the feeble gaslight.

"Drop your knife, Jack," said Sherlock Holmes of Baker Street.

The Ripper backed away. Behind him was the wall of the court, eight feet high. No escape that way. The only access to the court was the passageway through which they had just passed, and between the entrance to the passage and the Ripper himself stood one of the most accomplished swordsmen in Europe.

Holmes's blade snaked out—caught the scarf that hid the Ripper's face, flung it into a corner of the courtyard.

Quickly the Ripper flung his arm across his face.

"You forfeit the game, Jack?" Holmes asked quietly.

The Ripper shrugged his massive shoulders. "What else can I do?" he growled in his deep voice. He dropped his knife. And then the Ripper sprang.

With an agility amazing in a man so big, he seized Holmes around the knees. The detective, taken completely unaware, fell back, his head striking on the stone of the doorstep behind him.

For a moment, all was quiet in the squalid court.

Slowly the Ripper arose from his knees. On the cobblestones at his feet lay the razor-keen, nine-inch knife. He bent and retrieved it. Slowly he advanced on the prostrate body of the unconscious detective.

From the shadows that shrouded the top of the courtyard wall, a heavy body launched itself.

Full on the Ripper it dived, knocking him off his feet and pinning him to the cobblestones. The man who had dived from the wall twisted the knife from the Ripper with one hand, and with the other he delivered a smashing blow to the Ripper's jaw. Blood ran from the corners of the Ripper's mouth. The man from the wall seized the Ripper by both shoulders, raised the bulky body effortlessly, and smashed the Ripper's head against the cobblestones. The Ripper lay on his back as if dead. The man from the wall stared down at him. The Ripper was easy to recognize, even in the dim light of the courtyard.

The man who had leaped from the wall turned to Holmes, felt his pulse.

From a pocket of his greatcoat he removed a flask, forced brandy between the detective's lips. Holmes opened his eyes. His right hand groped for the sword cane that lay beside him. Then he recognized his rescuer.

"My dear Watson!" Sherlock Holmes cried.

Holmes, his head bandaged expertly by his friend the doctor, reached for and lit his briar pipe, threw himself into the armchair by the fire in the old sitting room in Baker Street.

"It is a pity," he said to Watson, seated opposite him, "that, while you have all the facts in your journal, the public will never know of them. Scotland Yard can hardly admit that the Ripper who has terrorized the entire East End of London for so many months is one of its own men—an inspector, at that, and a rising one. But let me ask you this. How did you come to be in that courtyard off Cable Street? You gave me your solemn promise that you would not follow me."

"Nor did I," Watson said. "I followed Athelney Jones. You did not ask, nor did I give, any promise about that."

"You suspected him, Watson?"

"More than that, Holmes. I knew when I followed him that Athelney Jones was the Ripper."

"But how, Watson, how?"

It was early on the morning of Sunday, November 11, 1888.

"You will recall," said Dr. Watson, "that when Inspector Jones called upon us on"—he glanced at his watch—"on what is now the day before yesterday, he told us of the seventh Ripper murder —that of Mary Jane Kelly. Do you also recall what he ended by saying: 'None of those living in the court at No. 26 Dorset Street saw anything of Mary Jane Kelly after eight o'clock. She was seen in Commercial Street just before the closing of the public-house.' Then he said: 'And to think, Mr. Holmes, that only ten hours before she had been so plump, so rosy, so happy that she was singing—'"

"I am afraid that I do not yet see—" Sherlock Holmes began.

"The *Times* next morning—which you had not read when I picked it up after breakfast, for it was fresh and folded—stated that about one o'clock a person living in the court opposite to the one occupied by the murdered woman had indeed heard her singing. The song was *Sweet Violets*.

"As you deduced, I walked to the post office that morning and sent a wire. It was to the *Times*. I asked for the reply to be sent to me at the post office, and it was quick in coming. Only one person—other, of course, than the Ripper himself—had heard the singing, a stevedore named Becket. Becket told the correspondent from the *Times* that he had talked to no one else. He had not been at home when the police had come to question him. Only the *Times* reported that Becket had heard Mary Jane Kelly singing. Unless Inspector Athelney Jones was himself the Ripper for whom he professed to be hunting, how then did he know—*a day before the* Times *was published*—that Mary Jane Kelly, shortly before her hideous death, was plump, rosy, *singing?*

"You deduced that I sent a telegram from the Wigmore Street Post-office. In point of fact, I dispatched three—to the *Times*, to young Stamford, to Superintendent Arnold, the latter two after I had received my reply from the *Times*. Young Stamford was kind enough to check the records of Saint Bartholomew's for me. Athelney Jones had indeed at one time attended lectures in surgery—it was part, he declared, of the training that had enabled him to become, in comparatively little time, a Scotland Yard inspector. He would have, then, that anatomical knowledge that would seem to be required by the man who called himself Jack the Ripper. My telegram to Superintendent Arnold was likewise a simple question: Did Inspector Athelney Jones have a private office at the Commercial Road Police Station? Superintendent Arnold replied that Inspector Jones did. It had an entrance from the Police Station itself, of course, but it also had a second door which led into the alley in back of the Commercial Road. You will recall that I felt strongly that the Ripper must have some private place in Whitechapel where he could remove all signs of his fearful deeds. . . .

"Under the circumstances, I thought it wise to shadow the inspector. When I heard you, in your disguise as a streetwalker, say, 'I live off Cable Street,' I guessed where the Ripper would strike next, took a short cut through the street behind the courtyard wall, piled up boxes, climbed to the top of the wall, and waited the few moments it took you, limping, to arrive. The rest, of course, you know as well as I do."

Holmes took the pipe from his mouth.

"Extraordinary, my dear Watson," he said.

"Elementary, my dear Holmes," said Dr. John H. Watson.

XVI. THE SECOND MRS. WATSON: 1889–90

After my marriage and my subsequent start in private practice, the very intimate relations which had existed between Holmes and myself became to some extent modified. He still came to me when he desired a companion in his investigations . . .

JOHN H. WATSON, M. D.

Miss Mary Morstan, daughter of the late Captain Arthur Morstan of the 34th Bombay Infantry, and John H. Watson, M.D., of 221B Baker Street, London, were married on Wednesday, the first of May, 1889, at Saint Mark's Church in Camberwell. Mrs. Cecil Forrester was the matron of honor. Mr. Sherlock Holmes, also of 221B Baker Street, was of course the best man.

In the preceding April, Holmes and Watson had shared with Miss Violet Hunter[1] the adventure of the Copper Beeches. "A little problem," Holmes called it, but the "most interesting" which had come his way in some months. For Watson, however, it ended in a disappointment. Miss Hunter was a governess, as his own Mary had been—Miss Hunter was obviously as interested in Holmes the man as she was in Holmes the detective—how delightful, Watson thought, if in the coming May there should be a *double* wedding. But, as he wrote rather wistfully at the end of his account of the case, his friend Holmes "manifested no further interest in Miss Hunter when once she had ceased to be the centre of one of his problems."

Alone in Baker Street, Holmes brooded.

[1] During his long professional career, Mr. Sherlock Holmes of Baker Street was always particularly eager to assist clients with the name of Violet. It had been, of course, the Christian name of his own mother.

How different, he thought, had been the second marriage of his friend, Dr. Watson, and that earlier marriage at which Holmes had also officiated—the marriage of Irene Adler to the lawyer Godfrey Norton.

The more the detective pondered, the more convinced he became that here was no genuine union. Quietly, he set an investigation in motion.

Mme. Adler-Norton, he soon found, was leading a miserable existence. The handsome Norton had shown himself to be a scoundrel of the deepest dye—as a man, he was a drunken brute; as a lawyer, he was an unscrupulous shyster. Irene had been forced to return to the operatic stage—her not inconsiderable earnings were at once wrested from her by her "husband."

As for the clergyman who had performed the supposed marriage—he had been ordained, indeed, but he had been unfrocked as well, as Holmes soon discovered.

His evidence gathered, Holmes carried it to Lestrade.

"A faked marriage is no marriage at all," Holmes pointed out. "It is a very serious felony."

"As Mr. Godfrey Norton will discover before I have finished with him!" the little inspector cried, his brown eyes snapping. "He'll have time to think things out during the next ten years or so, if I am not mistaken."

Lestrade was not mistaken.

"Miss Adler is free of that rascal now," he told Holmes in the old room at Baker Street a short time later. "And I have kept my word to you—she does not suspect that you had any hand in this undertaking."

"That is as I wished it," Holmes said, and he reached out for the cocaine bottle.

Shortly after his second marriage, Watson bought a connection in the Paddington district. Old Mr. Farquhar, from whom he purchased it, had at one time an excellent general practice, but his age, and an affliction of the nature of St. Vitus's dance from which he suffered, had very much thinned it.

"The public," Watson wrote,[2] "not unnaturally, goes upon the principle that he who would heal others must himself be

[2] In "The Stockbroker's Clerk."

whole, and looks askance at the curative powers of the man whose own case is beyond the reach of his drugs. Thus, as my predecessor weakened his practice declined, until when I purchased it from him it had sunk from twelve hundred to little more than three hundred a year. I had confidence, however, in my own youth and energy, and was convinced that in a very few years the concern would be as flourishing as ever."

Watson's confidence was confirmed by Holmes's first visit.[3]

"Your neighbor is a doctor too," Holmes stated, nodding at the brass plate on the house next to Watson's.

"Yes, he bought a practice, as I did."

"An old-established one?"

"Just the same as mine. Both have been here ever since the houses were built."

"Ah, then you got hold of the better of the two."

"I think I did. But how do you know?"

"By the steps, my boy," Holmes chuckled. "Yours are worn three inches deeper than his."

The July which immediately succeeded Watson's marriage to Mary Morstan was made memorable, he tells us, by three cases of interest in which he was privileged to study the methods of his friend Mr. Sherlock Holmes.

The first of these, however, dealt with interests of such importance, and implicated so many of the first families in the kingdom, that, Watson felt, "the new century will have come before the story can be safely told."

It is a great pity that Watson never told the story, and that painstaking research by many eminent scholars cannot add to the few details that Watson has given us about it, for "no case in which Holmes was ever engaged has illustrated the value of his analytical methods so clearly or has impressed those who were associated with him so deeply. I still retain an almost verbatim report of the interview in which he demonstrated the true facts of the case to Monsieur Dubuque, of the Paris police, and Fritz von Waldbaum, the well-known specialist of Danzig,

[3] On Saturday, June 15,.1889. A week previously Holmes and Watson had shared the case which Watson was to chronicle under the title of "The Boscombe Valley Mystery." But in this case, Holmes did not *visit* Watson— he wired to the doctor to meet him at Paddington Station.

both of whom had wasted their energies upon what proved to be side issues."

The second of the July 1889 cases is also lost to us—Watson has left us only the title under which he recorded it in his notes[4]— but the third of the July 1889 cases[5]—the very abstruse and complicated mystery of the Naval Treaty—Watson recounted in *The Strand Magazine,* October–November 1893, and in *Harper's Weekly,* October 14–October 21, 1893.

Percy Phelps, who had been at school with Watson, had later risen to a high position in the Foreign Office, and was trusted and honored there until a horrible misfortune came suddenly to blast his career. Could Watson bring his celebrated friend, Mr. Sherlock Holmes, to Briarbrae, in Woking, to learn the details?

Holmes was glad to come, and learned from Phelps that he had been entrusted with a secret treaty between England and Italy. The document was of the utmost importance, and the document had been stolen from Phelps under such circumstances that it seemed impossible that even Holmes could help him.

"You have implicit faith in Holmes?" Phelps asked Watson eagerly.

"I have seen him do some very remarkable things."

"But he has never brought light into anything quite so dark as this?"

"Oh yes," said Watson reassuringly. "I have known him to solve questions which presented even fewer clues than yours."

It was only the next day that Holmes invited Phelps and Watson to breakfast at Baker Street.

"Mrs. Hudson has risen to the occasion," Holmes said, uncovering a dish of curried chicken. "Her cuisine is a little limited, but she has as good an idea of breakfast as a Scotswoman. What have you there, Watson?"

"Ham and eggs."

---

[4] As "The Adventure of the Tired Captain." It should be noted here, however, that Mr. Rolfe Boswell believes this case and that of "The Adventure of the Missing Three-Quarter" to be one and the same. See *The Baker Street Journal,* Vol. II, No. 2, p. 161.

[5] Actually, the *fourth* of the July 1889 cases. On Tuesday, July 30, 1889, as "The Adventure of the Naval Treaty" began, Holmes was engaged in solving an adventure in which Watson did not share—that of the Very Commonplace Little Murder. See Appendix I: The Chronological Holmes

"Good! What are you going to take, Mr. Phelps? Curried fowl, eggs, or will you help yourself?"

"Thank you, but I can eat nothing," Phelps said.

"Oh, come! Try the dish before you!"

"Thank you, I would really rather not."

"Well, then," said Holmes, with a mischievous twinkle, "I suppose that you have no objection to helping me?"

Phelps raised the cover, and as he did so he uttered a scream, and sat there staring with a face as white as the plate at which he looked. Across its center lay a little cylinder of blue-gray paper.

"The treaty!" Phelps cried, catching it up, devouring it with his eyes, pressing it to his bosom and shrieking out in his delight.

"There! there!" said Holmes, patting him upon the shoulder. "It was too bad to spring it upon you like this, but Watson here will tell you that I can never resist a touch of the dramatic."

While Watson's practice increased steadily, August of 1889 found him with a sadly depleted bank account. Mary he had sent for a holiday in the glades of the New Forest and on the beach at Southsea; he longed to be with her, but he returned instead to Baker Street to spend a fortnight with Holmes. We owe to that visit the account he has given us of the strange, though peculiarly terrible, chain of events which he called "The Cardboard Box."

By Saturday, September 7, 1889, Mary had returned from her holiday and Watson was back at work. "Of all the problems which have been submitted to my friend Mr. Sherlock Holmes for solution during the years of our intimacy," he wrote, "there were only two which I was the means of introducing to his notice. One of these was the case of Colonel Warburton's madness; the other, that of Mr. Hatherley's thumb." The latter case, Watson wrote, was strange in its inception and dramatic in its details— even though "it gave my friend fewer openings for those deductive methods of reasoning in which he achieved such remarkable results."

Then, in mid-September, came "one of the strangest cases which ever perplexed a man's brains"—that of "The Crooked Man."

One thing still bothered Watson as the case came to a close. "If the husband's name was James," he asked as he and Holmes walked down to the station, "and the other was Henry, what was that talk about David?"

Holmes chuckled.

"That one word, my dear Watson, should have told me the whole story had I been the ideal reasoner which you are so fond of depicting," he said. "It was evidently a term of reproach."

"Of reproach?" Watson asked.

"Yes, David strayed a little now and then, you know, and on one occasion in the same direction as Sergeant James Barclay. You remember the small affair of Uriah and Bathsheba? My Biblical knowledge is a trifle rusty, I fear, but you will find the story in the first or second of Samuel."

Watson's practice grew more and more demanding. He saw less and less of Holmes, and in the year 1890 there were only three cases of which he retained any record.

In March of that year there was the chaotic affair at Wisteria Lodge—chaotic because it covered two continents and concerned two groups of mysterious persons. "It will not be possible," Holmes said to Watson, "for you to present it in that compact form which is dear to your heart."

In September of that same year there was the adventure of the race horse, Silver Blaze. It is a memorable case—most memorable, perhaps, for Holmes's observation to Inspector Gregory:

"Is there any other point to which you would wish to draw my attention?" Gregory asked.

"To the curious incident of the dog in the nighttime," Holmes replied.

"The dog did nothing in the nighttime," the inspector retorted.

"That," said Sherlock Holmes, "that was the curious incident."

Three months later, in December, came "a very sweet little problem"—that of the Beryl Coronet. "I would not have missed it for a great deal," Holmes said—perhaps because it enabled him to be of service once again to a man Holmes did not like, but whom no loyal Englishman could help but serve—"a name which is a household word all over the earth—one of the highest, noblest, most exalted names in England."

Yet we should not leave the year 1890 without remarking the relationship between Mr. Sherlock Holmes of Baker Street and his distinguished contemporary, Mr. George Bernard Shaw.

That Sherlock Holmes was no stranger to George Bernard Shaw is certain. Hesketh Pearson, the British biographer, reports in his *G. B. S., a Postscript,* that Shaw, at the age of eighty-eight, inveighed against Holmes, saying: "Sherlock was a drug addict without a single amiable trait, [but] Watson was a decent fellow."

What first brought Holmes and Shaw together? What caused the animosity between them?

As Mr. Rolfe Boswell has written,[6] "Sarasate is the link . . ."

Pablo de Sarasate (1844–1908) was of course the great Spanish violin virtuoso, and Holmes was one of his warmest admirers.

In 1887 Holmes had interrupted the very intriguing investigation of the League of the Red-Headed Men to hear Sarasate play at St. James's Hall. "I observe that there is a good deal of German music on the program," he remarked to Watson at the time, "which is rather more to my taste than Italian or French. It is introspective, and I want to introspect."

Watson tells us that all that October afternoon Holmes sat in the stalls wrapped in perfect happiness, gently waving his long thin fingers in time to the music, his face gently smiling, his eyes languid and dreamy.

Sarasate played in London again in October 1890. We may be sure that Holmes attended the first of his concerts, as would George Bernard Shaw, then the music critic of the *World,* signing his columns for the first time with the initials G.B.S.[7]

Holmes was a devotee of the stringed instruments; Shaw, on the other hand, held that the human voice was by far the greatest medium for making music. His review of Sarasate's opening concert was caustic: "Sarasate," the redheaded, red-bearded Irishman

---

[6] In "Sarasate, Sherlock and Shaw," in *The Baker Street Journal,* Vol. II, No. 1, New Series, January 1952, pp. 22–29.

[7] As music critic of the *Star,* a year earlier, Shaw had signed his reviews "Corno di Bassetto," the Italian name for the basset horn, the tenor clarinet pitched in F, usually made curved for convenience in handling.

wrote, "set up by the autumn holidays, left all criticism behind him. . . . He also left Cusins behind him by half a bar or so all through the two concertos, the unpremeditated effects of syncopation resulting therefrom being more curious than delectable."

"Doubtless," as Mr. Boswell points out, "such glib comment riled Sherlock Holmes, who had forgotten more about violin-playing than G.B.S. would ever know. Very probably a sharp letter of protest went out from 221B Baker Street to the *World*'s editor-in-chief, pointing out that Sarasate's series of five brilliant concerts at Barcelona earlier in the month had not been exactly in the category of autumnal holiday-making."

It is to be deeply regretted that the breach between Sherlock Holmes and George Bernard Shaw was never healed. The two men had much in common, as well as much to dispute about, and both had the distinction of being among the longest-lived men of their generation.[8]

[8] Shaw, born in 1856, died in 1950 at the enviable age of ninety-four.

XVII. THE FINAL PROBLEM?: FRIDAY, APRIL 24–MONDAY, MAY 4, 1891

It is with a heavy heart that I take up my pen to write these the last words in which I shall ever record the singular gifts by which my friend Mr. Sherlock Holmes was distinguished.

JOHN H. WATSON, M.D.

During the winter and the early spring of 1891, Watson saw in the papers that Holmes had been engaged by the French Government upon a matter of supreme importance, and he received two notes from Holmes, one dated from Narbonne and the other from Nîmes, from which he gathered that Holmes's stay in France was likely to be a long one.

It was with some surprise, then, that Watson saw his friend walk into his consulting room upon the evening of April 24, 1891. To Watson, Holmes looked even paler and thinner than usual. With scarcely a word to the doctor, Holmes edged his way around the wall, flung the shutters together, and bolted them securely.

"You are afraid of something?" Watson asked.

Holmes flung himself into an armchair. "Well," he said, "I am."

"Of what?"

"Of an air gun."

"My dear Holmes, what do you mean?"

"The air gun is no airy nothing," Holmes said, smiling, "in the hands of Colonel Sebastian Moran. But tell me—is Mrs. Watson in?"

"She is away upon a visit. I am quite alone."

"Then it makes it easier for me to propose that you should come away with me on a visit to the Continent."

It was not Holmes's nature to take an aimless holiday, and something about his pale, worn face told Watson that his nerves were at their highest tension. Holmes saw the question in Watson's eyes, and, putting his finger tips together and his elbows upon his knees, he offered an explanation.

"You have heard me speak of Professor Moriarty?" he asked.

"The famous scientific criminal, as famous among crooks as—"

"My blushes, Watson," Holmes murmured.

"I was about to say 'as he is unknown to the public.' "

"A touch, Watson—a distinct touch!" Holmes laughed. "You are developing a certain unexpected vein of pawky humor, against which I must learn to guard myself."

"But what of Moriarty?" Watson asked eagerly.

"He has made a slip at last. Only a little slip, Watson, but more than he could afford. Three months ago I had my chance, and, starting from that point, I have woven my net around him until now it is all but ready to close. In three days, that is to say on Monday next, matters will be ripe, and the professor, with all the principal members of his gang, should be in the hands of the police. Then will come the greatest criminal trial of the century, the clearing up of over forty mysteries, and the rope for all of them—but if we move prematurely, you understand, they may slip out of our hands at the last moment.

"Now, if I could have done this without the knowledge of Professor Moriarty, all would have been well. But he was far too wily for that. He saw every step which I took to draw my toils around him. Again and again he strove to break away, but as often I headed him off. I tell you, my friend, that if a detailed account of that silent contest could be written, it would take its place as the most brilliant piece of thrust-and-parry work in the history of detection. Never have I risen to such a height, and never have I been so hard pressed by an opponent. He cut deep, and yet I just undercut him. This morning the last steps were taken, and three days only were wanted to complete the business. I was sitting in my room thinking the matter over, when the door opened and Professor Moriarty stood before me.

"My nerves are fairly shockproof, Watson, but I must confess to a start when I saw the very man who had been so much in my thoughts standing there on my threshold. His appearance was of course quite familiar to me. He peered at me with great interest in his puckered eyes, his face protruding forward, oscillating, as usual, from side to side in that curiously reptilian fashion.

" 'You have less frontal development as a man than I should have expected from knowing you as a boy,' he said at last. 'By the way, Master Sherlock, it is a dangerous habit to finger loaded firearms in the pocket of one's dressing gown.'

"The fact is that upon his entrance I had instantly recognized the extreme personal danger in which I lay. The only conceivable escape for him lay in silencing my tongue. In an instant I had slipped the revolver from the drawer into my pocket, and was covering him through the cloth. At his remark I drew the weapon out and laid it cocked upon the table. He still smiled and blinked, but there was something about his eyes which made me very glad that I had it there.

" 'Pray take a chair,' I said, 'I can spare you five minutes if you have anything to say.'

" 'All that I have to say has already crossed your mind,' he said.

" 'Then possibly my answer has crossed yours,' I replied.

" 'You stand fast?'

" 'Absolutely.'

"He clapped his hand into his pocket, and I raised the pistol from the table. But he merely drew out a memorandum book in which he had scribbled some dates.

" 'You crossed my path on the 4th of January,' he said. 'On the 23rd you incommoded me; by the middle of February I was seriously inconvenienced by you; at the end of March I was absolutely hampered in my plans; and now, at the close of April, I find myself placed in such a position through your criminal persecution that I am in positive danger of losing my liberty. The situation is becoming an impossible one.'

" 'Have you any suggestion to make?' I asked.

" 'You must drop it, Master Sherlock,' he said, swaying his face about. 'You really must, you know.'

" 'After Monday,' I said.

" 'Dear me, Mr. Holmes, dear me!' he said—you recall, Watson, the insulting note he sent us at the ending of the strange case you have called in your journal *The Valley of Fear.* 'I am quite sure that a man of your intelligence will see that there can be but one outcome to this affair. It is necessary that you should withdraw. You have worked things in such a fashion that we have only one resource left. It has been an intellectual treat to me to see the way in which you have grappled with me in this affair, and I say, unaffectedly, that it would be a grief to your old tutor to take any extreme measures. You smile, sir, but I assure you that it really would.'

" 'Danger is part of my trade,' I remarked.

" 'This is not danger,' he said. 'It is inevitable destruction. You stand in the way not merely of an individual, but of a mighty organization, the full extent of which you, with all your cleverness, have been unable to realize. You must stand clear, Holmes, or be trodden under foot.'

" 'I am afraid,' I said, rising, 'that in the pleasure of this conversation I am neglecting business of importance which awaits me elsewhere.'

"He rose also and looked at me in silence, shaking his head sadly.

" 'Well, well,' he said at last. 'It seems a pity, but I have done what I could. I know every move of your game. You can do nothing before Monday. It has been a duel between us for years. Now you hope to place me in the dock. I tell you that I will never stand in the dock. You hope to beat me. I tell you that you will never beat me. If you are clever enough to bring destruction upon me, rest assured that I shall do as much for you.'

" 'You have paid me several compliments, Professor Moriarty,' I said. 'Let me pay you one in return when I say that if I were assured of the former eventuality, I would, in the interests of the public, cheerfully accept the latter.'

" 'I can promise you the one but not the other,' he snarled, and so turned his rounded back upon me and went peering and blinking out of the room.

"That was my singular interview with Professor Moriarty, Watson. I confess that it left an unpleasant effect upon my mind. His soft, precise fashion of speech leaves a conviction of sincerity which a mere bully could not produce. Of course you will say: 'Why not take police precautions against him?' The reason is that I am well convinced that it is from his agents that the blow would fall. I have the best of proofs that it would be so."

"You have already been assaulted?"

"My dear Watson, Professor Moriarty is not a man who lets the grass grow under his feet. I went out about midday to transact some business in Oxford Street. As I passed the corner which leads from Bentinck Street on to the Welbeck Street crossing a two-horse van furiously driven whizzed round the corner and was on me like a flash. I sprang for the footpath and saved myself by the fraction of a second. The van dashed round from Marylebone Lane and was gone in an instant. I kept to the pavement after that, Watson, but as I walked down Vere Street a brick came down from the roof of one of the houses, and was shattered to fragments at my feet. I called the police and had the place examined. There were slates and bricks piled upon the roof preparatory to some repairs, and they would have me believe that the wind had toppled over one of these. Of course I knew better, but I could prove nothing. I took a cab after that and reached my brother Mycroft's rooms in Pall Mall, where I spent the day. Now I have come round to you, and on the way I was attacked by a rough with a bludgeon. I knocked him down, and the police have him in custody, but I can tell you with absolute confidence that no possible connection will ever be traced between the gentleman whose front teeth have been loosened by my knuckles and the retiring mathematical coach."

"You must spend the night here," Watson said.

"No, my friend, you would find me a dangerous guest. I have my plans laid, and all will be well. Matters have gone so far now that they can move without my help as far as the arrest goes. It is obvious, therefore, that I cannot do better than to get away for the few days which remain before the police are at liberty to act. It would be a great pleasure to me, therefore, if you would come to the Continent with me."

"I have, as you know, a neighbor doctor who will be happy to take care of my practice for a week or so," Watson said. "I should be glad to come."

"And to start tomorrow morning?"

"If necessary."

"Oh yes, it is most necessary. Then these are your instructions, and I beg, my dear Watson, that you will obey them to the letter, for you are now playing a double-handed game with me against the cleverest rogue and the most powerful syndicate of criminals in Europe, if not the world. Now, listen. You will send whatever luggage you intend to take by a trusty messenger to Victoria Station tonight. In the morning you will send for a hansom, desiring your man to take neither the first nor the second which may present itself. Into this third hansom you will jump, and you will drive to the Strand end of the Lowther Arcade, handing the address to the cabman upon a slip of paper, with the request that he will not throw it away. Have your fare ready, and the instant your cab stops, dash through the Arcade, timing yourself to reach the other side at a quarter-past nine. You will find a small brougham waiting close to the curb, driven by a fellow with a heavy black cloak tipped at the collar in red. Into this brougham you will step, and you will reach Victoria in time for the Continental express."

"But where shall I meet you?"

"At the station. The second first-class carriage from the front will be reserved for us."

In the morning, Watson obeyed Holmes's instructions to the letter. A hansom was procured with such precautions as would prevent its being one which was placed ready for him, and Watson drove immediately to the Lowther Arcade, through which he hurried at top speed. A brougham was indeed waiting with a very massive driver wrapped in a dark cloak, who, the instant that Watson had stepped in, whipped up the horse and rattled off to Victoria Station. As soon as Watson had alighted at the station, the driver turned the carriage and dashed away without so much as a look in Watson's direction.

Watson's luggage was waiting for him, and he had no difficulty in finding the carriage Holmes had indicated. His only anxiety now was the nonappearance of Holmes. The station clock marked only seven minutes from starting time. In vain Watson searched among the groups of travelers and leave-takers for the figure of his friend. There was no sign of him. Watson spent several minutes in assisting a venerable Italian priest, who was endeavoring to make a porter understand, in his broken English, that his luggage was to be booked through to Paris. Then he returned to the second first-class carriage from the front, where he found that the porter, in spite of the "Engaged" sign in the carriage window, had given him the decrepit Italian priest as a traveling companion. Watson shrugged his broad shoulders resignedly and continued to look out anxiously for his friend. The doors had been shut and the whistle blown, when—

"My dear Watson," said a well-known voice, "you have not even condescended to say good morning to me."

Watson turned in astonishment. The aged ecclesiastic had turned his face toward Watson. For an instant the wrinkles were miraculously smoothed away, the nose drew down from the chin, the lower lip ceased to protrude and the mouth to mumble. The dull eyes regained their fire, and the drooping figure expanded. The next instant the role of an Italian priest had been resumed. Holmes had gone as quickly as he had come.

"Good heavens!" Watson cried. "How you startled me!"

"Every precaution is still necessary," Holmes whispered. "I have reason to think they are hot upon our trail. Ah, there is Moriarty himself!"

The train had already begun to move as Holmes spoke. Glancing back, Watson saw a tall man pushing his way furiously through the crowd and waving his hand as if he desired the train to stop. It was too late, however. The train was rapidly gathering momentum, and an instant later it shot clear of the station.

"With all our precautions, you see that we have cut it rather fine," Holmes said, laughing. He rose, threw off the black cassock and hat which had formed his costume, and packed them away in a handbag.

"Have you seen the morning paper, Watson?"

"No."

"They set fire to our rooms in Baker Street last night. No great harm was done."

"Holmes, this is intolerable!"

"They must have lost my track completely after their bludgeon man was arrested. Otherwise they could not have imagined that I had returned to my rooms. They have evidently taken the precaution of watching you, however, and that is what has brought Moriarty to Victoria. You could not have made any slip coming?"

"I did exactly what you advised."

"Did you find your brougham?"

"Yes, it was waiting."

"Did you recognize your coachman?"

"No."

"It was my brother Mycroft. It is an advantage to get about in such a case with all the various kinds of helps that a brother like Mycroft can manage. But we must plan what we are to do about Moriarty now."

"As this is an express, and as the boat runs in connection with it, I should think that we have shaken him off very effectively."

"My dear Watson, you evidently did not realize my meaning when I said that Moriarty may be taken as being quite on the same intellectual plane as myself. You do not imagine that if I were the pursuer I should allow myself to be baffled by so slight an obstacle. Why, then, should you think so meanly of him?"

"What will he do?"

"What I should do. Engage a special. This train stops at Canterbury. And there is always at least a quarter of an hour's delay at the boat. He will catch us there."

"One would think that we were the criminals. Let us have him arrested on his arrival."

"It would be the ruin of the work of three months. We should get the big fish, but the smaller would dart right and left out of the net. On Monday we should have them all. No, an arrest is inadmissible."

"What then?"

"We shall get off at Canterbury."

"And then?"

"Well, then we must make a cross-country journey to Newhaven, and so over to Dieppe. Moriarty will again do what I should do. He will get on to Paris, mark down our luggage, and wait for two days at the depot. In the meantime we shall treat ourselves to a couple of carpet bags, encourage the manufactures of the countries through which we travel, and make our way at our leisure into Switzerland, via Luxembourg and Basle."

At Canterbury, therefore, they alighted. In an hour there would be a train to Newhaven. Holmes pointed up the line.

"Already, you see," he said.

Far away among the Kentish woods there arose a thin spray of smoke. A minute later a carriage and engine could be seen flying along the open curve which leads to the station. Holmes and Watson had hardly time to take their places behind a pile of luggage when the special passed with a rattle and a roar, beating a blast of hot air into their faces.

"There he goes," Holmes said, as they watched the carriage swing and rock over the switch points. "There are limits, you see, to our friend's intelligence. It would have been a *coup de maître* had he deduced what I would deduce and acted accordingly."

"And what would he have done had he overtaken us?"

"There cannot be the least doubt that he would have made a murderous attack upon me. It is, however, a game at which two may play. The question now is whether we should take a premature lunch here, or run our chance of starving before we reach the buffet at Newhaven."

They made their way to Brussels that night and spent two days there, moving on upon the third day as far as Strasbourg. On the Monday morning Holmes had telegraphed to the London police, and in the evening they found a reply waiting for them at their hotel. Holmes tore it open, and then with a bitter curse hurled it into the grate.

"I might have known it," he groaned. "He has escaped!"

"Moriarty?"

"Yes, he has given them the slip. They have secured the whole gang with the exception of him."

But Scotland Yard was wrong.

Imagine a face, gaunt and swarthy, with the brow of a philosopher above and the jaw of a sensualist below. Imagine, between, cruel blue eyes with drooping, cynical lids, a fierce, aggressive nose, thin and projecting above a huge grizzled mustache, a mouth scored at the ends by deep, savage lines.

It is the face of Colonel Sebastian Moran.

The son of Sir Augustus Moran, C.B., at one time the British Minister to Persia, educated at Eton and Oxford, once of Her Majesty's Indian Army—the 1st Bangalore Pioneers—Colonel Sebastian Moran is the best shot in the empire, with a bag of tigers never rivaled.

He is also, after Professor James Moriarty, the most dangerous criminal in London.

But Colonel Sebastian Moran, the old shikari, is not at the moment in London. For Colonel Sebastian Moran is Professor Moriarty's chief of staff, and now, like his chief, he is on the Continent—bent on the destruction of Sherlock Holmes.

For a charming week Holmes and Watson wandered up the Valley of the Rhône, and then, branching off at Leuk, they made their way over the Gemmi Pass, still deep in snow, and so, by way of Interlaken, to Meiringen.

"It was a lovely trip," Watson wrote, "the dainty green of the spring below, the virgin white of the winter above; but it was clear to me that never for one instant did Holmes forget the shadow which lay across him. In the homely Alpine villages or in the lonely mountain passes, I could still tell, by his quick glancing eyes and his sharp scrutiny of every face that passed us, that he was well convinced that, walk where we would, we could not walk ourselves clear of the danger which was dogging our footsteps.

"Once, I remember, as we passed over the Gemmi, and walked along the border of the melancholy Daubensee, a large rock which had been dislodged from the ridge upon our right clattered down and roared into the lake behind us. In an instant Holmes had raced up on to the ridge, and, standing upon a lofty pinnacle, craned his neck in every direction. It was in vain that our guide assured him that a fall of stones was a common chance in the spring-time at that spot. He said nothing, but he smiled at me with the air of a man who sees the fulfillment of that which he expected . . ."

It was on the third of May that they reached the little village of Meiringen, where they put up at the 'Englischer Hof. At the advice of the landlord, they set off, on the afternoon of the fourth, with the intention of crossing the hills and spending the night at the hamlet of Rosenlaui.

First, however, they would make a small detour. The world-famous falls of the Reichenbach lay halfway up the hill, and Holmes desired to see them.

Now he and Watson stood at the brink. Below them the torrent, swollen by the melting snow, plunged into a tremendous abyss, from which the spray rolled up like the smoke from a burning house. The shaft into which the river hurled itself was an immense chasm, lined by glistening, coal-black rock, and narrowing into a creaming, boiling pit of incalculable depth, which brimmed over and shot the stream onward over its jagged lip.

Watson looked at the long sweep of green water roaring down, and the thick flickering curtain of spray hissing up, and shuddered. "This is a fearful place," he said.

"The path ends here," Holmes replied. "Let us return as we came."

They had turned to do so, when they saw a Swiss lad running along the path with a letter in his hand. It bore the mark of the 'Englischer Hof, and was addressed to Watson.

"What is it?" Holmes asked.

"An English lady at the hotel," Watson answered. "She has been taken with a sudden hemorrhage, and wishes to see an English doctor."

"You must return to Meiringen," Holmes said. "I will walk over the hill to Rosenlaui, where you can rejoin me this evening." He sat with his back against a rock and his arms folded, gazing down at the rush of waters below him.

Near the bottom of the descent, Watson turned and looked back. He could not see the fall, but he could see the curving path which wound over the shoulder of the hill and led to the brink. Along this a man was walking rapidly, his black figure outlined against the green behind him.

Watson hurried on upon his errand.

At Meiringen the landlord was standing at the door of his hotel.

"Well," said Watson, as he hurried up, "I trust that the lady is no worse?"

The landlord looked at him with surprise.

"You did not write this?" Watson asked, pulling the letter from his pocket. "There is no sick Englishwoman at the hotel?"

"Certainly not," the landlord cried. "But it has the hotel mark upon it! It must have been written by that tall Englishman who came in just after you had gone. He said—"

But Watson was already running down the village street, making for the path he had so recently descended.

"Good afternoon, Mr. Sherlock Holmes."

The detective looked up. Hands folded behind his back, feet planted wide, Professor James Moriarty stood blocking the narrow pathway that was the only road to safety. Holmes read an inexorable purpose in the master criminal's gray eyes.

"A somber spot," the professor continued. "A fitting spot for our last meeting."

Holmes said nothing.

"You are not an easy man to trace," the professor went on. "You must admit that having traced you is a tribute to the efficiency of my organization."

"An organization now ended."

The professor smiled thinly.

"Ended, temporarily, in England, perhaps," he admitted. "Thanks to your impertinent interference, Holmes. But here on the Continent I still have friends and valued allies. I shall perhaps remain here for a year or two. And then I shall return to a London made healthier by your absence."

The professor took a slow step forward.

Holmes sighed. "I may leave a note for my friend?" he asked.

The professor paused, then after a moment he nodded his agreement. "But make it, if you please, a short note, Mr. Holmes."

Holmes tore some leaves from his notebook and wrote:

My dear Watson. I write these few lines through the courtesy of Mr. Moriarty, who awaits my convenience for the final discussion of those questions which lie between us . . .

I am pleased to think that I shall be able to free society from any further effects of his presence, though I fear that it is at a cost which will give pain to my friends, and especially, my dear Watson, to you . . .

Indeed, if I may make a full confession to you, I was quite convinced that the letter from Meiringen was a hoax, and I allowed you to depart on that errand under the persuasion that some development of this sort would follow.

Tell Inspector Patterson that the papers which he needs to convict the gang are in the pigeon-hole M, done up in a blue envelope and inscribed "Moriarty." I made every disposition of my property before leaving England, and handed it to my brother Mycroft. Pray give my greetings to Mrs. Watson, and believe me to be, my dear fellow,

Very sincerely yours,

Sherlock Holmes.

Holmes folded the papers and placed them beneath his silver cigarette case on top of a rock that jutted into the path. Moriarty at his heels, he walked to the end of the pathway.

Holmes turned. Instantly, the professor sprang. His long, ape-like arms locked around the detective, forced him close to the edge of the chasm. For an instant they tottered together upon the brink of the fall. Then Holmes, with a lightning movement, broke the professor's grip. Quickly he stepped back. The professor's foot slipped on the spray-dampened rock. For a second he kicked madly and clawed the air with his hands. Then, with a horrible scream, he plunged over the brink. Holmes saw him fall for a long way, strike a rock, bound off, splash into the water. Minutes passed, and there was no further sign of the professor.

Before the master criminal's body had reached the bottom of the fall, Holmes had formed a plan. The professor was dead, he was sure, but Moriarty was not the only man who had sworn the death of Holmes. There were at least three others—the sinister Colonel Moran, the foremost of the three—whose desire for vengeance would only be increased by the death of their leader. If they were in London, Inspector Patterson would take them. But if one or more of them had come with Moriarty to the Continent . . .

Very well, let the world think him dead. Then these men, if they were still at liberty, would feel safe to take chances. They would lay themselves open, and sooner or later, he, Holmes, would destroy them.

But there was now an immediate problem. Holmes could not return along the path without leaving tracks in the wet ground that would betray him. He stood up and examined the rocky wall behind him. A few small footholds presented themselves, and some halfway to the top there were indications of a ledge. Holmes started the climb. Far beneath him the fall roared. Not a fanciful man, he still seemed to hear the voice of the professor screaming at him out of the abyss. The slightest mistake here would be fatal. Time and again tufts of grass came away in Holmes's hand. More than once his foot slipped in the wet notches of the rock. Still he struggled upward. At last he reached the ledge, several feet deep and covered with green moss. There he could lie unseen.

And there he was stretched when Dr. John H. Watson found himself at the Reichenbach Fall again.

In vain the doctor shouted. His only answer was his own voice reverberating in a rolling echo from the cliffs around him. The sight of Holmes's alpenstock, leaning against a rock, turned Watson cold and sick. He stood for a minute or two, trying to collect himself. Then he lay on his face and peered over the brink, the spray shooting up around him. He shouted again, but only the weird, half-human cry of the fall was borne back to him. Then the glitter of Holmes's cigarette case caught the doctor's eye. Beneath it he found Holmes's note. The writing was as firm and clear as though it had been written at the detective's desk in the old sitting room in Baker Street.

Slowly Dr. Watson read the note, and then, dazed with horror, he turned and stumbled down the path that led to the village.

On the ledge above the fall, Holmes pushed himself up on his elbows. His adventures, he imagined, had reached their end, but surprises were still in store for him.

A huge rock, falling from above, boomed past him, struck the path, bounded over into the chasm. A second later, another stone struck the ledge within a foot of the detective's head.

Holmes looked up. A grim face glared down at him, malevolence blazing in its cold blue eyes.

Holmes had been right, then. Moriarty had not come to the Continent alone. At least one confederate had kept guard while the professor attacked—and that confederate was the formidable Colonel Moran.

Again Holmes saw the face of the big-game hunter peer over the cliff. Again a rock twice the size of his head sang past him. Swiftly, Holmes swung himself over the edge of the ledge, hung by his hands, groped for a foothold. With infinite caution—the descent was far worse than the ascent—the detective lowered himself, inch by inch, down the almost sheer face of the cliff.

Torn and bleeding, he landed at last on the path. The watcher from above saw Sherlock Holmes of Baker Street disappear into the gathering darkness. With a curse, Colonel Moran threw a final, futile stone.

ENTR'ACTE. DR. WATSON, WRITER

[The] public . . . has shown some interest in those glimpses which I have occasionally given them of the thoughts and actions of a very remarkable man . . .

JOHN H. WATSON, M.D.

Heartbroken, weary, and mourning the death of the best and wisest man whom he had ever known, Dr. John H. Watson returned to England.

"Your merits should be publicly recognized," he had told Holmes at the close of the first adventure he and the detective had ever shared together. "You should publish an account of the case. If you won't, I will for you."

"You may do what you like, Doctor," Holmes had replied carelessly.

It was a long and arduous task, but Watson had his satisfaction. In December 1887, *Beeton's Christmas Annual* had carried, as its feature article, the chronicle which Watson had written and entitled, most strikingly, *A Study in Scarlet*.

Three years later, in 1890, he had given the public another adventure, the memorable *Sign of the Four*.

Now, in 1891, Dr. Watson sought to lose himself once more in the work of writing—difficult work, he found, for an ex-army surgeon turned general practitioner. But he knew no better way to pay tribute to the memory of his friend.

There arose a difficulty.

Watson's literary agent, Dr. Conan Doyle,[1] only recently re-

[1] Later Sir Arthur Conan Doyle (1859–1930). Though his ancestors were of the Irish landed gentry, Sir Arthur's grandmother, like Holmes's, was of French extraction. His grandfather, John Doyle, was a brilliant political cartoonist in the early 1800's; his uncle, Richard Doyle, drew the cover for *Punch* which was used until a few years ago; his uncle, Henry Doyle, was

turned from Vienna, had taken lodgings for himself and his family at No. 23 Montague Place, Russell Square. There Watson went to consult him.

Doyle had placed the *Study in Scarlet* for Watson, and had himself added the narrative "The Country of the Saints," to bring the doctor's manuscript up to book length. A skillful writer and a shrewd thinker, Dr. Conan Doyle had only recently written *The White Company*, which was even then appearing as a serial in *The Cornhill Magazine*.

Dr. Conan Doyle was happy to advise his friend Dr. John H. Watson.

"The situation as I see it is this," he said, leaning back in the armchair in which he did his own writing and puffing clouds of smoke from his Dublin clay. "You need an income far greater than your pension provides to support yourself and Mary. Yet your Paddington practice is a busy one. It has increased steadily since you bought it from old Farquhar. It leaves you no time, no energy, in which to write.

"Now, I seem to remember that during your first marriage your earlier practice—in Kensington, I believe it was—was never very absorbing.[2] Why not sell your Paddington practice and use the proceeds to repurchase the practice in Kensington? It will give you a living, at least—and still permit you to give the world more accounts of your remarkable friend."

It was good advice, and Watson followed it.

But now, in Kensington, he faced another difficulty.

So many of the cases he wished to put before the public— among them, "A Scandal in Bohemia," "The Red-Headed League," "A Case of Identity" and "The Five Orange Pips"— these and others had taken place during the period of his first marriage.

To speak so often of his first wife in the public prints would be a blow to Mary—a constant reminder that, in Watson's affections, she was second to another.

Watson found a solution. He would insert in certain of his accounts small statements, little references, that would make it

---

the director of the National Gallery of Ireland; his uncle, James Doyle, the compiler of *The Chronicle of England*.

[2] See "The Red-Headed League."

appear that these cases had taken place *after* the adventure of the Sign of the Four and his meeting with Mary. Then, when he spoke of "his wife," the reader, Watson reasoned, would naturally assume that the wife was Mary.[3]

It was a deception, and Watson, an honorable man, despised deception. But better to confound the reader than to wound Mary.

So Watson began to write, and the memoirs that had been simmering in his brain for so long began to pour forth.

It is no exaggeration to say that the entire world was electrified by the appearance, in *The Strand Magazine* for July 1891, not two months after Holmes's disappearance, of the first of these long-suppressed adventures.

From then until December 1893, two round dozen of them in all came in a steady stream from the faithful pen of Dr. John H. Watson.

[3] Thus, in "A Scandal in Bohemia," Watson speaks of "the well-remembered door" of 221 Baker Street, "which must always be associated in my mind with my wooing . . ." In "The Red-Headed League," the police official, Peter Jones, is made to refer to "that business of the Sholto murder, and the Agra treasure . . ." Again in "A Case of Indentity," Watson tells us that he "looked back" to "the weird business of the Sign of the Four"—and in "The Five Orange Pips," Holmes supposedly mentions the Sign of the Four as a "possibly more fantastic" case.

XVIII. MEETING IN MONTENEGRO: JUNE 1891

"Your son . . . has carried himself in this matter as I should be proud to see my own son do, should I ever chance to have one."

SHERLOCK HOLMES.

In the year 1891, Cettigne (Cetinje), capital of the isolated and all but inaccessible principality of Montenegro, was a city of perhaps three thousand inhabitants. But it held the governmental offices. It was the site of the new palace, housing the somewhat Ruritanian court of Prince Nicholas. And it boasted a theater-*cum*-opera house.

No railroads passed through Montenegro in the 1890's. The border was crossed by little except goat trails in the mountain passes. The little port of Antivari—it could be reached by one of the ships of the Puglia Line, sailing infrequently from Bari in Italy—was, practically, the only entrance to the country.

From Antivari, a precipitous road connected the port with Rieka and Cettigne, and up this road, on a fine day in June of the year 1891, toiled a carriage. It brought within it a tall, lean, hawk-nosed man who went by the name of Sigerson and who claimed to be a Norwegian.

Cettigne, Sherlock Holmes reasoned, was a city where one who had cause to believe that he was being hunted day and night by the redoubtable Colonel Moran might, for a time at least, feel some degree of security.

By the telegraph line to Belgrade and Vienna, he could easily keep in touch with his brother Mycroft—for, in all the world, only Mycroft and Moran knew that Sherlock Holmes still lived.

This was essential, for Holmes needed funds. And a little discreet bribery, plus a simple but effective disguise—a recently grown mustache and hair dyed black—would ensure that no news of his presence in Montenegro would reach the world outside.

All in all, Holmes was satisfied with the situation.

For Irene Adler, things had gone well since Inspector Lestrade, as she supposed, had freed her from her false marriage to the brute Norton.

Still an international beauty, still an operatic contralto of considerable merit, she had found her return to the stage none too difficult. For the moment, perhaps, La Scala and the Warsaw Opera were impossibilities, but someday—someday soon, perhaps . . .

Meantime, her own woman again, she rose to new heights as the featured member of her smaller company. Late in 1890 the troupe had gone on tour. Early 1891 found it in Eastern Europe. And now, in the June of 1891, it played the opera house in Cettigne, capital of Montenegro.

It was on the third night of *Rigoletto*—Irene in the role of Maddalena—that a note was handed to the contralto between the acts in her dressing room.

"An old acquaintance," it read, "would be given great pleasure if Miss Adler would consent to sup with him after the opera. Miss Adler will perhaps recall this acquaintance if he mentions that she once in 1887 wished him a good-night in Baker Street in London, adding his name. In Montenegro, however, he prefers to be known simply as

"Sigerson."

Irene Adler smiled. Across the bottom of the note she wrote: "Miss Irene Adler will be pleased to sup this evening with one she well remembers as a formidable antagonist in 1887."

"Take this to Monsieur Sigerson," she told the boy who had delivered the message, and returned to her dressing table.

It was comfortable in the great bed, comfortable, but lonely, too. It was a paradox: to be always alone, and yet never quite alone.

What did the calendar say? March 1892. She had lived for four-and-thirty years now. And what full years they had been! They had held all the good things that any years could hold— fortune and fame, and, more than fortune and fame put together, love.

There had been all the world to play in, and the chords that came forth in the playing were warm and sonorous. But of all that whole, wide, wonderful world, what a place to have picked to be born in! And what a place to have picked to *give* birth in! New Jersey! It was, she supposed, a place that you could learn to love, when you came to know it, especially if you had been born there. But why couldn't it have been some romantic spot in England or France or Spain or Italy? Montenegro would have been best of all. It was a lovely land, though full of strange people with stranger ways.

It had happened right there in Cettigne, and he had been sitting in that same box at the opera, night after night, almost within reach, and she had never recognized him. He had dyed his hair, of course, and he had grown that hateful mustache, but still she had never recognized him. And then the note came.

It was a charming villa he had found, there on the outskirts of Cettigne.

She had soon persuaded him to wash the dye from his hair, and then the mustache had gone. Sherlock was himself again. He had objected, of course, but by now he could deny her nothing. Then she had insisted that he have his photograph taken. It was ridiculous, she said, that he, the world's greatest detective, had never been photographed. "Besides," she said, "you carry always a photograph of me that I gave, not to you, but to a king. If you carry my photograph, I must carry a photograph of you." Holmes, still demurring, had nonetheless sat for the photograph.

Yes, these had been the happiest months of Irene Adler's entire life.

And then the fierce old man had come. She had seen his tall and stooping figure in the village square. He was English, certainly. The brow—like Shakespeare's! The cruel blue eyes—the jutting nose—the savage mouth! What had Sherlock said? That he had been a famous hunter of tigers. Now he hunted a man.

What should she do?

She herself must leave Montenegro soon, for now she carried her own secret. A false trail? One that would lead Sherlock away from Montenegro, out of danger—but in a very different direction from the one she herself planned to take?

The scheme had worked, but it had been most difficult. And what a dreadful journey to America! And first there had been the letter to compose—as hard to write, without letting certain things show through, as that other, the Briony Lodge letter. . . .

How dark it had become! And growing darker.

But the dark would be gone again with the rising sun. And its rays, slanting across the quiet room, would strike upon a photograph on the stand beside her bed. And the figure the sunlight would illuminate was not the figure of a barrister. Nor was it the figure of a king.[1]

We can be positive that the baby was a boy.

For consider:

There lives and works in New York City today a very famous man.

He was born in the United States, but Montenegro, he has said, was his "boyhood home." He joined its army while "still a boy."

A member of the American Historical Association in good

---

[1] The only photograph of Sherlock Holmes ever taken is reproduced, for the first time, as the jacket illustration of this volume.
Some explanation is perhaps required here.
As Holmesian scholars in the U.S. are now aware, "Irene Adler" was the stage name adopted by Miss Clara Stephens of Trenton, New Jersey, sister of Miss Eliza P. Stephens, the mother of the late, great, dearly beloved Sherlockian, James Montgomery.
In mid-1950, sorting over some family papers, Mr. Montgomery came unexpectedly upon an old photograph, carefully tucked away between two pieces of cardboard. With it was a faded old letter, which disclosed that *this* photograph was none other than that taken of "Irene Adler" and "the King of Bohemia."
Mr. Montgomery made this revelation, and actually *reproduced* the photograph in question, as a part of his 1950 Christmas greeting to fellow members of The Baker Street Irregulars, Inc. See his *Art in the Blood* and *What Is This Thing Called Music (or Body and Soul)*.
That Mr. Montgomery subsequently discovered other photographs and letters—including the photograph of Holmes and an account of Holmes's part in the Jack the Ripper murders, imparted to "Irene Adler" by Holmes himself—has not hitherto been revealed.

standing, who has examined "the source documents according to the approved methods of historical research," has established the year of this man's birth as "between 1892 and 1895."[2]

Another scholar, Dr. John D. Clark, has narrowed these dates to "late in 1892 or early 1893."[3]

Like Sherlock Holmes, this man is a professional detective, and he is often consulted by the official police in criminal cases. His home and office are an old brownstone house on the south side of Thirty-fifth Street, between Tenth and Eleventh avenues. Its address is 506 West Thirty-fifth. Its telephone number is Bryant 9-2828.

The name this man goes by is obviously an alias, a pseudonym. But it is surely no coincidence that the Christian name he uses contains the *er-o* of Sherlock, his surname the *ol-e* of Holmes.[4]

Three people only call this man by his Christian name. He himself calls only two people, not employees, by their Christian names.

Like Sherlock Holmes, this detective is assisted by a man of action who acts also as his biographer. The assistant, like Dr. John H. Watson, uses as his literary agent a celebrated author.

In his youth, this famous detective, like Sherlock Holmes, was an athlete.

Like Sherlock Holmes, this man is a gastronome, with a fine taste in food and wines.

Like Sherlock Holmes, this man has an (apparent) insensitiveness to women.

Like Sherlock Holmes, this man has done confidential work for his government. Before the Second World War, he worked for the U.S. State Department. During the Second World War he was consulted by the FBI on at least two occasions and by G-2 repeatedly.

Mentally, his resemblance to Sherlock Holmes is remarkable. As remarkable is his physical—and temperamental—resemblance to *Mycroft* Holmes.

[2] See "The Easy Chair," by Bernard De Voto, in *Harper's Magazine*, July 1954, pp. 8–15.

[3] For Dr. Clark's article, see *The Baker Street Journal*, Vol. VI, No. 1, New Series, January 1956, pp. 5–11.

[4] See "The Great O-E Theory," in *In the Queen's Parlor*, by Ellery Queen; New York: Simon & Schuster, 1957, pp. 4–5.

Like Mycroft Holmes, this man is large and stout. His body is "absolutely corpulent." His face, "though massive," has a "sharpness of expression." His hand, like that of Mycroft Holmes, could well be described as "broad," "flat," "like the flipper of a seal."

Like Mycroft Holmes, this man has little energy. From year's end to year's end, he takes as little exercise as possible. For him, the art of the detective begins and ends in reasoning from an armchair. He will almost never visit the scene of a crime—"a planet might as well leave its orbit." He lets others do any leg work that must be done.

It is significant to note that the celebrated author who serves as literary agent to this famous detective's assistant will neither confirm nor deny that the detective's father was none other than Sherlock Holmes of Baker Street.

"As the literary agent of [name deleted]," he wrote on June 14, 1955, in a letter to the editor of *The Baker Street Journal,* "I am of course privy to many details of [name deleted]'s past which to the general public . . . must remain moot for some time. If and when it becomes permissible for me to disclose any of those details, your distinguished journal would be a most appropriate medium for the disclosure. The constraint of my loyalty to my client makes it impossible for me to say more now.

"With my best respects,

        "Sincerely,

            "Rex Stout."

XIX. VENTURE INTO THE UNKNOWN: 1891-93

"I travelled for two years in Tibet, therefore, and amused myself by visiting Lhasa and spending some days with the head Lama. You may have read of the remarkable explorations of a Norwegian named Sigerson, but I am sure that it never occurred to you that you were receiving news of your friend . . ."

SHERLOCK HOLMES.

Mycroft Holmes, like his brother Sherlock, believed that work was the best antidote to sorrow.

Not for another four years would Dr. Watson learn the whole truth about Mycroft's unique position: "You are right in thinking that he is under the British Government," Sherlock Holmes would say to Watson in 1895.[1] "You would also be right in a sense if you said that occasionally he *is* the British Government."

Now, in August 1891, Sherlock sorrowed for his lost Irene. Very well; Mycroft, on behalf of the British Government, would find work for his brother.

Then, as in more recent years, Russian intrigue on the northern borders of India was continuous, and a source of great concern to Britain. Tibet was being infiltrated by Mongols and Buriats, acting as agents for Russia. Mycroft, *as* the British Government, would be delighted to have a trained observer, versed in the ways of international espionage, on the ground, to give him a true report on conditions in that vital but inaccessible border country.

"We may fairly infer," writes Mr. A. Carson Simpson,[2] that

[1] "The Adventure of the Bruce-Partington Plans."
[2] On Page 10, Vol. II, of his great work, *Sherlock Holmes's Wanderjahre;* Philadelphia: International Printing Company; Vol. I, 1953; Vol. II, 1954; Vol. III, 1955; Vol. IV, 1956.

Sherlock Holmes "went to Tibet with 'a message to Garcia.' How else can we account for his 'spending some days with the head Lama' at Lhasa?"

We may conjecture, then, though diplomatic secrecy does not permit us to verify, that the British Government would do everything it could to smooth Holmes's way through the British-controlled or dominated territory he would have to traverse en route. Therefore, with Mr. Simpson as our guide, let us join Holmes on his venture into the unknown at Darjeeling, 7160 feet above sea level in the imposing mountains of Northern India.

At Darjeeling, Holmes had a short but busy stay, recruiting and outfitting the men and animals for his adventure, buying and packing such stores as tea and flour, sugar and potatoes. Much of this had already been attended to, on orders from Mycroft to the India Office; the other necessary items Holmes had obtained in Bombay and Calcutta.

At Darjeeling also Holmes received the permit necessary to enter and travel in Tibet—an imposing document, dated in the Year of the Iron Female Hare, signed by the Head Lama, Regent during the minority of the Dalai Lama and abbot of the great Ten-gye-ling Monastery in Lhasa, then one of the four major monasteries in Tibet. It opened up to Holmes the land north of those giants of the Himalaya mountain range which Holmes could see from the hill station where he assembled his expeditionary force. No doubt he speculated, as he worked, on what he would find beyond them.

Once ready to go, Holmes dropped 6450 feet in his eighteen-mile trip by cart road to the valley of the Teesta River. This he crossed at the Teesta Bridge on the following day and started his sixty-mile trip, over a narrow and crude pony track, to the Tibetan frontier.

The monsoon had already set in. There were heavy, driving rains each day. The Teesta Valley was low, narrow, scorching hot, devoid of the slightest breeze. In this stifling, steamy atmosphere, Holmes first encountered that ultimate in irritants, the Himalayan leech.

On stones and blades of grass along the path, the leeches in multitudes sat waiting for their meal of blood. They clung to any animal or human being who passed. Holmes's mules suffered severely, and drops of blood on the stones of the path became frequent from their bleeding wounds.

All that first evening Holmes himself was busy picking leeches from his clothes, hands, legs, head. They climbed up the sides of his tent and dropped down into his food, his cup, and onto his plate. They varied in size from great striped horse leeches to tiny leeches as thin as a pin—these, when gorged, would swell to the size of a finger.

It was a baptism of blood, and, having undergone it, Holmes was peculiarly qualified, in 1894, to uncover the truth of "the repulsive story of the red leech and the terrible death of Crosby, the banker."[3]

Contending with leeches all the way, Holmes followed the pony track through Yalimpong, gradually climbing along the river to Rangpo, where he left it and entered Sikkim. The very conditions which favored the leeches brought their compensation, for his way now led through a tropical forest of evergreen oaks, tree ferns, pandanus, hibiscus, daturas, bougainvillaeas, festooned with orchids and flowering creepers and with large and brilliantly colored butterflies flitting across the path in profusion.

Here began the steep climb to the Tibetan frontier. Near Gnatong, the path reached the zone of many-colored rhododendrons. Soon after, Holmes crossed the 13,390-foot Jelep La (Pass) on the frontier, and made the steep descent into the Chumbi Valley. The beginning of the climb up the valley to the settlement of Chumbi was easy, and the foliage—consisting largely of birch, sycamore, willow, wild roses, iris, and wild strawberry—was a welcome change from that on the Sikkim side of the pass.

---

[3] "The Adventure of the Golden Pince-Nez." Unfortunately, Dr. Watson did not see fit to give us any particulars about this case; it was perhaps too horrible for a Victorian public. Mr. Simpson suggests that Crosby encountered a gigantic leech—a mutation, or "sport"—that was to drain *all* of the blood from his system, leaving only a shrunken corpse. He does not, however, exclude the possibility that the term "leech" was used in its extended meaning of "physician," and that the "red" refers to the color of his hair, the color of his clothes, his association with bloodletting, or his political complexion, "in which case he would naturally select the capitalist Crosby as his victim."

Holmes climbed rapidly to Phari Dzong, forty miles from the Jelep La and even higher.

Holmes was traveling now across the high Tibetan Plain, with the monsoon rains behind him, and experiencing the typical dry Tibetan climate, with brilliant sunshine, blue skies, still mornings, and strong afternoon winds blowing the dust into everything.

At Gyantsa the trade route to western Tibet diverged, but Holmes, of course, continued toward Lhasa. Just a hundred miles farther along, he crossed the Tsangpo by the famous ancient iron-chain suspension bridge—a single span of about 150 yards, suspended from iron chains of one-foot links, between tall masonry piers. Intended only for pedestrians, it had a footway of one-foot-wide planks lashed end to end, suspended from the chains by yak-hair cables.

Near here the Tsangpo joined the Kyi River, and this Holmes followed for another thirty-five miles to Lhasa. There his first act was to call upon the head Lama and present him with the traditional white silk scarf.

We know that Holmes visited Tibet on behalf of the British Government, but this still leaves a question unanswered. Why did the regent, the head Lama, take the unprecedented course of inviting Holmes to come to Lhasa to see him?

Mrs. Winifred M. Christie has submitted[4] that only one hypothesis will explain that invitation: the regent knew Holmes's true identity, and invited him to Lhasa to discover the truth about a creature which, by 1891, had come to concern him, a creature some of his people called *metoh-kangmi,* which has been translated into English as "Abominable Snowman."[5]

While the Snowman did not explode into the European consciousness until 1921, when his tracks were seen on a 22,350-foot pass by members of the First Everest Expedition, the tradition of this formidable being existed much earlier in Tibet and disquieting stories were told about him. None at that time claimed

[4] "On the Remarkable Explorations of Sigerson," *The Sherlock Holmes Journal,* Vol. I, No. 2, September 1952, pp. 39–44.

[5] "Abominable" is not an exact rendition of the Tibetan term. Authorities contend that "filthy," "disgusting," or "demon" might be a better translation.

to have seen him and lived. He was known only by his footprints in the snow.

"What more natural, therefore," Mr. Simpson writes, "than for the regent to turn to the world's greatest authority on footprints? We know that [Holmes] was ahead of his time in this, as in other methods of scientific crime detection. His monograph 'Upon the Tracing of Footsteps, with Some Remarks upon the Use of Plaster of Paris as a Preserver of Impresses' . . . was translated into the French by François le Villard of the French detective service."[6]

As for the regent, he had good reason for wanting to know more about the Snowman. As Sir Charles Bell writes, in *Tibet, Past and Present* (Oxford, 1924, p. 21):

"According to their Legend the Tibetans are descended from a monkey. The latter, who was an incarnation of Chen-re-zi, the Compassionate Spirit, met a she-devil, who addressed him thus: 'By reason of my actions in my former life I have been born in a demon race, but, being in the power of the god of lust, I love you greatly.' After much hesitation and after consulting his spiritual guide, the Compassionate One married her and they had six children. The father fed these on sacred grain, with the result that by degrees the hair on their bodies decreased, and their tails became shorter and finally disappeared. So says the Tibetan chronicle: Pu-tön Rim-po-che's Chö-chung, folio 10."

"The Lama," Mr. Simpson adds, "was, of course, concerned to know whether or not the Snowmen were atavistic cousins of the Tibetans of his day."

What were they like, these Snowmen? Perhaps the best account of them to date is given by Captain John Noel, in *The Story of Everest* (Boston, 1927, pp. 110–12):

"They lived high up on Everest, and at times came down and wrought havoc in the villages. . . . One must speak of them with great respect, otherwise they will bring bad luck and perhaps even come down and raid and kill, because they are known to kill men, carry off women, and to bite the necks of yaks and drink their blood. The ordinary Tibetan peasant . . . tells of their strange rovings in the snow, of the long hair which falls over their

[6] In 1888 (*The Sign of the Four*). Its first publication, in English, was in 1878.

eyes, so that if you are chased by a Sukpa[7] you must run downhill; then the long hair will get into his eyes and you can escape from him. . . . The King of the Sukpas is supposed to live on the very top of Everest, whence he can look down upon the world below, and choose upon which herd of grazing yaks he will descend. Yak-herds say that the Sukpa can jump by huge bounds at a time; that he is much taller than the tallest man; and that he has a hard tail upon which he can sit. The men he kills he will not eat. He just bites off the tips of their fingers, toes and noses, and leaves them."

The Second Everest Expedition (1922) found no footprints left by the Snowmen, but were assured by the abbot of the Rongbuk Lamasery that there were at least five of these beings in the Upper Rongbuk Valley and its glaciers.

In 1925, however, a European, N. A. Tombazi, actually saw a Snowman near the Zemu Gap in Sikkim. "I soon perceived the object, two or three hundred yards down the valley," Tombazi wrote (in *Account of a Photographic Expedition to the Southern Glaciers of Kangchenjunga in the Sikkim Himalaya,* Bombay, 1925, pp. 55–57). "There was no doubt that its outline was like that of a human being; it walked upright. . . . Against the snow it looked dark, and apparently it wore no clothes. . . . I examined the footprints, which resembled those of a human being, although they were only six or seven inches in length. The five toes and instep were clearly visible, but the imprint of the heel was very slight. The prints were undoubtedly those of a biped. From enquiries I gathered that no human being had been in this area since the beginning of the year."

Footprints of the Snowman were photographed in 1951 by Eric Shipton of the Mount Everest Reconnaissance Expedition, at about 19,000 feet on the Nepal side of Everest, and found to be just about the length of the head of his ice ax.

The Swiss expedition of the next year measured the tracks as well, and found them to be 29 cm. long, 12 cm. wide and 51 cm. apart.

The London *Daily Mail* expedition of 1954 saw several scalps of the Snowmen in monasteries, where they were used in ceremonial

[7] Another native name for this awesome creature. It is also known as the *Yeti.*—W.S.B.-G.

dances. According to the official historian of the expedition,[8] the Sherpas of Nepal—an intelligent, logical-minded, hardheaded, and trustworthy people—all agree that the Snowman is about 5½ feet tall, with a high pointed head and a hairless face, but with a body covered with stiff, reddish, four-inch-long hair. He has a distinctive call, which has been compared to that of a sea gull, but much louder. This is, of course, the smaller of the two types of Snowman: Izzard reports that the *Daily Mail* expedition found that there are two types—the larger *dzu-teh* of Tibet and adjacent Sikkim and the smaller *mih-teh* of Nepal.

But all of this would come much later. When Holmes undertook to investigate the Snowman for the head Lama in 1891, only one European, Lieutenant Colonel L. Austine Waddell, had seen its footprints—on a high pass in Sikkim in 1889—and his account of the discovery, *Among the Himalayas,* would not be published until nine years later, in 1898.

We may be sure that Holmes, while discussing Snowmen with the head Lama, also asked him for instruction in Lamaistic Buddhism.

It will be remembered that Holmes, in September 1888, during his investigation of the Sign of the Four, discoursed upon the Buddhism of Ceylon "as though he had made a special study of it."

Perhaps his interest was first aroused by his part in solving the singular tragedy of the Atkinson Brothers at Trincomalee in early 1887 or late 1886. In any case, an authority on the southern form of Buddhism, he would now be anxious to learn more about the northern, or Tibetan, form.

"Knowing his indomitable determination," Mr. Simpson writes, "can we doubt that he . . . carried his studies far enough to be an Arhanta, an adept?"

Mr. Simpson holds that the changes in Holmes after 1894, noted by so many Sherlockian commentators, are clearly due to this.

"Among the changes in Holmes which support this explanation," Mr. Simpson continues, "is his renunciation of the cocaine

[8] Ralph Izzard, *The Abominable Snowman;* Garden City, N.Y.: Doubleday & Company, Inc., 1955. See also Charles Stonor, *The Sherpa and the Snowman;* London: Hollis & Carter, 1955.

habit. There is no instance of his taking this, or any other, narcotic after his Return. . . . The knowledge which he gathered from the lamas of Tibet would enable him to attain tranquility of mind without the aid of a Lethean drug. . . .

"Significant, too, is the change in [Holmes's] drinking habits after his Return, in view of the Tibetan opposition to the use of alcohol.[9] While he was not changed into a total abstainer, he became an extreme moderate. Before he went to Tibet, there are many references to his drinking, which included whisky and brandy. In the . . . adventures which took place after the Return, however, covering a score of years, there are only four instances of his taking a drink, and in no case did he imbibe ardent spirits. . . .

"A further confirmation of the influence of Buddhist doctrine is to be found in the fact that, after his Return, he only once killed a living thing. . . .[10]

"Our conclusion is reenforced, too, by an attitude clearly inspired by lamaistic teachings. . . . In 'The Adventure of the Abbey Grange' [Holmes says] 'Once or twice in my career I feel that I have done more real harm by my discovery of the criminal than ever he had done by his crime. I have learned caution now, and I had rather play tricks with the law of England than with my own conscience.' . . .

"We must remember that, to the lama, Nirvana is not extinction, as the primitive Buddhists hold, but a hereafter of eternal fulfillment at the Ten Points of Space. [Holmes's] recognition of this, as well as of the doctrines of Karma and of the Acquisition of Merit, are clearly shown by his words to Mrs. Ronder in 'The Adventure of the Veiled Lodger': 'The ways of fate are indeed hard to understand. If there is not some compensation hereafter, then the world is a cruel jest.'

"And later, in the same story: 'Your life is not your own. Keep your hands off of it. . . . The example of patient suffering is in itself the most precious of all lessons to an impatient world.'

9 All the same the Tibetans make a beer called *chang,* which makes Snowmen who get at it quite drunk.—W.S.B.-G.

10 And Holmes in this case regarded himself as the executioner of a sinister, destructive organism See "The Adventure of the Lion's Mane." —W.S.B.-G.

"Again, Holmes is seen to accept the doctrine of the unreality of the external world and of what we think of as tangible, physical things, when he says in 'The Adventure of the Retired Colourman': 'Is not all life pathetic and futile? . . . We reach. We grasp. And what is left in our hands at the end? A shadow.' This is sometimes called the doctrine of illusion.

"Still more significant are the closing words of 'The Adventure of the Cardboard Box':[11] 'What is the meaning of it, Watson? What object is served by this circle of misery and violence and fear? It must tend to some end, or else our universe is ruled by chance, which is unthinkable. But what end? There is the great standing perennial problem to which human reason is as far from an answer as ever.'

"Here is a clear recognition of one of the cardinal principles of Lamaistic Buddhism—that true understanding is impossible by one's own unaided reasoning; the guidance of a teacher is necessary. Here, too, is an obvious reference to the doctrine of the Round (or Wheel) of Existence, in which the individual is condemned to suffer, to a greater or less degree, through a series of reincarnations in varied forms. He can escape the Round only by acquiring that profound realization of the Tradition which is called Enlightenment, and which elevates him to Buddhahood. . . ."

The head Lama would surely tell Holmes that one of the most suitable teachers of the doctrine was the abbot of the Rocky Valley Inner Monastery at Rongbuk. This was situated only sixteen miles from Mount Everest, where Holmes was going, in any event, to investigate the Snowman.

Another place which Holmes would naturally visit in the course of his explorations, and where he would receive spiritual guidance of the highest order, was the Monastery of the Mount of Blessing—Ta-shi Lhün-po—the seat of the Pan-chen Rim-po-che, or Ta-shi Lama; this great dignitary ranks almost with the Dalai Lama.

Holmes, then, would retrace his steps to the Chak-sam Bridge

[11] Since this adventure demonstrably took place *before* Holmes's visit to Tibet, it is another example of his early interest in Buddhism in all its forms, and his deep reading therein.—W.S.B.-G.

and a bit beyond, then take the northern branch of the east-west trade route, following the Tsangpo for some miles. The two branches unite near Shigatse; then, a bit farther on, the caravan trail to Katmandu diverges. Holmes would follow this through Shekar Dzong to Tingri Dzong. There he would turn to the south, following the river valley to Rongbuk—a trip of some 375 miles from Lhasa.

How far Holmes climbed Mount Everest is an insoluble problem. Mr. Simpson thinks it unlikely that he reached the summit, "but he may well have gone as far as the North Col, or perhaps even higher," in his pursuit of the Snowman. This, of course, as Mr. Simpson so rightfully notes, made Holmes "the first European—and probably the first man—to set foot on the sacred ground of the highest mountain in the world. To the British Empire, therefore, belongs the credit for the first partial ascent, as well as for finishing the job on that memorable May 29, 1953, over sixty years later."

Holmes was well fitted for the task, for, as Watson tells us,[12] "Few men were capable of greater muscular effort . . . he was absolutely untiring." He was "exceptionally strong in the fingers"[13]—a great asset for mountain-climbing—and he "was always in training."[14] He was a good runner and therefore strong-winded: "We had run two miles, I suppose, before Holmes at last halted."[15] We recall, too, that at the Reichenbach Fall, Holmes climbed to a difficult ledge from which he watched Watson's search for him.

"Where did he get this flair?" asks Mr. Simpson. "Apparently from the same source as his 'art in the blood' "—his maternal forebears, the Vernets. Eric Shipton, the noted climber, says: 'Since the first World War, French mountaineers have been in the forefront in the field of Alpine achievement. They have been very largely responsible for the astonishing advance in climbing technique during the last thirty years. The [name] . . . Vernet . . . will live among the greatest in the history of mountaineering.' "[16]

---

12 "The Yellow Face."
13 "The Adventure of the Beryl Coronet."
14 "The Adventure of the Solitary Cyclist."
15 "The Adventure of Charles Augustus Milverton."
16 Introduction to Maurice Herzog's *Annapurna* (New York, 1953, p. 5). Mr. Simpson adds that "a notion of the great climbing ability and attain-

It would be idle to speculate on the contents of Holmes's report on the Abominable Snowman. Until the Government of Tibet sees fit to release it to the world, we may only be sure that Holmes solved the mystery to his own complete satisfaction, and to that of the head Lama.

There seems little doubt, however, that Holmes found the Snowman to be a mild, inoffensive creature. With his new respect for animal life, Holmes would surely keep its existence a secret so that it should not be shot by sportsmen or imprisoned in zoos by scientists, let alone exterminated, as so many other rare animals have been in recent years and are being today.

Holmes tells us that he next "passed through Persia" and "looked in at Mecca." Seldom have we had a better example of his dry humor, for Persia in that year 1893 was seething with unrest, and all strangers, particularly Englishmen and Russians, were regarded with suspicion. As for Mecca, it was then in the midst of a civil war.

Holmes then "paid a short but interesting visit to the Khalifa at Khartoum," the results of which he communicated to the Foreign Office. Here Watson's report is in error. The Khalifa[17] was not at Khartoum in 1893—that historic city had been leveled to the ground in 1885, and the Khalifa had taken up his residence in nearby Omdurman, where he held forth embattled until 1898, when General Kitchener overthrew him and returned the seat of affairs once more to Khartoum.

Returning then to Europe, Holmes spent some months in research into the coal-tar derivatives, which he conducted in a laboratory at his beloved Montpellier in the South of France. But his interest in crime never slackened; with avidity he scanned the French journals. And thus it was, early in April 1894, that Sherlock Holmes learned of the death of the Honorable Ronald Adair, second son of the Earl of Maynooth,[18] murdered between

---

ments of this Jean Vernet , . . can be obtained from his writings, *Au coeur des Alpes,* Grenoble, 1951, for example." It is surely also significant that Holmes, like Sir Edmund Hillary, was a tall, lean man, and that Holmes, in later life, like Sir Edmund, was a *beekeeper.*

[17] The Mohammedan ruler of the Sudan south of Egypt and Libya.

[18] The Earl of Maynooth was at that time governor of one of the Australian colonies.

the hours of ten and eleven-twenty on the night of March 30, under what Holmes's journal called "most unusual and inexplicable circumstances."

The facts were these:

After dinner on March 30, Adair had played a rubber of whist at one of his clubs, the Bagatelle. He had returned exactly at ten to the apartment he shared with his mother and sister at No. 427 Park Lane. His mother and sister were out, but the servant deposed that she had heard Adair enter the front room on the second floor, generally used as his sitting room. She had lit a fire there; it smoked; she had opened the window. No sound was heard from the room until eleven-twenty, when Lady Maynooth and her daughter returned.

Lady Maynooth went to her son's sitting room to say good night; the door was locked on the inside, and she had received no answer to her cries or knocking. Help was obtained; the door was forced. The Honorable Ronald Adair was found lying near the tea table. His head had been horribly mutilated by an expanded revolver bullet (Holmes's gray eyes narrowed), but no weapon of any sort was found in the room. On the table lay two bank notes for £10 each and £17 10s. in silver and gold. There were some figures also upon a sheet of paper, with the names of some club friends opposite to them. From this it was conjectured that before his death the young man had been trying to make out his losses or winnings at cards.

A minute examination served only to make the case more complex. No reason could be given why Adair should have fastened the door upon the inside. There was no possibility that the murderer could have done this and then escaped by the window, for the drop was at least twenty feet and a bed of crocuses in full bloom lay beneath, undisturbed. No one could have climbed to the window without leaving traces. Had a man fired through the open window? It would be a remarkable shot who could inflict with a revolver so deadly a wound. Again, no one had heard a shot.

An inquest would of course be held. Certain to be called were the three men with whom Adair had played whist at the Bagatelle Club on the evening of the thirtieth.

They were Mr. Murray and Sir John Hardy.

And—Holmes gripped the paper so tightly that his knuckles went white.

And the famous big-game hunter, Colonel Sebastian Moran.

XX. THE RETURN OF SHERLOCK HOLMES: THURSDAY, APRIL 5, 1894

The crime was of interest in itself, but that interest was nothing to me compared to the inconceivable sequel . . .
JOHN H. WATSON, M.D.

Dr. John H. Watson's close intimacy with Mr. Sherlock Holmes had interested him very deeply in crime. He never failed to read with care the various problems which came before the public during the years 1891–94, and he even attempted on several occasions to employ Holmes's methods in their solution, though, he tells us," "with indifferent success."[1]

But no other crime of which he had recently read so appealed to him as that of the tragedy of Ronald Adair. All day as he drove upon his rounds he turned the matter over in his mind, yet found no explanation which seemed to him satisfactory.

That evening he strolled across Hyde Park and found himself about six o'clock at the Oxford Street end of Park Lane. A group of loafers upon the pavement, all staring up at a certain window, directed him to the house he had come to see. A tall, thin man with colored glasses, whom Watson strongly suspected

---

[1] Watson, as usual, is being overly modest. Despite the continual attempt in his chronicles to play down his own perspicacity, it is impossible for him to disguise completely the fact that he is by no means a fool. To give one example out of many that might be cited: In *The Hound of the Baskervilles,* Watson makes a series of "perfectly sound" (as Holmes called them) deductions about Dr. James Mortimer from an examination of that gentleman's walking stick. As Holmes also declared at the time: "I am bound to say that in all the accounts which you have been so good as to give of my own small achievements you have habitually underrated your own abilities. . . ."

of being a plain-clothes detective, was pointing out some theory of his own, while the loafers crowded around to listen to what he said. Watson got as near as he could, but the man's observations seemed to him absurd. He stepped back in disgust. As he did so he struck against an elderly man and knocked several books from his arm. Some poor bibliophile, Watson thought, as he bent to pick up the books and noted the title of one of them —*The Origin of Tree Worship*. Without thanks for Watson's courtesy, but rather with a snarl of contempt, the old collector turned upon his heel, and Watson saw his bowed back and long white side whiskers disappear into the throng.

Watson had not been back in his study in Kensington for five minutes when the maid announced a caller. To Watson's surprise, it was the old book collector, his precious volumes wedged under his arm.

"You're surprised to see me, sir," the old man croaked. "Well, I've a conscience, sir, and when I chanced to see you go into this house, I thought to myself, I'll just step in and see that kind gentleman, and tell him that if I was a bit gruff in my manner there was not any harm meant, and that I am much obliged to him for picking up my books."

"You make too much of a trifle," Watson said. "May I ask how you knew who I was?"

"Well, sir, if it isn't too great a liberty, I am a neighbor of yours, for you'll find my little bookshop at the corner of Church Street, and very happy to see you, I am sure. Maybe you collect yourself, sir? Here's *British Birds,* and *Catullus,* and *The Holy War*—a bargain, every one of them. With five volumes you could just fill that gap on the second shelf. It looks a bit untidy, does it not, sir?"

Watson turned his head to look at the cabinet behind him. When he turned again, Sherlock Holmes was standing smiling at him across his study table.

For the first and last time in his life, Dr. John H. Watson fainted.

"My dear Watson," said the well-remembered voice, "I owe you a thousand apologies. I had no idea you would be so affected."

"Holmes!" Watson cried. "Is it really you? Can it be that you are indeed alive? Is it possible that you succeeded in climbing out of that awful abyss?"

Holmes chuckled. "Well," he said, "I had no great difficulty getting out of it, for the very simple reason that I was never in it." Stretching—"It is no joke for a tall man to take a foot off his stature for several hours"—Holmes told Watson the entire story. "And now, my dear fellow," he concluded when the long tale was over, "if I may ask for your co-operation, we have a hard and dangerous night's work ahead of us. You'll come with me?"

"When you like and where you like!"

"This is indeed like old times!" Holmes cried. And then his face sobered. "I have read in the journals about Mary," he said. He laid a hand on Watson's shoulder. "Work, Watson, as I well know myself, is the best antidote to sorrow, and I have a piece of work for both of us tonight. Still, we have time for a mouthful of dinner. And we have three years of the past to discuss. Let that suffice until half-past nine, when you and I shall once again start off upon an adventure—the notable adventure of the empty house."

It was indeed like old times when, at half-past nine, Dr. Watson found himself seated once again beside Sherlock Holmes in a hansom cab, his revolver in his pocket and the thrill of adventure in his heart.

Holmes's hawklike features were cold and stern and silent in the light of the street lamps, his brows drawn down and his thin lips compressed.

Holmes stopped the cab at the corner of Cavendish Street, and, as they stepped out, Watson saw him glance searchingly to right and left. Then, with an assured step, he rapidly led Watson through a network of mews and stables whose very existence the doctor had never guessed.

They emerged at last into a small road, lined with gloomy old houses, which led them into Manchester and then to Blandford Street. Here Holmes turned swiftly down a narrow passage, passed through a wooden gate into a deserted yard, and then, taking a key from his pocket, opened the back door of a house. Holmes and Watson entered together, the detective closing the door softly behind them.

The place was pitch dark, but it was evident to Watson that they were in an empty house. His feet creaked over bare planking, and his outstretched hand touched a wall from which the paper hung in ribbons. Holmes's cold, thin fingers closed around his wrist, led him forward through a long hall until he could dimly see the fanlight over the door. Here Holmes turned suddenly to the right. They found themselves in a large, square, empty room, heavily shadowed in the corners, but faintly lit in the center from the lights of the street beyond. Holmes put his lips close to Watson's ear.

"Do you know where we are?" he whispered.

Watson stared through the murky window. "Why, surely this is Baker Street!" he said.

"Exactly. We are in Camden House, which stands opposite to our old quarters."

"But why are we here?"

"Because Camden House commands so excellent a view of No. 221. Draw a little nearer to the window, Watson, taking every precaution not to show yourself, and then look up at our old rooms."

Watson crept forward and looked across at the bow window. As his eyes fell upon it, he gave a cry of amazement. The blind was down, and a strong light was burning in the room. The shadow of a man, seated in a chair, was thrown, hard and black, against the blind. There was no mistaking the figure—the shadow was that of Sherlock Holmes!

"Good heavens!" Watson cried. "It's marvelous!"

"The credit should go to Monsieur Oscar Meunier, of Grenoble, who spent some days doing the molding from a photograph with which I provided him—the only photograph, Watson, that I have ever allowed to be taken. The result is a bust in wax, which I arranged myself during a short visit to Baker Street this afternoon."

"But why, Holmes, why?"

"Because, my dear Watson, I had the strongest possible reason for wishing a certain person to think that I was there when I am really elsewhere. He knew—and *only* he, except for my brother Mycroft, knew—that Sherlock Holmes was still alive. He lost my trail once, in Montenegro, but he knew that sooner or later I should come back to my rooms. He has had them watched continuously, and this morning his sentinel saw me arrive. The sentinel is a harmless enough fellow—a garrotter by trade, and a remarkable performer upon the jew's-harp. I cared nothing for him. But I cared a great deal for the much more formidable person who was behind him, the bosom friend of Moriarty, the man who dropped the rocks over the cliff at Reichenbach, the most cunning and dangerous criminal now at large in London. That is the man who is after me tonight, Watson, and that is the man who is quite unaware that we are after *him*."

Watson, his eyes still fastened upon the lighted window, clutched Holmes's arm and pointed upward.

"The shadow moved!" he cried.

"Of course it moved," Holmes replied. "Am I such a farcical bungler that I should erect a dummy and expect one of the sharpest men in Europe to be deceived by it? We have now been in this room for two hours, and Mrs. Hudson has made some change in the figure eight times. She works it from the front, so that her shadow may never be seen. Ah!"

Holmes drew in his breath with a shrill, excited intake. In the dim light Watson could see that his head was thrown forward, his whole attitude rigid with attention. Then a low, stealthy sound came to Watson's ears, not from the direction of Baker Street, but from the back of the very house in which they lay concealed. A door opened and shut. An instant later steps crept down the passage—steps which were meant to be silent, but which reverberated harshly through the empty house. Holmes crouched back against the wall, and Watson did the same, his hand closing upon the handle of his revolver. The vague outline of a man stood for an instant in the open door. Then, crouching, menacing, the man crept forward into the room. The sinister figure stole over to the window, and very softly and noiselessly raised it for half a foot. As he sank to the level of the opening, the light of the street lamp, no longer dimmed by the dusty glass, fell full upon his face. The man seemed to be beside himself with excitement. His cold blue eyes glittered, his features worked convulsively. From the pocket of his overcoat, the man drew a bulky object. He busied himself in some task which ended with a loud, sharp click, as if a spring or bolt had fallen into place. Still kneeling upon the floor, he bent forward and threw all his weight and strength upon some lever. There was a long, whirling, grinding noise, ending once more in a powerful *click*. The man straightened himself then, and Watson saw that he held in his hand a sort of gun, with a curiously misshapen butt. He opened it at the breech, put something in, and snapped the breech lock. Then, crouching down, he rested the end of the barrel upon the ledge of the open window. His long mustache drooped over the stock, and his eye gleamed as it peered along the sights. With a sigh of satisfaction, the man cuddled the butt into his shoulder. His finger tightened on the trigger. Then there was a strange, loud whiz and a long, silvery tinkle of broken glass.

At that instant Holmes sprang like a tiger onto the marksman's back. The man was up in an instant. With convulsive strength he seized Holmes by the throat, but Watson struck him hard on the back of the head with the butt of his revolver, and the man dropped flat upon his face. Watson fell upon him, held him fast as Holmes blew a shrill call upon a police whistle. Instantly there was the clatter of running feet upon the pavement outside, and two policemen in uniform, with one small, sharp-featured plain-clothes detective, rushed through the front entrance and into the room.

"That you, Lestrade?" Holmes asked.

"Yes, Mr. Holmes. I took the job myself. It's good to see you back in London, sir."

"I thought you needed a little irregular help," Holmes laughed. "Three undetected murders in one year won't do, Lestrade! But I must admit that you handled the Molesey Mystery with less than your usual—well, that's to say, you handled it very well."

The prisoner, breathing hard, with a constable holding each arm, fixed his cruel blue eyes on Holmes. "You fiend!" he muttered. "You clever, clever fiend!"

"Ah, Colonel," Holmes said, arranging his rumpled collar. " 'Journeys end in lovers' meetings,' as the old play says. This, gentlemen, is Colonel Sebastian Moran, whom I have not had the pleasure of seeing since he favored me with some small attentions as I lay on a ledge above the Reichenbach Fall."

Colonel Moran sprang forward with a snarl of rage, but the constables dragged him back.

"You may or may not have just cause for arresting me," he said, "but at least there can be no reason why I should have to submit to the gibes of this person. If I am in the hands of the law, let things be done in a legal way."

"Well, that's reasonable enough," Lestrade said. "Anything further you have to say, Mr. Holmes, before we go?"

Holmes had picked up the powerful air gun from the floor and was examining its mechanism with great interest.

"An admirable and unique weapon," he said. "Noiseless and of tremendous power. I knew Von Herder, the blind German mechanic, who constructed it to the order of the late Professor Moriarty. For years I have been aware of its existence, though I have never before had an opportunity of handling it. I commend it very specially to your attention, Lestrade, and also the bullets which fit it."

"You can trust us to look after it, Mr. Holmes," Lestrade said, as the whole party moved toward the door. "Anything else?"

"Only to congratulate you most heartily. With your usual mixture of cunning and audacity, you have got him."

"Got whom, Mr. Holmes?"

"Why, the man the whole force has been seeking in vain— Colonel Sebastian Moran, who shot the Honorable Ronald Adair with an expanding bullet from an air gun through the open window of the second floor of No. 427 Park Lane, upon the 30th of last month. Colonel Moran and young Adair had between them won a considerable amount of money at cards. Then Adair discovered that Moran had been cheating. Adair threatened to expose him. That would mean ruin for Moran. He therefore murdered Adair, who at the time had locked his door and was endeavoring to work out how much of his winnings he should return to those who had been cheated by his partner. Well, Colonel Moran will trouble us no more. The air gun will embellish the Black Museum at Scotland Yard. And once again Mr. Sherlock Holmes of Baker Street is free to devote his life to examining those interesting little problems which the complex life of London presents so plentifully."

XXI. THE GAME'S AFOOT AGAIN:
1894–95

I have never known my friend to be in better form . . .
JOHN H. WATSON, M.D.

All was once again as it had been.

To Watson, reading *The Time Machine* in the pages of the *New Review* in 1895, it seemed almost as if he and Holmes had been transported from 1888 to 1894 in the amazing device invented by the fertile brain of Mr. H. G. Wells.

Watson, at Holmes's request, had sold his practice and returned to share the old quarters in Baker Street. "A young doctor, named Verner, had purchased my small Kensington practice," he wrote,[1] "and given with astonishingly little demur the highest price that I ventured to ask—an incident which only explained itself some years later, when I found that Verner was a distant relation of Holmes's, and that it was my friend who had really found the money."[2]

Thanks to the supervision of Mycroft Holmes and the immediate care of Mrs. Hudson, the Baker Street rooms were as they had been, the old landmarks all in place. There were the chemical corner and the acid-stained deal-topped table. There upon a shelf was the row of formidable scrapbooks and books of reference which so many of Holmes's fellow-citizens would have been glad to see burned. The violin case, the pipe rack, the coal

---

[1] In "The Adventure of the Norwood Builder."
[2] Settling later in San Francisco, Dr. Horace Verner, Holmes's cousin on his mother's side (*Verner* is of course an Anglicized form of *Vernet*), was himself to become a remarkable investigator of the *outré*. See "The Anomaly of the Empty Man," in Anthony Boucher's *Far and Away*.

scuttle which contained the cigars—even the Persian slipper which held the pipe tobacco—all met Watson's approving eye as he glanced about him.

And Holmes, now forty years of age, had mellowed rather than changed. He no longer engaged in the indoor pistol practice which had once disturbed Watson. He seemed less the confirmed misogynist that Watson had once thought him—the man "who never spoke of the softer emotions, save with a gibe and a sneer," the man who found "all emotions abhorrent to his cold, precise, but admirably balanced mind." Best of all, Holmes had now given up completely even the occasional use of cocaine, a habit that Watson had earlier feared might someday check his friend's remarkable career.

Lestrade came again to the rooms at 221 Baker Street in the years that followed Holmes's return. To Baker Street also in these years came young Stanley Hopkins, a product of Eton and Oxford, one of the first university men who were later to make Scotland Yard the world's greatest organization for the prevention and detection of crime. It was Hopkins who was a midnight visitor to 221B on a wild, tempestuous night toward the close of November 1894.

"Did you see anything of the Yoxley case in the latest editions?" he asked. "I can make neither head nor tail of it!"

But to Holmes, it was "a simple case, and yet in some ways an instructive one."[3]

It took Watson three massive manuscripts to record their work for the year 1894 alone. Glancing through them, his eye might fall on his account of the Addleton tragedy and the singular contents of the ancient British barrow. The famous Smith-Mortimer succession case came also within this period, as did the tracking and arrest of Huret, the Boulevard Assassin—an exploit which won for Holmes an autograph letter of thanks from the French President, M. Casimir-Périer,[4] and awarded him with the Order of the Legion of Honor.

[3] See "The Adventure of the Golden Pince-Nez."

[4] His unpopularity as President of the Republic was such that in the autumn of 1894 threats were made to murder him, his wife, and his children. He had reason to be anxious, too: the previous President, Sadi Carnot, had been himself assassinated on May 30, 1894. Unquestionably it was the President himself whose life Holmes saved from the Boulevard Assassin, Huret.

This was also the year of the shocking affair of the Dutch steamship *Friesland*—a shocking affair, indeed, as Mr. Ray Kierman has demonstrated.[5] Holmes's cousin on his father's side, the notorious Professor George Edward Challenger, had brought to London nothing less than a living pterodactyl as proof of his visit to Maple White Land on the borders of Brazil and western Bolivia. Panic followed the exhibition of the monster out of the earth's prehistory, and the creature, alarmed, had escaped from the Queen's Hall.

Holmes, with Watson, had attended his cousin's exhibition. His quick mind instantly perceiving that the beast might be intercepted by prompt action, he had chartered the *Friesland* and placed the vessel in the very path that the creature must pursue in its flight back to the upper reaches of the Amazon.

There seems little doubt that Holmes lured the monster to the very decks of the *Friesland,* and there fought it, nor little doubt that Watson, in the nick of time, when the pterodactyl had Holmes down for a last prod of its vile and lethal beak, stepped forward and sent a bullet through the brainless skull of the creature from his Adams .450, "more than once a good friend in need."

It was a story Watson burned to tell, but Holmes's nature "was always averse to anything in the shape of public applause, and he bound me in the most stringent terms to say no further word of the affair."

Nor would Holmes allow Watson to chronicle the very abstruse and complicated problem concerning the peculiar persecution of John Vincent Harden, the well-known tobacco millionaire; the investigation of the sudden death of Cardinal Tosca, an inquiry which Holmes carried out at the express desire of His Holiness the Pope;[6] or the arrest of Wilson, the notorious canary trainer, which removed a plague spot from the East End of London.

Still, there were stories Watson *could* tell, and tell them he did: the adventures of "The Three Students" and "The Solitary Cyclist," of "Black Peter" and "The Norwood Builder."

[5] In *The Baker Street Journal,* Vol. II, No. 2, New Series, April 1952, pp. 103–7.

[6] This was the *second* investigation which Holmes had carried out for Pope Leo XIII (1810–1903). In 1888 (see Appendix I) he had brought to a successful conclusion the case Watson called the Little Affair of the Vatican Cameos (*The Hound of the Baskervilles*).

Then, in the third week of November 1895:

"Well, well! What next!" Sherlock Holmes exclaimed, tearing open a telegram. "Brother Mycroft is coming around."

"Why not?" Watson asked.

"Why not? It is as if you met a tramcar coming down a country lane. Mycroft has his rails, and he runs on them. What upheaval can possibly have derailed him?"

"Does he not explain?"

Holmes handed over his brother's telegram.

" 'Must see you over Cadogan West. Coming at once. Mycroft,' " Watson read aloud. "I have heard that name—Cadogan West." He plunged among the litter of newspapers upon the sofa. "I have it!" he cried. "Cadogan West was the young man who was found dead on the Underground on Tuesday morning."

Holmes sat up at attention, his pipe halfway to his lips.

"This must be serious, Watson! That Mycroft should break out in such an erratic fashion! A planet might as well leave its orbit. Let us have the facts."

"The man's full name was Arthur Cadogan West. He was twenty-seven years of age, unmarried, and a clerk at Woolwich Arsenal."

"Government employ. Behold the link with brother Mycroft."

"He left Woolwich suddenly on Monday night. Was last seen by his fiancée, Miss Violet Westbury, when he left her abruptly in the fog about seven-thirty that evening. There was no quarrel between them and she can give no motive for his action. The next thing heard of him was when his dead body was discovered by a plate layer named Mason, just outside Aldgate Station on the Underground."

"When?"

"The body was found at six on the Tuesday morning. It was lying wide of the metals upon the left hand of the track as one goes eastward, at a point close to the station, where the line emerges from the tunnel in which it runs. The head was badly crushed—an injury which might well have been caused by a fall from the train. The body could only have come on the line in that way. Had it been carried down from any neighboring street, it must have passed the station barriers, where a collector is always standing. This point seems absolutely certain."

"Very good. The case is definite enough. The man, dead or alive, either fell or was thrown from a train. So much is clear. Continue."

"The trains which travel the lines of rail beside which the body was found are those which run from west to east, some being purely Metropolitan, and some from Willesden and outlying junctions. It can be stated for certain that this young man, when he met his death, was traveling in this direction at some late hour of the night, but at what point he entered the train it is impossible to state."

"His ticket, of course, would show that."

"There was no ticket in his pockets."

"No ticket! Dear me, Watson, this is really very singular. According to my experience it is not possible to reach the platform of a Metropolitan station without showing one's ticket. Presumably, then, the young man had one. Was it taken from him in order to conceal the station from which he came? It is possible. Or did he drop it in the carriage? That also is possible. But the point is of curious interest. I understand that there was no sign of robbery?"

"Apparently not. There is a list here of his possessions. His purse contained two pounds fifteen. He had also a checkbook on the Woolwich branch of the Capital and Counties Bank. Through this his identity was established. There were also two dress-circle tickets for the Woolwich Theater, dated for that very evening. Also a small packet of technical papers."

Holmes gave an exclamation of satisfaction.

"There we have it at last, Watson! British Government—Woolwich Arsenal—technical papers—Brother Mycroft. The chain is complete. But here he comes, if I am not mistaken, to speak for himself."

A moment later the portly figure of Mycroft Holmes was ushered into the room. At his heels came Lestrade.

"A most annoying business, Sherlock," Mycroft Holmes said when he had struggled out of his overcoat and subsided into an armchair. "I extremely dislike altering my habits. In the present state of Siam[7] it is most awkward that I should be away from

---

[7] In 1893 France had forced Siam to cede all territory east of the Mekong River, including most of Laos and a part of Cambodia. Great Britain, which

the office. But it is a real crisis. I have never seen your old friend, the Prime Minister,[8] so upset. As to the Admiralty—it is buzzing like an overturned beehive. Have you read up on the case?"

"We have just done so. What were those technical papers?"

"Ah! That's the point! Fortunately, it has not come out. The papers which this wretched youth had in his pocket were the plans of the Bruce-Partington submarine."

Sherlock Holmes and Dr. Watson sat expectant.

"Well? You have surely heard of it?"

"Only as a name."

"I may tell you that its importance can hardly be exaggerated. It has been the most jealously guarded of all Government secrets. The plans are exceedingly intricate. They comprise some thirty separate patents, each essential to the working of the whole. They are kept in an elaborate safe in a confidential office adjoining the arsenal, with burglar-proof doors and windows. Under no circumstances were the plans to be taken from the office. If the chief constructor of the Navy desired to consult them, even he was forced to go to the Woolwich office for the purpose. And yet here we find them in the pockets of a dead junior clerk in the heart of London."

"But you have recovered them."

"No, Sherlock, no! That's the pinch. Ten papers were taken from Woolwich. There were seven in the pockets of Cadogan West. The three most essential are gone—stolen, vanished. You must drop everything, Sherlock. Never mind your petty problems of the police court. It's a vital international problem that you have to solve. In all your career you have never had so great a chance of serving your country."

---

at that time controlled Burma, feared a French move westward toward Burma. France on her part equally feared a British move eastward from Burma. Thanks to the diplomacy of Mycroft Holmes, this awkward situation was resolved in 1896, when France and England agreed to recognize Siam as an independent nation.

[8] This was, of course, Robert Arthur Talbot Gascoyne-Cecil, third Marquess of Salisbury (1830–1903), then serving for the third time as Prime Minister (1885; 1886–92; 1895–1902). It will be remembered that Holmes had won the Prime Minister's liking and deep respect for his work in the (first) Adventure of the Second Stain in October 1886.

An hour later, Holmes, with Watson and Lestrade, stood with an expression of strained intensity upon his keen, alert face, staring at the rails that curved out of the tunnel just above Aldgate Station. His lips tightened, his brows concentrated, Holmes turned to the courteous, red-faced old gentleman who represented the railway company.

"This is where the young man's body lay, then," the detective said. "It could not have fallen from above—there are all blank walls. Therefore, it could only have come from a train, and that train, so far as we can trace it, must have passed about midnight on Monday. There are switch points here, and a curve, too."

"What is it, Mr. Holmes?" Lestrade asked. "Do you have a clue?"

"An idea, an indication, no more. But the case is certainly growing in interest. Watson, we have done all we can here. We need not trouble you any further, Lestrade. I think our investigation must now carry us to Woolwich."

At London Bridge, Holmes wrote a telegram to his brother, which he handed to Watson before dispatching. "See some light in the darkness," Watson read, "but it may flicker out. Meanwhile, please send by messenger to Baker Street a complete list of all foreign spies or international agents known to be in England, with full address. Sherlock."

"Things are dark to me," Watson said, as he and Holmes took their seats in the Woolwich train.

"The end is dark to me also, but I have hold of one idea which may lead us far. Cadogan West met his death elsewhere, and his body was placed on the roof of a railway carriage."

"On the roof!"

"Remarkable, is it not? But consider the facts. Is it a coincidence that it is found at the very point where the train switches and sways as it comes round on the points? Is not that the place where an object on the roof might be expected to fall off? The switch points would affect no object inside the train. Either the body fell from the roof, or a very curious coincidence has occurred. But now consider the question of the blood."

"There was no blood on the line."

"Because the body had bled elsewhere. Each fact is suggestive in itself. Together they have a cumulative force."

"And the ticket, too!"

"Exactly. That would explain the absence of a ticket." Holmes relapsed into a silent reverie, which lasted until the slow train drew up at last in Woolwich Station. There Holmes called a cab and drew a paper from his pocket.

"Mycroft has jotted down a few essential names and addresses upon this sheet," Holmes said. "I think that we will call first on Sir James Walter, the famous Government agent who is the official guardian of the Bruce-Partington papers. He is one of two who have a key to the safe. I may add that the papers were undoubtedly in his office during working hours on Monday, and that Sir James left for London about three o'clock, taking his key with him. He was at the house of Admiral Sinclair during the whole of the evening."

"Has the fact been verified?"

"Yes, by his brother, Colonel Valentine Walter, who testified to his departure from Woolwich, and by Admiral Sinclair himself, who testified to his arrival in London."

"Who was the other man with a key?"

"The senior clerk and draftsman, a Mr. Sidney Johnson."

The house of Sir James Walter was a handsome villa with green lawns stretching down to the Thames. A butler answered their ring.

"Sir James, sir!" he said, with solemn face. "Sir James died this morning. Perhaps you would care to step in, sir, and see his brother, Colonel Walter."

They were ushered into a dim-lit drawing room, where an instant later they were joined by a tall, handsome, light-bearded man of fifty.

"It was this horrible scandal," he said. "My brother, Sir James, was a man of very sensitive honor, and he could not survive such an affair. It broke his heart. He was always so proud of the efficiency of his department."

"You cannot throw any light upon the affair?"

"I know only what I have heard or read."

"This is indeed an unexpected development. Well, Watson, let us turn now to the Cadogan Wests."

A small but well-kept house in the outskirts of the town sheltered the bereaved mother, dazed with grief. At her side was a white-faced young lady, Miss Violet Westbury, the fiancée of the dead man and the last to see him upon the fatal night.

"Was your fiancé in want of money?" Holmes asked.

"No, his needs were simple and his salary ample. He had saved a few hundreds, and we were to marry at the New Year."

"No signs of any mental excitement?"

The girl colored and hesitated. "Yes," she said at last. "I had a feeling that there was something on his mind."

"For long?"

"Only for the last week or so. Once or twice it seemed to me that he was on the point of telling me something."

"Tell us of that last evening."

"We were to go to the theater. The fog was so thick that a cab was useless. We walked, and our way took us close to the office. Suddenly, with an exclamation, Arthur darted away in the fog. I waited but he never returned. Next morning, after the office opened, they came to inquire. About twelve o'clock we heard the horrible news."

Holmes shook his head sadly.

"Come, Watson," he said, "our ways lie elsewhere. Our next stop must be the office from which the papers were taken."

Sidney Johnson, the senior clerk, was a thin, gruff, bespectacled man of middle age, his cheeks haggard, his hands twitching from the nervous strain to which he had been subjected.

"It is bad, Mr. Holmes, very bad!" he said. "That West, of all men, should have done such a thing! I can see no other way out of it. And yet I would have trusted him as I trust myself."

"At what hour was the office closed on Monday?"

"At five."

"Did you close it?"

"I am always the last man out."

"Where were the plans?"

"In the safe. I put them there myself."

"Suppose that Cadogan West wished to make his way into the building after hours. He would need three keys, would he not?"

"To reach the papers, he would. The key of the outer door, the key of the office, and the key of the safe."

"Only Sir James Walter and you had those keys?"

"I had no keys of the doors—only of the safe."

"Sir James's key went with him to London?"

"He said so."

"And your key never left your possession?"

"Never."

Holmes examined the lock of the safe, the door of the room, and finally the iron shutters of the window. On the lawn outside the window was a laurel bush with several of its branches snapped or twisted. Holmes examined them carefully with his lens, and then some dim, vague marks on the earth beneath. Finally he asked the chief clerk to close the iron shutters.

"You see, Watson," he said, "that they hardly meet in the center. It would be possible for anyone outside to see what was going on in the room."

One more piece of information Holmes added to his knowledge before he and Watson left Woolwich: the clerk in the ticket office had seen Cadogan West upon the Monday night. Alone, he took a single third-class ticket and went by the eight-fifteen to London Bridge.

"Our scent runs cold here," Holmes said. "My instinct now is to work from the other end. If Mycroft has given us a list, we may be able to pick our man."

Back at Baker Street, a note awaited them. Holmes glanced at it and handed it to Watson, who read:

"There are numerous small fry, but few who would handle so big an affair. The only men worth considering are Adolph Meyer, of 13 Great George Street, Westminster; Louis La Rothière, of Camden Mansions, Notting Hill; and Hugo Oberstein of 13 Caulfield Gardens, Kensington. The latter was known to be in town on Monday, and is now reported as having left." The note was signed "Mycroft."

Holmes had spread out his big map of London, and leaned eagerly over it. "Well, well," he said presently. "Things are turning a little in our direction at last. I am going out now. It is only a reconnaissance. I will do nothing serious without my trusted comrade and biographer at my elbow. Do you stay here, and begin your narrative of how we saved the State."

Shortly after nine o'clock that night, a messenger arrived at Baker Street with a note for Watson: "Am dining at Goldini's

Restaurant. Please join me there at once. Bring a jemmy, a dark lantern, a chisel, and a revolver. S.H."

Holmes sat at a little round table near the door of the restaurant.

"Have you had something to eat?" he greeted Watson. "Then join me in a coffee, a curaçao and a cigar. Have you the tools?"

"In my overcoat."

"Excellent. Now, Watson, it must be evident to you that there is only one possible way in which this young man's body could have been placed on the roof of the train. You are aware that the Underground trains run clear of tunnels at some points in the West End. As I have traveled on the Underground I have occasionally seen windows just above my head. Suppose that a train halted under such a window. Would there be any difficulty in laying a body upon the roof?"

"To me it seems most improbable."

"We must fall back upon my old axiom: when all other contingencies fail, whatever remains, however improbable, must be the truth. Here all other contingencies *have* failed. Then my map told me that a leading international agent, who had just left London, lived in a row of houses which abutted upon the Underground. Mr. Hugo Oberstein, of 13 Caulfield Gardens, became my objective. A helpful official at Gloucester Road Station allowed me to ascertain that the backstair windows of Caulfield Gardens do indeed open upon the line. Even more essential: owing to the intersection of the line with one of the larger railways, Underground trains are frequently held motionless for some minutes at that very spot."

"Splendid, Holmes! You have got it!"

"So far, Watson, so far. Well, having seen the back of Caulfield Gardens, I visited the front. Oberstein has indeed gone to the Continent. We cannot tell what correspondence may be in his rooms. We will therefore visit them tonight."

"Could we not get a warrant and legalize it?"

"Hardly on the evidence."

Watson's answer was to rise from the table.

"Then we are bound to go," he said.

The little fan of yellow light from Holmes's lantern shone upon a low window at the rear of Oberstein's apartment. Holmes threw it open, and as he did so there was a low, harsh murmur, growing steadily into a loud roar as the train dashed past in the darkness. Holmes swept his light along the window sill. It was thickly coated with soot from the passing engines, but the black surface was blurred and rubbed in places.

"You can see where they rested the body, Watson. And here is a blood mark. The demonstration is complete."

Holmes settled down to a systematic investigation of the flat. Swiftly and methodically he turned over the contents of drawer after drawer and cupboard after cupboard, but no gleam of success brightened his austere face.

"The cunning fox has covered his tracks," he said at last. "This is our last chance."

It was a small tin box which stood upon the writing desk. Holmes prized it open with his chisel. Inside was an envelope containing newspaper advertisements.

"*Daily Telegraph* agony column, by the print and paper," Holmes said. "No dates, but messages arrange themselves. This must be the first: 'Hoped to hear sooner. Terms agreed to. Write fully to address given on card. Pierrot.' Next comes: 'Too complex for description. Must have full report. Stuff awaits you when goods delivered. Pierrot.' Next comes: 'Matter presses. Must withdraw offer unless contract completed. Make appointment by letter. Will confirm by advertisement. Pierrot.' Finally: 'Monday night after nine. Two raps. Only ourselves. Do not be suspicious. Payment in hard cash when goods delivered. Pierrot.' A fairly complete record, Watson! If we could only get at the man at the other end! Well, there is nothing more to be done here. I think we might drive round to the office of the *Daily Telegraph* and so bring a good day's work to a conclusion."

"Have you seen Pierrot's advertisement today?" Holmes said to Watson at breakfast.

"What, another one?"

"Yes. Here it is: 'Tonight. Same hour. Same place. Two taps. Most vitally important. Your own safety at stake. Pierrot.' I think, Watson, that if Mycroft and Lestrade could make it convenient to come with us about eight o'clock to Caulfield Gardens we might possibly get a little nearer to a solution."

By nine o'clock, the four were seated in Oberstein's study.

An hour passed, and yet another. Eleven struck. Then Holmes raised his head with a sudden jerk. "He is coming," he said.

They heard a furtive step outside, then two sharp taps with the knocker. Holmes rose, opened the outer door. The gas in the hall was a mere point of light. As a dark figure slipped by him, Holmes closed the door and fastened it. A moment later the man stood before them. Holmes followed him closely, and as the man turned with a cry of surprise and alarm, he caught him by the collar and threw him back into the room. The man staggered and fell senseless upon the floor. His broad-brimmed hat flew from his head, his cravat slipped down from his lips, and they saw the light beard and soft, handsome features of Colonel Valentine Walter.

"The younger brother of the late Sir James Walter, the head of the Submarine Department," Holmes said. "He is coming to. I think you had best leave the examination to me."

The man groaned and sank his face in his hands. They waited, but he was silent.

"I can assure you," said Holmes, "that every essential is already known. We know that you were pressed for money, that you took an impression of the keys which your brother held, that you entered into a correspondence with Oberstein, who answered your letters through the advertisement columns of the *Daily Telegraph*, signing himself 'Pierrot.' We are aware that you went down to the office in the fog on Monday night, but that you were seen and followed by young Cadogan West. He saw your theft, but could not give the alarm, as it was just possible that you were taking the papers to your brother in London. Like the good citizen he was, he followed you in the fog, and kept at your heels until you reached this very house. There he intervened, and then it was, Colonel Walter, that to treason you added the more horrible crime of murder."

"Before God I swear that I did not!" cried the wretched prisoner. "It was Oberstein. He struck the boy on the head with a life preserver, and within five minutes Cadogan West was dead.

Oberstein kept three of the papers I had brought him. The others he stuffed in West's pockets. We waited half an hour at the window before a train stopped. Then we had no difficulty in lowering West's body on to the top of it."

There was a silence in the room. It was broken by Mycroft Holmes.

"Did Oberstein give you no address?" he asked.

"He said that letters to the Hôtel du Louvre, Paris, would eventually reach him."

"Then," said Sherlock Holmes, "sit at this desk and write to my dictation. 'Dear Sir. With regard to our transaction, you will no doubt have observed by now that one essential detail is missing. I have a tracing which will make it complete. This has involved me in extra trouble, however, and I must ask you for a further advance of five hundred pounds. I will not trust it to the post, nor will I take anything but gold or notes. I would come to you abroad, but it would excite remark if I left the country at present. Therefore I shall expect to meet you in the smoking room of the Charing Cross Hotel at noon on Saturday.' That will do very well. I shall be much surprised if it does not fetch our man."

"And it did," Watson wrote. "Oberstein, eager to complete the coup of his lifetime, came to the lure and was safely engulfed for fifteen years in a British prison. In his trunk were found the Bruce-Partington plans, which he had put up for auction in all the naval centers of Europe.

"Colonel Walter died in prison towards the end of the second year of his sentence.

"As to Holmes, I learned some weeks afterwards that my friend had spent a day at Windsor, whence he returned with a remarkably fine emerald tiepin. When I asked him if he had bought it, he answered that it was a present from a certain gracious lady in whose interests he had once been fortunate enough to carry out a small commission. He said no more; but I fancy that I could guess at that lady's august name . . ."

XXII. THE CROWDED YEARS: 1896–1902

"Mr. Holmes, if ever you put forward your full powers, I implore you to do so now . . ."
DR. THORNEYCROFT HUXTABLE.

"From the years 1894 to 1901 inclusive," Dr. Watson wrote,[1] "Mr. Sherlock Holmes was a very busy man. It is safe to say that there was no public case of any difficulty in which he was not consulted during those eight years, and there were hundreds of private cases, some of them of the most intricate and extra- ordinary character, in which he played a prominent part. Many startling successes and a few unavoidable failures were the outcome of the long period of continuous work. As I have preserved very full notes of all those cases, and was myself personally engaged in many of them, it may be imagined that it is no easy task to know which I should select to lay before the public. I shall, however, preserve my former rules, and give the preference to those cases which derive their interest not so much from the brutality of the crimes as from the ingenuity and dramatic quality of the solutions."

"When one considers," he wrote elsewhere,[2] "that Mr. Sherlock Holmes was in active practice for twenty-three years, and that during seventeen of these I was allowed to co-operate with him and to keep notes of his doings, it will be clear that I have a mass of material at my command. The problem has always been, not to find, but to choose. There is the long row of year-books which fill a shelf, and there are the dispatch-cases

[1] In "The Adventure of the Solitary Cyclist."
[2] In "The Adventure of the Veiled Lodger."

filled with documents, a perfect quarry for the student, not only of crime, but of the social and official scandals of the late Victorian era. Concerning these latter, I must say that the writers of agonized letters, who beg that the honour of their families or the reputation of their famous forebears may not be touched, have nothing to fear. The discretion and high sense of professional honour which have always distinguished my friend are still at work in the choice of these memoirs, and no confidence will be abused. I deprecate, however, in the strongest way the attempts which have been made lately to get at and destroy these papers. The source of these outrages is known, and if they are repeated I have Mr. Holmes's authority for saying that the whole story concerning the politician, the lighthouse and the trained cormorant will be given to the public. There is at least one reader who will understand."

And again:[3]

"Somewhere in the vaults of the bank of Cox & Co., at Charing Cross, there is a travel-worn and battered tin dispatch-box with my name . . . painted upon the lid. It is crammed with papers, nearly all of which are records of cases to illustrate the curious problems which my friend Mr. Sherlock Holmes had at various times to examine. Some, and not the least interesting, were complete failures, and as such will hardly bear narrating, since no final explanation is forthcoming. A problem without a solution may interest the student, but can hardly fail to annoy the casual reader. Among these unfinished tales is that of Mr. James Phillimore, who, stepping back into his house to get his umbrella, was never more seen in this world. No less remarkable is that of the cutter *Alicia,* which sailed one spring morning into a small patch of mist from which she never again emerged, nor was anything further ever heard of herself and her crew.[4] A third case worthy of note is that of Isadora Persano, the well-known journalist and duellist, who was found stark staring mad with a matchbox in front of him which contained

[3] In "The Problem of Thor Bridge."

[4] It is, of course, well known that the entire crew of the brig *Mary Celeste,* but not the ship itself, did just about this in the year 1872. Of the many "explanations" that have been offered to the public, that of Dr. Watson's literary agent, which Dr. Conan Doyle titled "J. Habakuk Jephson's Statement," may have special interest.

a remarkable worm, said to be unknown to science. Apart from these unfathomed cases, there are some which involve secrets of private families to an extent which would mean consternation in many exalted quarters if it were thought possible that they might find their way into print. I need not say that such a breach of confidence is unthinkable, and that these records will be separated and destroyed now that my friend has time to turn his energies to the matter. There remain a considerable residue of cases of greater or less interest which I might have edited before had I not feared to give the public a surfeit which might react upon the reputation of the man whom above all others I revere. In some I was myself concerned and can speak as an eye-witness, while in others I was either not present or played so small a part that they could only be told as by a third person . . ."

It was late in October 1896 that Watson, at his club, received a hurried note from Holmes asking for his immediate attendance at Baker Street. "Your presence," it said, "may be useful."

From Mrs. Merrilow, of South Brixton, he and Holmes heard the queer story of the Veiled Lodger. For seven years, it seemed, Mrs. Merrilow had had such a lodger, a Mrs. Ronder, and only once in those seven years had Mrs. Merrilow seen Mrs. Ronder's face.

"And I wish to God I had not!" cried Mrs. Merrilow.

To Watson, it was somehow a rather different Holmes who solved, in one day, this tragic case. "He sat upon the floor like some strange Buddha . . ." Watson wrote.[5]

Only a month later came the case that Watson was to chronicle as "The Adventure of the Sussex Vampire."

"For a mixture of the modern and the medieval, of the practical and of the wildly fanciful," said Sherlock Holmes, "I think this is surely the limit."

Then, in December of that memorable year 1896:

"Mr. Sherlock Holmes?" said Cyril Overton, the enormous young man from Trinity College, Cambridge. "I've been down to Scotland Yard. I saw Inspector Stanley Hopkins. He advised

[5] Whether or not Holmes ever revealed to Watson the depth of his Buddhistic studies, the fruit of his two years in Tibet, is a point debated by Sherlockian commentators.

me to come to you. Godfrey Staunton is simply the hinge that the whole team turns on. And tomorrow we play Oxford. And Godfrey's disappeared, and I don't believe he's ever coming back . . ."

To Holmes, the Oxford *and* the Cambridge man, the problem of this missing three-quarter seemed paramount.

Oxford won the match (by a goal and two tries), but Holmes, with the help of Pompey, the pride of the local draghounds, solved the problem.

"Come, Watson," he said at the end, and they passed from a house of grief into the pale sunlight of a winter day.

"Come, Watson, come!" Holmes cried again, on a bitterly cold and frosty morning in the January of 1897. "The game is afoot! Not a word! Into your clothes and come!"

Ten minutes later they were both in a cab and rattling through the silent streets on their way to Charing Cross Station and one of the most extraordinary adventures in Watson's large collection—the case he titled "The Adventure of the Abbey Grange." Stanley Hopkins, it seems, was baffled again. "I should be very glad of your immediate assistance in what promises to be a most remarkable case," he had written to Holmes. "It is something quite in your line. . . . I beg you not to lose an instant. . . ."

"Hopkins has called me in seven times, and on each occasion his summons has been entirely justified," Holmes said. "I fancy that every one of his cases has found its way into your collection, and I must admit, Watson, that you have some power of selection which atones for much which I deplore in your narratives.[6] Your fatal habit of looking at everything from the point of view of a story instead of as a scientific exercise has ruined what might have been an instructive and even classical series of demonstrations. You slur over work of the utmost finesse and delicacy in order to dwell upon sensational details

6 Holmes referred to the fact that of the seven cases which he had so far cleared up for Hopkins, Watson had written accounts of only three: "The Adventure of Black Peter," "The Adventure of the Golden Pince-Nez," "The Adventure of the Missing Three-Quarter." Of course, Watson was also to write an account of the present case, the eighth in which Holmes had helped Hopkins.

which may excite but cannot possible instruct the reader."

"Why do you not write them yourself?" said Watson with some bitterness.

"I will, my dear Watson, I will," Holmes replied. "At present I am, as you know, fairly busy, but I propose to devote my declining years to the composition of a textbook which shall focus the whole art of detection into one volume."

Not since the spring of 1887 had Holmes labored as he labored in the spring of 1897.

For the second time in his long professional career, his iron constitution showed symptoms of giving way. It was in the March of that year that Dr. Moore Agar ordered Holmes to surrender himself to complete rest. At Poldhu Bay, in Cornwall, he settled down to a study of the ancient Cornish language,[7] broken by long walks and solitary meditations upon the moor. "In every direction upon these moors there were traces of some vanished race," Watson wrote. "The glamour and mystery of the place, with its sinister atmosphere of forgotten nations, appealed to the imagination of my friend . . ." Undoubtedly, Holmes was reminded of his life in a neolithic hut on Dartmoor during his investigation of the Hound of the Baskervilles, and of his boyhood explorations of the strange and mysterious moors of Yorkshire.

The holiday in Cornwall led, as we know, to a case that Holmes claimed to be the strangest he had ever been called upon to handle.[8] As in "The Adventure of the Abbey Grange," Holmes could not find it in his heart to turn the malefactor over to the law.

"I think you must agree, Watson, that it is not a case in which we are called upon to interfere. Our investigation has been independent, and our action shall be so also. You would not denounce the man?"

"Certainly not," Watson answered.

So in these later years we see again the deep influence upon Sherlock Holmes of his Buddhistic learning.

[7] Holmes's theory was that it was akin to the Chaldean, and had been largely derived from the Phoenician traders in tin.
[8] "The Adventure of the Devil's Foot."

Holmes, entirely recovered, returned to Baker Street in the May of 1897, and as before a steady stream of clients climbed the seventeen steps that led to the detective's sitting room.

Holmes's curious faculties, Watson felt, had never been keener. Again and again the doctor was to find himself astonished by his friend's inferences and conclusions.

"So, Watson," Holmes said suddenly, after some hours of silence, on a morning in August 1898, "you do not propose to invest in South African securities?"

The doctor gave a start of amazement. This intrusion into his most intimate thoughts was inexplicable.

"How on earth do you know that?" he asked.

"By an inspection of the groove between your left forefinger and thumb."

"I see no connection."

"Very likely not. But I can quickly show you a close connection. Here are the missing links of the very simple chain: 1. You had chalk between your left forefinger and thumb when you returned from your club last night. 2 You put chalk there when you play billiards to steady the cue. 3. You never play billiards except with Thurston.[9] 4. You told me four weeks ago that Thurston had an option on some South African property which would expire in a month, and which he desired you to share with him. 5. Your checkbook is locked in my drawer, and you have not asked for the key.[10] 6. You do not propose to invest your money in this manner."

"How absurdly simple!" Watson cried.

"Quite so," said Holmes, a trifle nettled. "Every problem becomes very childish when once it is explained to you. Here is an interesting unexplained one. See what you can make of that, friend Watson." Holmes tossed a sheet of paper upon the table.

[9] Unquestionably Julian Thurston, of Thurston and Coy, Catharine Street, the Strand, one of the chief makers of billiard tables in England. The great championship billiard matches were held in London at this time in Thurston's Hall. It speaks highly of Watson's ability at billiards that he was good enough to play with one of the great billiards masters of the day.

[10] Why was Holmes the custodian of Watson's checkbook? Watson himself gives us the answer—in "The Adventure of Shoscombe Old Place"—when he says that his love of gambling led him at one time to pay for racing "with half my wound pension."

"Why, Holmes, it is a child's drawing!" Watson cried.

It was not a child's drawing. It was a sample of a remarkable cipher—and the beginning of that "very pretty" case, "The Adventure of the Dancing Men."

Its opening was followed—on the very next day—by the case Watson called "The Adventure of the Retired Colourman." It seemed at first to be so simple as to be hardly worth Holmes's attention, but it rapidly assumed a very different aspect.

"It's as workmanlike a job as I can remember," Inspector MacKinnon said to Holmes at the end.

Holmes shrugged. "Well, well, file it away in our archives, Watson. Someday the true story may be told."

The year 1899 was made memorable for Watson by "an absolutely unique experience"—Holmes's clash with "that king of blackmailers, Charles Augustus Milverton.

"I've had to do with fifty murderers in my career," Holmes said, "but the worst of them never gave me the repulsion which I have for this fellow."

The case repulsed Holmes in another way.

"You would not called me a marrying man, Watson?" he said to his friend at one point.

"No, indeed!"

"You will be interested to hear that I am engaged."

"My dear fellow! I congrat—"

"To Milverton's housemaid."

"Good heavens, Holmes!"

"It was a most necessary step. I am a plumber with a rising business, Escott by name.[11] I have walked out with her each evening, and I have talked with her. Good heavens, those talks! However, I have got all I wanted. I know Milverton's house as I know the palm of my hand."[12]

In the June of the following year, 1900, Holmes was called upon by Lestrade to solve the very curious problem precipitated

11 We have another example of Holmes's sense of mischievous humor in this use of his old stage name.

12 Lest it be thought that this was cruel strategy for Holmes to use, it should be pointed out that "Escott the plumber" had a hated rival who would certainly cut him out the instant his back was turned.

by the disappearance of the famous Black Pearl of the Borgias,[13] and the October of that same year brought him a visit from the American Gold King, Neil Gibson, and the "murder as if by magic" that Watson would call "The Problem of Thor Bridge."

Watson, in the winter of 1900–01 and the following spring, was much too busy writing his narrative of *The Hound of the Baskervilles*[14] to share many cases with Holmes, but his narrative was in the hands of the publishers by the May of 1901, and he was able to take part in a case destined to become a classic in the annals of criminology—that of the Priory School.

"We have had some dramatic entrances and exits upon our small stage at Baker Street," Watson wrote, "but I cannot recall anything more sudden and startling than the first appearance of Dr. Thorneycroft Huxtable, M.A., Ph.D., etc."

The adventure of the Priory School[15] was followed, in May of 1902, by that of Shoscombe Old Place—a singular incident, but one which ended upon a happier note than Sir Robert Norberton's actions perhaps deserved. Sir Robert's horse, Shoscombe Prince, won the Derby, Sir Robert netted eighty thousand pounds in bets, his creditors held their hands until the race was over, when they were paid in full, and enough was left to re-establish Sir Robert in a fair position in life.[16]

---

13 "The Adventure of the Six Napoleons."

14 It appeared in *The Strand Magazine*, issues of August 1901 through April 1902. So great was the public's interest in Watson's account that hundreds of men, women, and children queued up in long lines at *The Strand's* offices to buy a copy of the magazine on the first day each issue containing the story went on sale. "The story . . . was received with transports of rapture . . ." the late Fletcher Pratt wrote in his introduction to *The Later Adventures of Sherlock Holmes* (New York: The Limited Editions Club, 1952; reprinted in *Introducing Sherlock Holmes*). "George Newnes immediately published it in book form . . . in the largest edition thus far accorded to a Sherlock Holmes book, and there were more transports of rapture, which spread to the American edition brought out by McClure and Phillips in the same year."

15 As Watson called it. Holmes himself later revealed—in "The Adventure of the Blanched Soldier"—that its true name was the *Abbey* School, and that the "Duke of Holdernesse" of Watson's narrative was, in reality, the Duke of Greyminster.

16 Watson's account of this adventure was the last he was ever to write. His narrative appeared in *Liberty Magazine*, issue of March 5, 1927, and *The Strand Magazine*, issue of April 1927. Watson at that time was seventy-five years of age.

The adventure of the Three Garridebs—the case is to be dated in the June of 1902—"may have been a comedy, or it may have been a tragedy," Watson wrote. "It cost one man his reason, it cost me a blood-letting, and it cost yet another man the penalties of the law. Yet there certainly was an element of comedy."

And there was another element: in that instant when Killer Evans whisked out a revolver and fired two shots—in that instant when Watson felt a sudden hot sear as if a red-hot iron had been pressed to his thigh—in that same instant, he heard also the crash of Holmes's pistol as it came down on the Killer's head.

"You're not hurt, Watson?" Holmes cried. "For God's sake, say that you are not hurt!"

"It was worth a wound," Watson wrote, "it was worth many wounds—to know the depth of loyalty and love which lay behind that cold mask. The clear, hard eyes were dimmed for a moment, and the firm lips were shaking. For the one and only time I caught a glimpse of the great heart as well as the great brain. All my years of humble and single-minded service culminated in that moment of revelation . . ."

XXIII. THE THIRD MRS. WATSON: JULY 1902–OCTOBER 1903

The relations between us in those latter days were peculiar.
JOHN H. WATSON, M.D.

In the July of 1902—it was in that same month that Holmes solved the disappearance of Lady Frances Carfax—Dr. John H. Watson moved from Baker Street.

Dr. Watson—he was then only forty-nine—had fallen in love again.

With a mischievous twinkle in his eye, Holmes twitted his friend gently.

"You have some splashes on the left sleeve and shoulder of your coat, Doctor," he said. "It is clear that someone shared your cab in your drive this morning."

"I have no doubt the connection is a perfectly self-evident one to a logical mind," Watson said, "and yet I should be obliged to you if you would indicate it."

Holmes chuckled. "Had you sat in the center of a hansom you would probably have had no splashes, and if you had they would certainly have been symmetrical. Therefore it is clear that you sat at the side. Therefore it is equally clear that you had a companion."

"That is very evident."

"Absurdly commonplace, is it not?"

In the September of 1902, the old companions shared two cases. The first, to Watson, "was in some ways the supreme moment of my friend's career." No doubt Watson was deeply impressed by the fact that the man Holmes served once again in the case Watson called "The Adventure of the Illustrious Client" was now King Edward VII.[1] Holmes called the second[2] "an instructive" case. "There is neither money or credit in it," he added, "and yet one would wish to tidy it up."

Then, in October, Dr. Watson married for the third time. A few weeks later, with rooms in Queen Anne Street, he once again resumed the practice of medicine.

Holmes called it "the only selfish action which I can recall in our association." For it was clear, from the start of the courtship, that the third Mrs. Watson-to-be held views very different from those of Constance Adams and Mary Morstan. A husband's place, she felt, was in the home; a doctor's place, in his surgery. She let both partners know that in the future the occasions would be few indeed on which she would permit John to share one of Holmes's adventures.[3]

Still, Holmes was a man of habits, narrowed and concentrated habits, and Watson had become one of them. As an institution, Watson was like the shag tobacco, the old black pipe, the index books, the violin. When it was a case of active work, and a companion was needed upon whose nerve Holmes knew he could rely, the detective continued to call on his old friend.

"Come at once if convenient—if inconvenient come all the same, S.H.," he would wire. And Watson, wife notwithstanding, would come.

[1] We know, from "The Adventure of the Three Garridebs," that Holmes in the early June of that same year, 1902, had performed services for which he refused a knighthood. It is evident that Holmes never got over his dislike for "the King of Bohemia"—Albert Edward, Prince of Wales, later King Edward VII: he refused a knighthood from England while accepting the award of the Legion of Honor from France ("The Adventure of the Golden Pince-Nez").

[2] "The Adventure of the Red Circle."

[3] Sir Sydney Roberts early identified Watson's third wife as Miss Violet de Merville of "The Adventure of the Illustrious Client" (*Dr. Watson*, p. 27 *seq.*)—an identification which Mr. T. S. Blakeney convincingly demolished in *Sherlock Holmes: Fact or Fiction?* (p. 113 *seq.*)

The late Christopher Morley, on the other hand, was of the opinion that the third Mrs. Watson was Lady Frances Carfax, a view with which few Holmesians can agree.

Patient research continues. While it is hoped that the true identity of the third Mrs. Watson may someday be established beyond reasonable doubt, much about the lives of both Watson and Holmes must forever remain a mystery.

But in January 1903, Holmes was forced, at last, to write, for the first time, his own account of one of his experiences—"Watson had no note of it."[4]

Watson, however, in the spring and summer of 1903, was fortunate enough to visit Holmes at Baker Street on two occasions when the game was afoot.

"I had not seen Holmes for some days," he wrote,[5] "and had no idea of the new channel into which his activities had been directed. He was in a chatty mood that morning, however"—it was the morning of Tuesday, the 26th of May—"and had just settled me into the well-worn low armchair on one side of the fire, while he had curled down with his pipe in his mouth upon the opposite chair, when our visitor arrived. If I had said that a mad bull had arrived, it would give a clearer impression of what occurred . . ."

The visitor was Steve Dixie, the bruiser, come to frighten Holmes into refusing to take the Harrow Weald case. Of course such intimidation only made Holmes decide to take it up. He thought it a trifling affair, but it at least gave Watson an opportunity to meet the celebrated Isadora Klein, the richest and loveliest widow on earth.

Again, in the summer of 1903, it was pleasant to Dr. Watson to find himself once more in the untidy room on Baker Street which had been the starting point of so many remarkable adventures. He looked around him at the scientific diagrams on the wall, the acid-stained bench of chemicals, the violin case leaning in the corner. Finally, his eyes came around to the fresh and smiling face of Billy, the young but very wise and tactful page, who had helped a little to fill the gap of loneliness and isolation which now surrounded the saturnine figure of the great detective.

"It all seems very unchanged, Billy," Dr. Watson said. "I hope the same can be said of him?"

Billy glanced with solicitude at the closed door of the bedroom.

"I think he's in bed and asleep," he said.

---

[4] "The Adventure of the Blanched Soldier." It was not published until 1926—in the October 16 issue of *Liberty Magazine* and the November issue of *The Strand Magazine*.

[5] "The Adventure of the Three Gables."

It was seven o'clock in the evening of this lovely summer's day, but Dr. Watson was sufficiently familiar with the irregularity of his old friend's hours to show no surprise.

"That means a case, I suppose?"

"Yes, sir. He's very hard at it right now. I'm frightened for his health. He gets paler and thinner, and he eats nothing. 'When will you be pleased to dine, Mr. Holmes?' Mrs. Hudson asks. 'Seven-thirty, day after tomorrow,' says he. You know his way when he is keen on a case."

"Yes, Billy, I know."

"He's following someone. Yesterday he was out as a workman looking for a job. Today he was an old woman. Fairly took me in, he did, and I ought to know his ways by now."

"But what is it all about, Billy?"

Billy sank his voice. "I don't mind telling you, sir, but it should go no further. It's this case of the Crown Diamond . . ."

And how pleasant for Dr. Watson to be present as the final scene of the drama of the Crown Diamond was played.

"Lord Cantlemere, sir," said Billy.

"Show him up—this eminent peer who represents the very highest interests," Holmes said with a grin. "He is an excellent and loyal person, but rather of the old regime. Shall we make him unbend a little? Dare we venture upon a slight liberty? He knows, we may conjecture, nothing of what has occurred."

The door opened to admit a thin, austere figure with a hatchet face and drooping mid-Victorian whiskers of a blackness which hardly corresponded with the rounded shoulders and feeble gait. Holmes advanced affably, and shook an unresponsive hand.

"How do you do, Lord Cantlemere? It is chilly, for the time of the year, but rather warm indoors. May I take your overcoat?"

"No, I thank you. I will not take it off."

Holmes laid his hand insistently upon the sleeve.

"Pray allow me! My friend Dr. Watson would assure you that these changes of temperature are most insidious."

His Lordship shook himself free with some impatience.

"I am quite comfortable, sir. I have no need to stay. I have simply looked in to know how your self-appointed task was progressing."

"It is difficult—very difficult."

"I feared you would find it so. Every man has his limitations, Mr. Holmes, but at least it cures us of the weakness of self-satisfaction."

"Yes, sir, I have been much perplexed."

"No doubt."

"Especially upon one point. Possibly you could help me upon it?"

"You apply for my advice rather late in the day. I thought that you had your own all-sufficient methods. Still, I am ready to help you."

"You see, Lord Cantlemere, we can no doubt frame a case against the actual thieves."

"When you have caught them."

"Exactly. But the question is—how shall we proceed against the receiver?"

"Is this not rather premature?"

"It is well to have our plans ready. Now, what would you regard as final evidence against the receiver?"

"The actual possession of the stone."

"You would arrest him upon that?"

"Most undoubtedly, sir."

"In that case, my dear Lord Cantlemere, I shall be under the painful necessity of advising your arrest."

Lord Cantlemere was very angry. Fires flickered up into his sallow cheeks.

"You take a great liberty, Mr. Holmes. I am a busy man, sir, engaged upon important affairs, and I have no time for foolish jokes. I can tell you frankly, sir, that I have never been a believer in your powers, and that I have always been of the opinion that this matter would be far safer in the hands of the regular police. Your conduct confirms all my conclusions. I have the honor, sir, to wish you a very good night."

Holmes had swiftly changed his position and was between the peer and the door.

"One moment, sir," he said. "To actually go off with the Mazarin stone would be a more serious offense than to be found in temporary possession of it."

"Sir, this is intolerable! Let me pass!"

"Put your hand in the right-hand pocket of your overcoat."

"What do you mean, sir?"

"Come, come—do what I ask."

An instant later the amazed peer was standing, blinking and stammering, with the great yellow stone in his shaking palm.

"What! What! How is this, Mr. Holmes?"

"My old friend here will tell you that I have an impish habit of practical joking," Holmes said. "Also that I can never resist a dramatic situation. I took the liberty—the very great liberty, I admit—of putting the stone into your pocket at the beginning of our interview."

The old peer stared from the stone to the smiling face before him.

"Sir, I am bewildered. But—yes—this is indeed the Mazarin stone. We are greatly your debtors, Mr. Holmes. Your sense of humor may, as you admit, be somewhat perverted, and its exhibition remarkably untimely, but at least I withdraw any reflection I may have made upon your amazing professional powers. But how—"

"The details can wait," Holmes said. "No doubt, Lord Cantlemere, your pleasure in telling of this successful result in the exalted circle to which you return will be some small atonement for my practical joke. Billy, you will show His Lordship out. And tell Mrs. Hudson that I shall be glad if she would send up dinner for two."

XXIV. THE SUSSEX DOWNS: 1909

"It's surely time that I disappeared into that little farm of my dreams."

SHERLOCK HOLMES.

"From the point of view of the criminal expert," Holmes complained to Watson, "London has become a singularly uninteresting city since the death of the late-lamented Professor Moriarty.

"With that man in the field one's morning paper presented infinite possibilities. Often it was only the smallest trace, the faintest indication, and yet it was enough to tell me that the great malignant brain was there, as the gentlest tremors of the edges of the web remind one of the foul spider which lurks at the center. Petty thefts, wanton assaults, purposeless outrages—to the man who held the clue all could be worked into one connected whole. To the scientific student of the higher criminal world no capital in Europe offered the advantages which London then possessed. But now—"

It was time, Holmes had decided, to make one last bow, like the actor he had once been, and then retire gracefully from the stage on which he had played a leading role for so long.

It seemed, then, that the last bow was to have been the curious case of the creeping man, which Watson tells us was "one of the very last cases handled by Holmes before his retirement" to a life of study and beekeeping. Holmes was always of the opinion that Watson should someday publish the singular facts connected with Professor Presbury, if only, as he said, to dispel once and for all the ugly rumors which had agitated the University and were echoed in the learned societies of London. But there were obstacles in the way, and it was not until 1923 that Watson at last obtained permission to ventilate the facts. "Even now," he wrote, "a certain reticence and discretion have to be observed in laying the matter before the public." He masked the university as "Camford" in his account of the case, although there can be no doubt that the university was Oxford.[1]

Holmes brought the case to its successful, and sensational, conclusion in late September 1903. By October of that year, his agents had found a villa that suited him, at "Fulworth,"[2] on the southern slope of the Sussex Downs, five miles from Eastbourne.

For the last time, one day in November 1903, Mr. Sherlock Holmes walked down the seventeen steps up which, over the years, so many clients had climbed. It was good-by, forever good-by, to No. 221 Baker Street.[3] But with Holmes to the Sussex Downs, to act as housekeeper, went the faithful Martha Hudson.

"My villa is situated upon the southern slope of the Downs, commanding a great view of the Channel," Holmes wrote some years later. "At this point the coastline is entirely of chalk cliffs, which can only be descended by a single, long, tortuous path, which is steep and slippery. At the bottom of the path lie a hundred yards of pebbles and shingle, even when the tide is at full. Here and there, however, there are curves and hollows which make splendid swimming-pools filled afresh with each flow. This admirable beach extends for some miles in each direction . . .

"My house is lonely. I, my old housekeeper, and my bees have the estate all to ourselves."

We have Watson's word for it[4] that during this period of rest Holmes often refused the most princely offers to take up

[1] Holmes, it will be remembered, called Cambridge "this inhospitable town" in "The Adventure of the Missing Three-Quarter." In "The Adventure of the Creeping Man," on the other hand, he called "Camford" "This charming town."

[2] Watson is once more being discreet. But the late Christopher Morley identified "Fulworth" as the village of Cuckmere Haven, which lies between Seaforth and Eastbourne on the southern slope of the Sussex Downs.

[3] It seems beyond question that Holmes's decision to retire at a comparatively early age was influenced by the death on Thursday, October 8, 1903, of "Irene Adler."

[4] See his introduction to the volume *His Last Bow.*

various cases. His retirement, he had determined, was to be a permanent one. Yet it was a singular thing that a problem which was certainly as abstruse and unusual as any which he had faced in his twenty-three years of professional work should have come to him after his retirement.

An occasional weekend visit was the most that Holmes ever saw of Watson at this time, and Holmes, once again, was forced to act as his own chronicler. "I must needs tell my tale in my own plain way," he wrote, "showing by my words each step upon the difficult road which lay before me as I searched for the mystery of the Lion's Mane."

It was toward the end of July 1909[5] that a severe gale heaped the seas to the base of the cliffs, leaving a lagoon at the turn of the tide. But on the morning of which Holmes spoke in his chronicle, "the wind had abated, and all Nature was newly washed and fresh. It was impossible to work upon so delightful a day, and I strolled out before breakfast to enjoy the exquisite air. I walked along the cliff path which led to the steep descent to the beach. As I walked, I heard a shout behind me . . ."

It was Harold Stackhurst who called, the proprietor of a nearby coaching establishment, The Gables, with a staff of several masters and some score of young men preparing for various professions. Stackhurst himself was a well-known rowing Blue in his day, and an excellent all-around scholar. He and Holmes had been friendly from the day Holmes had come to the coast, and the two would occasionally drop in on one another in the evenings.

"What a morning, Mr. Holmes!" Stackhurst exclaimed. "I thought I should see you out."

"Going for a swim, I see."

"At your old tricks again," Stackhurst laughed, patting his bulging pocket. "Yes, McPherson started early, and I expect I may find him there."

Fitzroy McPherson was the science master, a fine upstanding young fellow whose life had been crippled by heart trouble following rheumatic fever. He was a natural athlete, however,

[5] Holmes's published account reads "Towards the end of July, 1907." This is a typographical error, as Dr. Ernest Bloomfield Zeisler has conclusively demonstrated. See *Baker Street Chronology*, "The Lion's Mane," pp. 134–36.

and excelled in every game which did not throw too great a strain upon him. Summer and winter he went for his swim, and Holmes had often joined him.

At this moment they saw the man himself. His head showed at the edge of the cliff, then his whole figure appeared at the top. He was staggering like a drunken man. Suddenly, with a terrible cry, he threw up his hands and fell upon his face to the ground. Holmes and Stackhurst rushed forward. McPherson was obviously dying. His eyes were sunken and glazed, his cheeks livid. One glimmer of life came into his face for an instant, and he muttered three words of warning.

"The Lion's Mane!" he whispered.

Then he half raised himself from the ground, threw his arms into the air, and fell forward on his side. Fitzroy McPherson was dead.

Holmes's quick eye noted that McPherson was dressed only in his burberry overcoat, his trousers, and an unlaced pair of canvas shoes. As he fell over, his burberry fell back, and Holmes saw that the man's entire back was covered with dark red lines as though he had been terribly flogged.

Holmes was kneeling, Stackhurst standing by the body, when a shadow fell across them. It was cast by the powerful body of Ian Murdoch, the mathematics coach at The Gables: a tall, dark man, so taciturn and aloof that he was looked upon as something of an oddity by the students, who would have made him their butt, except that there was some outlandish blood in the man which showed itself in occasional, ferocious outbursts of temper.

"Poor fellow! Poor fellow!" Murdoch murmured. "What can I do? How can I help?"

"You can hurry to the police station at Fulworth," Holmes replied. "Find Anderson, the village constable, and report this matter at once."

Holmes had hardly swallowed his first cup of tea one morning a few days later when Mrs. Hudson announced a visitor: Inspector Bardle of the Sussex Constabulary.

"I know your immense experience, sir," he said. "This is quite unofficial, of course, and need go no further. But I am fairly up against it in this McPherson case. The question is, shall I make an arrest?"

"Meaning Ian Murdoch?"

"Yes, sir. There is really no one else. If he didn't do it, then who did?"

"Consider," said Holmes, "all the gaps in your case. On the morning of the crime Murdoch can prove an alibi. He was with his students until the last moment. Then bear in mind the absolute impossibility that he could singlehanded have inflicted such terrible wounds on a man fully as strong as himself. Finally, there is the question of the instrument with which the injuries were inflicted."

"What could it have been but a scourge or a flexible whip of some sort?"

"Have you examined the marks?"

"I have seen them. So has the doctor."

"But I have examined them very carefully with a lens. This is my method in such cases." He stepped to the bureau and brought out an enlarged photograph. "Consider this weal which extends round the right shoulder. Do you observe nothing remarkable?"

"Can't say that I do."

"Surely it is evident that it is unequal in its intensity. There is a dot of extravasated blood here, and another there. What can they mean?"

"I have no idea. Have you?"

Holmes smiled. "Perhaps I have," he said.

There came a sudden interruption. Holmes's outer door was flung open, there were blundering footsteps in the passage, and Ian Murdoch staggered into the room, pallid, his clothes in wild disorder, clawing with his hands at the furniture to hold himself erect. "Brandy! Brandy!" he gasped, and fell groaning upon the sofa. Behind him came Stackhurst, hatless and panting.

"Yes, brandy!" Stackhurst cried. "This man is at his last gasp. It was all I could do to get him here. He fainted twice on the way."

Half a tumbler of brandy revived Murdoch. He pushed himself up on one arm and swung his coat off his shoulders. "For God's sake!" he pleaded. "Oil, opium, morphia! Anything to ease this agony!"

Holmes and Inspector Bardle cried out at the sight. Criss-crossed upon Murdoch's naked shoulder was the same strange pattern of red, inflamed lines which had been the deathmark of Fitzroy McPherson.

Holmes had years before abandoned the drug habit. No morphine was available, but pads of cotton-wool soaked in salad oil seemed to take the agony out of Murdock's strange wounds. At last his head fell heavily upon the cushion. It was half sleep and half faint, but it was ease from pain.

"My God!" Stackhurst cried. "What is it, Mr. Holmes?"

"Where did you find him?"

"Down on the beach. Exactly where poor McPherson met his end. He was at the edge of the water, reeling like a drunken man. I threw some clothes about him and brought him here at once. For heaven's sake, Mr. Holmes, use all the powers you possess! Spare no pains to lift the curse from this place! Can you, with all your world-wide reputation, do nothing?"

"I think I can, Stackhurst," Holmes replied quietly. "Come with me now. And you, Inspector, come along."

Leaving the unconscious man in the charge of Mrs. Hudson, the three went down to the deadly lagoon. On the shingle there was piled a little heap of towels and clothes, left by the stricken man. Slowly Holmes walked around the edge of the water, Stackhurst and Bardle in single file behind him. Most of the pool was quite shallow, but under the cliff where the beach was hollowed out it was four or five feet deep. It was to this part that a swimmer would naturally go. A line of rocks lay above it at the base of the cliff, and along this Holmes led the way, peering eagerly into the depths beneath him. He had reached the deepest and stillest part of the pool when his keen gray eyes caught the strange object for which he was seeking. It lay upon a rocky shelf some three feet under the water, a curious, vibrating hairy creature with streaks of silver among its yellow tresses.

"Behold," said Holmes, "the Lion's Mane."

There was a big boulder just above the ledge.

"It has done mischief enough," Holmes cried. "Help me, Stackhurst! Let us end this murderer forever."

They pushed the boulder until it fell with a tremendous crash into the water. When the ripples had cleared away they saw that it had settled upon the ledge below. From under the stone oozed a thick oily scum.

"Here is a book," said Sherlock Holmes, taking a small volume from the well-stocked shelves that covered three full walls of his study.

"It is *Out of Doors,* by the famous observer J. G. Wood.[6] Wood himself very nearly perished from contact with this vile creature, so he wrote with very full knowledge. *Cyanea capillata* is the miscreant's full name, and he is a jellyfish which is a fearful stinger—as deadly to a bather as a cobra to a jungle explorer. Wood says the creature nearly killed him, although he had only been exposed to it in the disturbed ocean and not in the narrow calm waters of a bathing pool. You cannot doubt, Inspector, that here is an account which completely explains the tragedy of poor Fitzroy McPherson."

"And incidentally exonerates me," remarked Ian Murdoch.

He and Stackhurst left Holmes's study with arms linked in friendly fashion. The inspector remained, staring at Holmes in silence with his oxlike eyes.

"Well, sir," he said at last, "you've done it again. I had read of you, but I never believed what I read. It's wonderful!"

Holmes shook his head ruefully.

"I was culpably slow at the start," he said. "Well, well, Inspector. I have often ventured to chaff you gentlemen of the police, but *Cyanea capillata* has very nearly avenged Scotland Yard."

---

[6] *Out of Doors: A Selection of Original Articles on Practical Natural History;* London: Longmans, Green and Co., 1874; new editions in 1882 and 1890. The Reverend John George Wood (1827–89), its author, wrote nearly sixty other books and many magazine articles, a number of them for children. It is likely that Holmes's obligation to Wood was even greater than has previously been acknowledged, since Wood was also the author of *Bees, Their Habits and Management* (London: G. Routledge & Co., 1853)—a subject to which we know that Holmes gave no little attention between 1904 and 1912.

XXV. HIS LAST BOW: SUNDAY, AUGUST 2, 1914

"Stand with me here upon the terrace, for it may be the last quiet talk that we shall ever have."

SHERLOCK HOLMES.

It was nine o'clock at night upon the second of August—the most terrible August in the history of the world.

The sun had long set, but one blood-red gash like an open wound lay low on the distant west. Above, the stars were shining brightly, and below, the lights of the shipping glimmered in the bay.

The two famous Germans stood beside the stone parapet of the garden walk, with the long, low, heavily gabled house behind them, and they looked down upon the broad sweep of the beach at the foot of the great chalk cliff on which Von Bork, like some wandering eagle, had perched himself four years before. They stood with their heads close together, talking in low, confidential tones. From below the glowing ends of their cigars might have been the smoldering eyes of some malignant fiend looking down in the darkness.

A remarkable man, this Von Bork—a man who could hardly be matched among all the devoted agents of the Kaiser. It was his talents which had first recommended him for the English mission, the most important mission of all, but since he had taken it over, those talents had become more and more manifest to the half-dozen people in the world who were really in touch with the truth. One of these was his present companion, Baron Von Herling, the chief secretary of the legation, whose huge hundred-horsepower Benz was blocking the country lane as it waited to carry its owner back to London.

"So far as I can judge the trend of events, you will probably be back in Berlin within the week," Von Herling was saying. "When you get there, my dear Von Bork, I think you will be surprised at the welcome you will receive. I happen to know what is thought in the highest quarters of your work in this country."

Von Bork laughed.

"They are not very hard to deceive," he remarked. "A more docile, simple folk could not be imagined."

"I don't know about that," said the other thoughtfully. "They have strange limits and one must learn to observe them. It is that surface simplicity of theirs which makes a trap for the stranger . . . Now you, with this sporting pose of yours—"

"No, no, don't call it a pose. A pose is an artificial thing. This is quite natural. I *am* a sportsman. I enjoy it."

"Well, that makes it the more effective. You yacht against them, you hunt with them, you play polo, you match them in every game . . . I have even heard that you go to the length of boxing with the young officers. And what is the result? Nobody takes you seriously. You are a 'good old sport,' 'quite a decent fellow for a German,' a hard-drinking, night-club, knock-about-town, devil-may-care young fellow. And all the time this quiet country house of yours is the center of half of the mischief in England, and the sporting squire the most astute secret-service man in Europe. Genius, my dear Von Bork—genius!"

"You flatter me, Baron. But certainly I may claim that my four years in this country have not been unproductive. Would you mind stepping inside for a moment?"

The door of the study opened straight onto the terrace. Von Bork pushed it back, and, leading the way, he clicked the switch of the electric light. He then closed the door behind the bulky form which followed him, and carefully adjusted the heavy curtains over the latticed window. Only when all these precautions had been taken did he turn his sunburned, aquiline face to his guest.

"Some of my papers have gone," he said, "with my wife and the household staff, who left yesterday for Flushing. I must, of course, claim the protection of our embassy for the others."

"Your name has already been filed as one of the personal suite. There will be no difficulties for you or your baggage. Of course, it is just possible that we may not have to go. England may leave France to her fate."

"And Belgium?"

"Yes, and Belgium, too."

Von Bork shook his head. "I don't see how that could be. There is a very definite treaty there. She could never recover from such a humiliation."

"She would at least have peace. For the moment."

"But her honor?"

"Tut, my dear sir. We live in a utilitarian age. Honor is a medieval conception. I should think they would be wiser to fight with allies than without them, but that is their own affair. This week is their week of destiny. But you were speaking of your papers." He sat in an armchair with the light shining on his broad bald head, while he puffed sedately at a cigar.

In a corner of the large oak-paneled, book-lined room stood a brass-bound safe. Von Bork detached a key from his watch chain, manipulated the double disc around the keyhole, inserted the key in the lock and swung open the heavy door.

"Look!" he said.

The secretary of the embassy gazed with absorbed interest at the rows of pigeonholes with which the safe was furnished. Each pigeonhole, stuffed with papers, had its label: "Harbour defences," "Aeroplanes," "Irish Civil War," "Egypt," "Portsmouth forts," "The Channel" . . .

"Colossal!" said the secretary. Putting down his cigar, he clapped his fat hands softly.

Von Bork bowed.

"And all in four short years!" the secretary continued. "Not such a bad show for the hard-drinking, hard-riding country squire."

"But the gem of my collection is coming," Von Bork said. "And there is the setting all ready for it." He pointed to a space over which "Naval signals" was printed. "Thanks to my checkbook and to the good Altamont, all will be well tonight."

The baron looked at his watch and gave a guttural exclamation of disappointment.

"Well, I can wait no longer. I had hoped to be able to return to the embassy with news of your great coup. Did Altamont name no hour?"

Von Bork pushed over a telegram:

> Will come without fail tonight and bring new spark plugs.
> Altamont.

"Spark plugs?"

"He poses as a motor expert, and I keep a full garage. In our code everything likely to come up is named for some spare part. If he talks of a radiator it is a battleship, of an oil pump a cruiser, and so on. Spark plugs are naval signals."

The secretary glanced again at the telegram. "Dispatched from Portsmouth at midday," he said. "By the way, what do you pay Altamont?"

"Five hundred pounds for this job. And of course he has a salary as well."

"The greedy rogue. They are very useful, these traitors, but still I grudge them their blood money."

"I grudge Altamont nothing. He is a wonderful worker. If I pay him well, he at least 'delivers the goods,' to use his own phrase. Besides he is not a traitor. He is an Irish-American."

"An Irish-American?"

"If you heard him talk you would not doubt it. Sometimes I can hardly understand him. He seems to have declared war on the King's English as well as on the English King. Must you really go? He may be here at any moment."

"I am sorry, but I have already overstayed my time. We shall expect you early tomorrow, and when you get that signal book through the little door on the Duke of York's steps you can put a triumphant 'Finis' to your record in England. What? Tokay?" He indicated a heavily sealed dust-covered bottle which stood with two high glasses upon a salver.

"May I offer you a glass before your journey?"

"No, I thank you. But it looks like revelry."

"Altamont has a nice taste in wines, and he took a fancy to my Tokay. He is a touchy fellow, and needs humoring in small things."

They had strolled out onto the terrace again, and along it to the farther end where, at a touch from the baron's chauffeur, the great car shivered and chuckled.

"Those are the lights of Harwich, I suppose," the secretary said, pulling on his dust coat. "How still and peaceful it all seems. There may be other lights within the week, and the English coast a less tranquil place! The heavens, too, may not be quite so peaceful if all that the good Zeppelin promises us comes true. But who is that?"

Behind them, only one window showed a light. In it there stood a lamp, and beside it, seated at a table, was an old woman in a country cap. She was bending over her knitting and stopping occasionally to stroke a large black cat curled on the floor beside her.

"That is Martha, the only servant I have left."

The secretary smiled.

"She might almost personify Britannia," he said, "with her complete self-absorption and her air of comfortable somnolence. Well, *au revoir*, Von Bork!"

With a final wave of his hand he sprang into the car, and a moment later the two golden cones from its headlights shot forward through the darkness. The secretary lay back in the cushions of the luxurious limousine, his thoughts so full of the impending European tragedy that he hardly observed that as his own car swung through the village street it nearly ran over a little Ford that was coming in the opposite direction.

Von Bork walked slowly back to the study when the last gleam of the motor lamps had faded into the distance. As he passed he observed that his old housekeeper had put out her lamp and retired.

There was a good deal of tidying up to do inside his study and he set himself to do it, until his keen, handsome face was flushed with the heat of the burning papers. A leather valise stood beside his table, and into this he began to pack very neatly and systematically the precious contents of his safe. He had hardly got started with the work, however, when his quick ears caught the sound of a distant car. Instantly he gave an exclamation of satisfaction, strapped up the valise, shut the safe, locked it, and hurried out onto the terrace. He was just in time to see the lights of a small car come to a halt at the gate. A passenger sprang out and advanced swiftly toward him, while the chauffeur—a heavily built, elderly man, with a gray mustache—settled down, like one who resigns himself to a long vigil.

"Well?" asked Von Bork eagerly, running forward to meet his visitor.

For answer the man waved a small brown-paper parcel triumphantly above his head.

"You can give me the glad hand tonight, mister," he cried. "I'm bringing home the bacon at last."

"The signals?"

"Same as I said in my wire. Every last one of them: semaphore, lamp code, Marconi—a copy, mind you, not the original. That was too dangerous. But it's the real goods, and you can bet on that."

"Come in," said Von Bork. "Except for my housekeeper, I am alone in the house. I was only waiting for this. Of course, a copy is better than the original. If an original were missing they would simply change the whole thing. You think it's all safe about this copy?"

The Irish-American had entered the study and stretched his long legs from the armchair. He was a tall, gaunt man of sixty, with clear-cut features and a small goatee which gave him a general resemblance to the caricatures of Uncle Sam. A half-smoked cigar hung from the corner of his mouth, and as he sat down he struck a match and relit it. "Making ready for the move, eh?" he asked as he looked around him. "Say, mister," he added, as his gray eyes fell upon the safe, "you don't tell me you've been keeping your papers in that?"

"Why not?"

"A contraption like that? And they reckon you to be some spy. Why, a Yankee crook would be into that in a minute with a can opener. If I'd known that any letter of mine was going to lie loose in a thing like that I'd have been a mug to write you at all."

"It would puzzle any crook to force that safe," Von Bork answered. "You won't cut that metal with any tool."

"But the lock?"

"It's a double combination lock. You know what that is?"

"Search me."

"You need a word as well as a set of figures before you can get the lock to work," Von Bork replied. He rose and showed a double-radiating disc around the keyhole. "This outer disc is for the letters, the inner one for the figures. So it's not quite as simple as you thought. It was four years ago that I had it made, and what do you think I chose for the word and the figures?"

"It's beyond me."

"Well, I chose *August* for the word and *1914* for the figures, and here we are."

The American's face showed surprise and admiration.

"Well," he said, "that *was* smart. You had it down to a fine thing."

"Yes, even then a few of us could guess the date. Here it is, and I'm shutting down tomorrow morning."

"Well, I guess you'll have to fix me up also. I'm not staying in this goldarned country all on my lonesome. In a week or less from what I see, John Bull will be on his hind legs and fair ramping. I'd rather watch him from over the water."

"But you're an American citizen."

"So was Jack James an American citizen, but he's doing time in pokey all the same. It cuts no ice with a British copper to tell him you're an American citizen. 'It's British law and order over here,' says he. By the way, mister, talking of Jack James, it seems to me you don't do much to cover your men."

"What do you mean?"

"Well, you're their boss, aren't you? It's up to you to see that they don't fall down. But they do fall down, and when did you ever pick them up? There's James—"

"It was James's own fault. You know that yourself. He was too self-willed for the job."

"James was a bonehead—I'll give you that. But then there was Hollis."

"The man was mad."

"Well, he did go a bit woozy towards the end. It's enough to make a man bughouse when he has to play a part from morning to night with a hundred guys all ready to set the coppers wise to him. But now there is Steiner—"

Von Bork started violently, and his sunburned face turned a

shade paler.

"What about Steiner?"

"Well, they got him, that's all. They raided his store last night, and he and his papers are all in Portsmouth jail. You'll go off and he, poor devil, will have to stand the racket, and lucky if he gets off with his life. That's why I want to get over the water as soon as you do."

Von Bork was a strong man, but it was easy to see that the news had shaken him.

"How could they have got on to Steiner?" he muttered. "That is the worst blow yet."

"Well, you nearly had a worse one, for I believe they are not far off me."

"You don't mean that!"

"Sure thing. My landlady down Fratton way had some inquiries, and when I heard of it I guessed that it was time for me to hustle. But what I want to know, mister, is how the coppers get to know these things? Steiner is the fifth man you've lost since I signed on with you, and I know the name of the sixth if I don't get a move on. How do you explain it, and ain't you ashamed to see your men go down like this?"

Von Bork flushed crimson.

"How dare you speak to me in such a way!"

"If I didn't dare things, mister, I wouldn't be working for you. But I'll tell you straight what's in my mind. I've heard that with you Germans when an agent has done his work you're not sorry to see him put away."

Von Bork sprang to his feet.

"Do you dare to suggest that I have given away my own agents?"

"I don't say that, mister, but there's a stool pigeon or a double-cross somewhere, and it's up to you to find out where it is. Anyhow I'm taking no more chances. It's me for little Holland, and the sooner the better."

Von Bork mastered his anger.

"We have been allies too long to quarrel now at the very hour of victory," he said. "You've done splendid work and taken risks and I can't forget it. By all means go to Holland, and you can get a boat from Rotterdam to New York. No other line will be safe a week from now. I'll take the signals book and pack it with the rest."

The American held the small parcel in his hand, but made no move to give it up.

"What about the dough?" he said.

"The what?"

"The boodle. The pay-off. The five hundred pounds. The gunner turned damn' nasty at the last, and I had to square him with an extra hundred dollars or it would have been no go for you and me. 'Nothin' doin'l' says he, and he meant it, too, but the last hundred did it. It's cost me two hundred pounds from first to last, so it isn't likely I'd give this up without getting my wad."

Von Bork smiled with some bitterness. "You don't seem to have a very high opinion of my honor," he said. "You want the money before you give up the book."

"Well, mister, it's a business proposition."

"All right. Have your way." Von Bork sat down at the table and scribbled a check. He tore it from the book, but refrained from handing it to his companion. "After all," he said, "since we are to be on such terms, Mr. Altamont, I don't see why I should trust you any more than you trust me. Do you understand?" he added, looking back over his shoulder at the American. "There's the check upon the table. I claim the right to examine that parcel before you pick up the check."

The American passed the parcel to Von Bork without a word. Von Bork undid the string and two wrappers of paper. Then he sat gazing for a moment in silent amazement at a small blue book which lay before him. Across the cover was printed in golden letters: *Practical Handbook of Bee Culture.*

The master spy had only an instant to glare at this strangely irrelevant inscription. The next he was gripped at the back of his neck by a grasp of iron, and a chloroformed sponge was held in front of his writhing face. . . .

"Another glass, Watson?" asked Mr. Sherlock Holmes, as he extended the bottle of Imperial Tokay.

The thick-set chauffeur, who had seated himself by the table, pushed forward his glass.

"It *is* good wine, Holmes," he rumbled, stroking a drop from his gray mustache.

"A remarkable wine, Watson! Our friend upon the sofa has assured me that it is from Franz Joseph's special cellar at the Schoenbrunn Palace. Might I trouble you to open a window? Chloroform vapor does not help the palate."

The safe was open, and Holmes was standing in front of it, removing dossier after dossier, swiftly examining each, and then packing it neatly in Von Bork's valise. The German lay upon the sofa sleeping stertorously with a strap around his upper arms and another around his legs.

"We need not hurry ourselves, Watson," Holmes said. "We are safe from interruption. Would you mind just touching the bell? There is no one in the house except Mrs. Hudson, who has played her part admirably. I got her the situation here when first I took the matter up. Ah, Mrs. Hudson, you will be glad to know that all is well."

The pleasant old housekeeper had appeared in the doorway. She curtseyed with a smile to Sherlock Holmes and then to Dr. Watson, but glanced with some apprehension at the man on the sofa.

"It is all right, Mrs. Hudson. He has not been hurt at all."

"I am glad of that, sir. According to his lights he has been a kind master. Imagine! He wanted me to go with his wife to Germany yesterday, but that would hardly have suited your plans, would it, sir?"

"No, indeed, Mrs. Hudson. So long as you were here I was easy in my mind. We waited some time for your signal tonight."

"It was the secretary, sir."

"I know. His car passed ours."

"I thought he would never go. I knew that it would not suit you, sir, to find him here."

"No, indeed. Well, it only meant that Dr. Watson and I waited half an hour or so until we saw your lamp go out and knew that the coast was clear. You can report to me tomorrow in London, Mrs. Hudson. I will be at Claridge's Hotel."

"Very good, sir."

"I suppose you have everything ready to leave?"

"Yes, sir. He posted seven letters today. I have the addresses as usual."

"Very good, Mrs. Hudson. I will look into them tomorrow. Good night. These papers," he continued, as their old landlady vanished, "are not of very great importance, for, of course, the information which they represent has been sent off long ago to the German Government. These are the originals which could not safely be got out of the country."

"Then they are of no use."

"I should not go so far as to say that, Watson. They will at least show our people what is known and what is not. I may say that a good many of these papers have come through me, and I need not add are thoroughly untrustworthy. It would brighten my declining years to see a German cruiser navigating the Solent according to the mine-field plans which I have furnished. But you, Watson"—he stopped his work and took his old friend by the shoulders—"I've hardly seen you in the light yet. How have the years used you? You look the same blithe boy as ever."

"I feel twenty years younger, Holmes. I have seldom been so happy as when I got your wire asking me to meet you at Harwich with the car. But you, Holmes—you have changed very little— save for that horrible goatee."

"These are the sacrifices one makes for one's country, Watson," Holmes said, pulling at his little tuft of chin whiskers. "Tomorrow it will be but a dreadful memory. With my hair cut and a few other superficial changes I shall no doubt appear at Claridge's tomorrow as I was before this American stunt—I beg your pardon, Watson, my well of English seems to be permanently defiled—before this American job came my way."

"But you had retired, Holmes. We heard of you as living the life of a hermit among your bees and your books in your little farm on the South Downs."

"Exactly, Watson. And here is one fruit of my leisured ease." He picked up the volume on bee culture from the table. "Alone I did it. Behold the fruit of pensive nights and laborious days, when I watched the little working gangs of bees as once I watched the criminal world of London."

"But how did you get to work again?"

"Ah, I have often marveled at it myself. Mycroft I could have withstood, even in his new and exalted capacity, but when the

Foreign Minister[1] and the Premier himself[2] also deigned to visit my humble home—well, things were going wrong, and no one could understand why they were going wrong. Agents were suspected or even caught, but there was evidence of some strong and secret central force. It was absolutely necessary to expose it. It has cost me two years, Watson, but they have not been devoid of excitement. When I say that I started my pilgrimage at Chicago, graduated in an Irish secret society at Skibbareen and so eventually caught the eye of a subordinate agent of Von Bork, who recommended me as a likely man, you will realize that the matter was complex. Since then I have been honored by Von Bork's confidence, which has not prevented most of his plans going subtly wrong and five of his best agents being in prison. I watched them, Watson, and I picked them as they ripened." While he spoke, Holmes was continuing his swift investigation of Von Bork's documents. "Hullo!" he added. "This should put another bird in the cage. I had no idea that the paymaster was such a rascal, though I have long had an eye upon him. Von Bork, you have a great deal to answer for."

Their prisoner had raised himself with some difficulty upon the sofa, and was staring at Holmes with a strange mixture of amazement and hatred.

"I shall get even with you, Altamont," he said, speaking with slow deliberation, "if it takes all my life I shall get level with you!"

"The old sweet song," Holmes said. "How often I have heard it in days gone by. It was a favorite ditty of the late-lamented Professor Moriarty. Colonel Sebastian Moran has also been known to warble it. And yet I live and keep bees upon the Sussex Downs."

"Curse you, you double traitor!" the German cried, straining against his bonds and glaring murder from furious eyes.

"No, no, it is not so bad as that," said Holmes, smiling. "As

---

[1] Grey of Fallodon, Edward Grey, 1st Viscount (1862–1933). As Britain's Foreign Secretary, 1905–16, he worked long but fruitlessly to avert war in Europe.

[2] Herbert Henry Asquith, 1st Earl of Oxford and Asquith (1852–1928), Prime Minister from 1908 through 1916. World War I brought his downfall in favor of David Lloyd George.

my speech surely shows you, Mr. Altamont[3] of Chicago had no existence in fact. I used him and he is gone."

"Then who are you?"

"It is really immaterial who I am, but since the matter seems to interest you, I may say that this is not my first acquaintance with the members of your family. I have done a good deal of business in Germany in the past, and my name is probably familiar to you."

"I would wish to know it," said the German grimly.

"Well, it was I who saved from murder, by the nihilist Klopman, the Count Von und Zu Grafenstein, who was your mother's eldest brother. It was I also—"

Von Bork sat up in amazement.

"There is only one man!" he cried.

"Exactly," said Sherlock Holmes.

Von Bork groaned and sank back on the sofa. "And most of my information came through you!" he cried. "What is it worth? What have I done? It is my ruin!"

"It is certainly a little untrustworthy," Holmes said. "It will require some checking, and you have little time to check it. Well, these papers are ready now, Watson. If you will be kind enough to unstrap our prisoner's legs, I think we may get started for London."

After a short, final struggle Von Bork was walked down the garden path and hoisted into the spare seat of the little car. His precious valise was wedged in beside him.

"I suppose you realize," Von Bork snarled, "that if your government bears you out in this treatment it becomes an act of war."

"What about your government and this treatment?" said Holmes, tapping the valise.

"You are a private individual. You have no warrant for my arrest. The whole proceeding is highly irregular."

"Highly," said Holmes.

"Kidnaping a German subject."

"And stealing his private papers."

---

[3] Holmes later told Watson that he found it amusing to take as his alias the same name that had been used by the convict Amory in Thackeray's *Pendennis*.

"Well, you realize your position, you and your accomplice here. If I were to shout for help as we pass through the village—"

"My dear sir, if you did anything so foolish you would give the village a new public house, with 'The Dangling Prussian' as its signpost. The Englishman is a patient creature, but his temper is a little inflamed at present. No, Herr Von Bork, you will go with us in a quiet, sensible fashion to Scotland Yard for a quiet, sensible talk with Commissioner Stanley Hopkins. And now, Watson, stand with me here upon the terrace, for it may be the last quiet talk that we shall ever have."

The two friends chatted in intimate conversation for a few minutes, recalling once again the days of the past, while the prisoner vainly wriggled to undo the bonds that held him. As they turned to the car, Holmes pointed to the moonlit sea, and shook a thoughtful head.

"There's an east wind coming, Watson."

"I think not, Holmes. It is very warm."

"Good old Watson! You are the one fixed point in a changing age. There's an east wind coming all the same, such a wind as never blew on England yet. It will be cold and bitter, Watson, and a good many of us may wither before its blast. But it's God's own wind nonetheless, and a cleaner, stronger land will lie in the sunshine when the storm has cleared. Start her up, Watson, for it's time we were on our way."

EPILOGUE. SHERLOCK HOLMES WALKS AT SUNSET: SUNDAY, JANUARY 6, 1957

. . . they still live for all that love them well; in a romantic chamber of the heart; in a nostalgic country of the mind: where it is always 1895.

VINCENT STARRETT.

The old—the very old—man walked along the cliff path.

Though he carried a stick, his back, despite his great age, was unbowed. His keen gray eyes were undimmed by the passing of the years. His hair, snow-white now, was still thick, combed straight toward the back of his head in the English fashion.

The old man was content.

His great work, the magnum opus of his latter years, was finished at last. Carefully wrapped, precisely addressed in his clear, copperplate handwriting, it lay on the study table. In the morning it would go to his publisher. He had been wrong to think that the fruit of twenty-three years of unceasing work as the world's first, and for so many of those years the world's only, consulting detective, could be contained in a single volume. His *Whole Art of Detection* would run at least to four. Its pages would contain all that he had learned from the cases that Watson had reported and those that Watson had been unable to report. Now at last the world would learn the truth about the Tarleton Murders; the case of Vamberry, the Wine Merchant; the adventure of the Old Russian Woman; the little matter of the Vatican Cameos; the summons to Norway; the commission from the Sultan of Turkey. Here, too, was the problem of the

Grosvenor Square Furniture Van, the singular affair of the Aluminium Crutch; Ricoletti of the Club Foot and His Abominable Wife; Bert Stevens, that terrible murderer; the missing Mr. Etherage; Colonel Upwood and his atrocious conduct at the Nonpareil Club; the unfortunate Mme. Montpensier and the Tired Captain; the Two Coptic Patriarchs and Old Abrahams and Isadora Persano, the well-known journalist and duelist.

The Whole Art of Detection—it would be his monument. How fitting that it should have been completed on this, his birthday. His one-hundred-and-third birthday!

How had he achieved such an age?

Tranquillity—the tranquillity of mind, the way of life, which he had learned in the lamaseries of far Tibet—that, of course, was part of the secret.

But there was a greater part.

It had seemed strange to some—Watson for one had never understood—why Holmes, after his retirement, should interest himself in beekeeping. *Practical Handbook of Bee Culture, with Some Observations upon the Segregation of the Queen*—that had been the full title of his volume. But that volume had contained only a little, only a very little, of all that he had learned. The results of his major experiments with the little workers—these were known, till now, to only one other than himself. Till now—for beside the package on the study table that contained his manuscript of *The Whole Art of Detection* lay a second, smaller package. As carefully wrapped, as precisely addressed as the first, it would go in the morning to the Royal Society. Here was all he had discovered in his years of "retirement" about that miraculous substance, royal jelly.

Royal jelly—the glandular secretion produced by nurse bees to feed the larvae immediately they had hatched from the egg. Royal jelly—produced by the pharyngeal glands of bees, much as the mammary glands of vertebrates produce milk. Royal jelly—fed in concentrated form to all bee larvae for the first three days after hatching, diluted with honey and pollen thereafter for those bees destined to become drones or workers. But the larvae destined to become queens—these were fed throughout the whole of the larval period on a concentrated diet of pure royal jelly.

Royal jelly, Holmes had reasoned, must be a substance of tremendous power, for on this diet alone the queen-bee larvae increased in weight fifteen hundred times in five days. And the experiments of Holmes, the chemist, had proved him right. Royal jelly, properly prepared and taken, could preserve and prolong the processes of human life.

"*Mens sana in corpore sano,*" the old man murmured. "Everything comes in circles, even the poet Juvenal."

The day was a pleasant one for a January in the South of England, but now, as the sun sank into the sea, the wind quickened. The old man on the cliff path drew his old-fashioned caped overcoat a little closer about his lean shoulders.

There was a bench beside the path ahead. He would take a moment's rest.

The old man stretched his long legs toward the cliff edge and gazed far out across the rolls of the Channel, their customary gray reddened by the sinking sun. Beneath him the waves pounded and broke against the chalk cliff.

The old man thought of his brothers.

Sherrinford. He wished he had known Sherrinford better. Still, he had been of great service to his eldest brother once, in 1896. Sherrinford—big, bluff, jovial Sherrinford—accused of murder! The idea was grotesque. Yet so much evidence seemed to point in his direction. Sherlock had found the facts that had cleared him, of course. But what a cesspool of ancient horrors the clearing had uncovered! Black magic, abroad in the twentieth century! The old man on the bench recalled the black corpse candles and the Hand of Glory, the seven scarlet handkerchiefs and the book that it was death to open. It had taken him almost a year to identify and extirpate the coven responsible for the mischief. Well, the facts of the matter would be known at last, in the pages of his *Whole Art of Detection.*

Thank God for Sherrinford, the old man thought. Without him, Mycroft, as the elder of two brothers, would have passed his days as the squire of a farmstead in Yorkshire. And England, and the world, had needed Mycroft.

What had he said to Watson so many years ago? "You would also be right in a sense if you said that occasionally he *is* the British Government."

With Mycroft alone he had so far shared the secret of the royal jelly. The substance had not only lengthened his brother's life almost beyond the bounds of believability. It had worked a miraculous transformation in the man, turned his lethargy into dynamic energy. Through two World Wars, Mycroft Holmes had been that most mysterious of men—the man at the very top of the British Secret Service.

The old man on the bench recalled his last meeting with Mycroft, in the Strangers' Room of the Diogenes Club, a few months before his brother's death.

"Even with your imagination, Sherlock," Mycroft had said, puffing at a huge cigar, sipping his fine old brandy, "I do not think you could picture me clambering ashore from a landing barge with my old friend Winston. 'I'm Mr. Bullfinch,' Winston said—for that was the code name agreed upon—'and I've come to see for myself how things are going in North Africa.' "

Well, Sherlock, too, had played some part in the great if terrible events that had begun on September 1, 1939. There was, he remembered, that morning when the young man who called himself a fusilier had rapped at his door to ask the way to Eastbourne.[1] It had been elementary to unmask the young man as Amos Boling, the American traitor and a trusted agent of German intelligence.

He remembered, too, his solution to the problem of that one-man invasion of Britain by the Nazi Rudolf Hess.[2]

Amos Boling and Rudolf Hess—not really worthy opponents, thought old Mr. Sherlock Holmes.

He thought of other opponents, far more worthy.

Dr. Grimesby Roylott, for example. He could see him now, standing on the bearskin hearthrug in the old sitting room at 221B, as he seized the poker, bent it into a curve with his great brown hands.

"See that you keep yourself out of my grip," Roylott had snarled. He hurled the twisted poker into the fireplace and strode out of the room.

[1] See "The Man Who Was Not Dead," by Manly Wade Wellman, in *Argosy Magazine,* issue of August 9, 1941, and *The Misadventures of Sherlock Holmes.*

[2] See "The Adventure of the Illustrious Impostor," by Anthony Boucher, in *The Misadventures of Sherlock Holmes.*

"I am not quite so bulky as he," Holmes had said to Watson, "but if he had remained I might have shown him that my grip was not much more feeble than his own."

As he spoke, he had picked up the steel poker and straightened it out again.

The hands of the old man, dreaming of the past, tightened on the handle of his stick.

John Clay, and the man who called himself Stapleton, and Inspector Athelney Jones, whom the world knew so much better by another, by a terrible, name . . .

And Colonel Sebastian Moran, that tiger of a man who hunted tigers and men . . .

And, most important of all, there had been, of course, Professor James Moriarty, the Napoleon of Crime.

The wind blew stronger. The waves beat more heavily on the shingle below.

The old man on the bench settled himself a little more firmly.

So many enemies. Culverton Smith and Charles Augustus Milverton and the German agent, Von Bork. And yet he still lived and kept his bees upon the Sussex Downs.

So many enemies—and so many rivals who were also, for the most part, friends. Youghal and MacDonald and Stanley Hopkins. And, in the earlier days, Gregson and Lestrade—"the best of the Scotland Yarders," that was how he had described them to Watson.

Good old Watson! Firm friend, trusted companion, British gentleman. Watson's death, in 1929, had been one of the greatest blows that the old man on the bench had ever borne.

Good old Watson! But the tales that Watson had written! What had he said, once, to Watson? "Detection is, or ought to be, an exact science, and should be treated in the same cold and unemotional manner. You have attempted to tinge it with romanticism, which produces the same effect as if you worked a love-story or an elopement into the fifth proposition of Euclid . . ."

The old man on the bench shook his head. It was as well that his fame would rest on his own *Whole Art of Detection,* never on those tales of Watson's.

Well, his work was done now, and well done. The world would

long remember the name of Sherlock Holmes.

It had grown much colder, and very dark.

The old man on the bench drew his caped overcoat still closer about him. The gray eyes closed. The white-maned head fell forward on his breast.

For the last time, the thin lips spoke.

"Irene," the old man said. "Irene."

Anderson of the Sussex Constabulary found him there in the morning.

Curtain

APPENDIX I.

THE CHRONOLOGICAL HOLMES

"The date being—?"

SHERLOCK HOLMES.

I. The Early Period: 1844–early January, 1881

April 1844	Siger Holmes invalided home to England.
Tuesday, May 7, 1844	Siger Holmes married Violet Sherrinford, third daughter of Sir Edward Sherrinford of Berkeley Square, London, at St. Sidwell's, Exeter.
Sunday, November 30, 1845	Sherrinford Holmes born.
Saturday, October 31, 1846	James Moriarty born at a yet-unidentified town in the West of England. He had two brothers, both curiously enough also named James.
Friday, February 12, 1847	Mycroft Holmes born.
Saturday, August 7, 1852	John Hamish Watson born. His father, Henry Watson, was a Hampshireman. His mother, the former Ella Mackenzie, was a native of eastern Scotland. Young John had an elder brother, Henry Watson, Jr., who died of drink in 1888. The Watsons were in comfortable circumstances. Mrs. Watson died when John was very young and Watson *père*

continued

went to Australia, taking his children with him. There Henry prospered and there John Watson spent his boyhood.

Friday, January 6, 1854

(William) Sherlock (Scott) Holmes born at the farmstead of Mycroft in the North Riding of Yorkshire.

July 1855

The Holmes family sailed to Bordeaux, traveled to Pau.

May 1858

The Holmes family traveled to Montpellier.

Tuesday, September 7, 1858

"Irene Adler"—Clara Stephens—born in Trenton, New Jersey.

June 1860

The Holmes family returned to England.

October 1860

Sir Edward Sherrinford died at the age of 73. The Holmes family sailed to Rotterdam, two months later settled in Cologne.

April 1861

The Holmes family began a Continental tour that lasted almost four years.

Saturday, May 4, 1861

Mary Morstan, daughter of Captain Arthur Morstan of the 34th Bombay Infantry, later the second Mrs. John H. Watson, born in India.

September 1864

The Holmes family returned to England, leased a villa in Kennington. Sherlock and Mycroft sent to a board school, Sherrinford to Oxford.

August 1865

Young John Watson returned to England for schooling at Wellington College, Hampshire.

Winter of 1865–66

Sherlock Holmes severely ill.

Spring 1866

Sherlock taken to Yorkshire, entered as a day boy at the grammar school near Mycroft.

September 1868	Siger, Violet, and Sherlock Holmes sailed to St. Malo, journeyed to Pau. Sherlock entered in the fencing salon of Maître Alphonse Bencin.
April 1871	The Holmes family returned to England, settled at the farmstead of Mycroft.
Summer 1872	Sherlock tutored by Professor James Moriarty.
September 1872	Watson chose the career of an army surgeon and enrolled at the University of London Medical School. As part of his training he worked in the surgery at St. Bartholomew's Hospital, London.
October 1872	Sherlock Holmes entered Christ Church College at Oxford.
Sunday, July 12–Tuesday, August 4 and Tuesday, September 22, 1874	Holmes was asked by his classmate Victor Trevor to try his hand at solving the case Watson was later to record under the title of "The *Gloria Scott*." "The first [case] in which I was ever engaged." "I had already formed [habits of observation and inference] into a system, although I had not yet appreciated the part they were to play in my life."
October 1874	Holmes entered Caius College, Cambridge.
July 1877	Holmes took rooms in Montague Street and began the private consultative practice that was to last for twenty-three years. "Months of inaction" followed. "You can hardly realize how long I had to wait." Holmes filled his too abundant leisure time by reading and writing.

June 1878	Watson took the degree of doctor of medicine at the University of London and proceeded to Netley to go through the course prescribed for surgeons in the Army.
June–August 1878	The Mullineaux Case.
September 1878	The Reckless Goings-On at the Suicide Club.
November 1878	Watson, attached to the Fifth Northumberland Fusiliers as assistant surgeon, sailed to India as the second Afghan War broke out.
Thursday, October 2, 1879	"The Musgrave Ritual." "There are points in it which make it quite unique in the criminal records of this or, I believe, of any other country. A collection of my trifling experiences would certainly be incomplete which contained no account of this very singular business."
Monday, October 13, 1879	Holmes made his first appearance on the London stage, playing Horatio in *Hamlet*.
Sunday, November 23, 1879	Holmes sailed for America with the Sasanoff Shakespearian Company, began an eight-month tour of the United States.
January 1880	The Case of Vanderbilt and the Yeggman ("The Adventure of the Sussex Vampire").
Spring 1880	Watson removed from his brigade and attached to the Berkshires (66th Foot).
Tuesday, July 6, 1880	The Dreadful Business of the Abernetty Family of Baltimore ("The Adventure of the Six Napoleons").

Tuesday, July 27, 1880	Battle of Maiwand. Watson, wounded, escapes to the British lines with the help of his orderly, Murray.
Thursday, August 5, 1880	Holmes embarked for his trip back to England from the United States.
Tuesday, August 31, 1880	Worn with pain, Watson was removed to the base hospital at Peshawar. Here he rallied, when he was struck down by enteric fever.
Sunday, October 21, 1880	For months, Watson's life was despaired of. When at last he came to himself and became convalescent, a medical board determined that not a day should be lost in sending him back to England. He was dispatched, accordingly, in the troopship *Orontes*.
Friday, November 26, 1880	Watson landed on Portsmouth jetty. He gravitated to London and stayed for some weeks at a private hotel in the Strand.
August 1880–early January 1881	The Tarleton Murders ("The Musgrave Ritual").
	The Case of Vamberry, the Wine Merchant ("The Musgrave Ritual").
	The Adventure of the Old Russian Woman ("The Musgrave Ritual").
	The Singular Affair of the Aluminium Crutch ("The Musgrave Ritual").
	Ricoletti of the Club Foot and His Abominable Wife ("The Musgrave Ritual").
	The Trifling Affair of Mortimer Maberley ("The Adventure of the Three Gables").

continued

The Taking of Brooks and Woodhouse ("The Adventure of the Bruce-Partington Plans").

The *Matilda Briggs* and the Giant Rat of Sumatra ("The Adventure of the Sussex Vampire").

The Case of Mrs. Farintosh, concerned with an opal tiara ("The Adventure of the Speckled Band").

Early January 1881

Watson made up his mind to take up quarters in some less pretentious and less expensive domicile. On the very day that he had come to this conclusion, he was standing at the Criterion Bar. . . . And later: "Dr. Watson, Mr. Sherlock Holmes," said Stamford, introducing them. Holmes and Watson met the next day and inspected the rooms at No. 221B Baker Street. They at once entered into possession.

II. The Partnership, to Dr. Watson's First Marriage: Early January 1881–Monday, November 1, 1886

Late February 1881

The Forgery Case (*A Study in Scarlet*).

Friday, March 4–Monday, March 7, 1881

A Study in Scarlet. "The finest study I ever came across." "A most extraordinary case—a most incomprehensible affair."

When I glance over my notes and records of the Sherlock Holmes cases between the years '82 and '90, I am faced by so many which present strange and interesting features, that it is no easy matter to know which to choose and which to leave.—John H. Watson, M.D., "The Five Orange Pips."

Friday, April 6, 1883

"The Adventure of the Speckled Band." "I cannot recall any [case] which presented more singular features."

January 1884–August 1886	Watson traveled to America, bought a practice in San Francisco, met and wooed Miss Constance Adams of that city.
March 1881–October 1886	The Delicate Case of the King of Scandinavia ("The Adventure of the Noble Bachelor").
	The Service for Lord Backwater ("The Adventure of the Noble Bachelor").
	The Case of the Woman at Margate ("The Adventure of the Second Stain").
	The Darlington Substitution Scandal ("A Scandal in Bohemia").[1] The Arnsworth Castle Business ("A Scandal in Bohemia").[2]
	The Little Problem of the Grosvenor Square Furniture Van ("The Adventure of the Noble Bachelor").
Wednesday, October 6–Thursday, October 7, 1886	"The Resident Patient." "It may be that, in the business which I am now about to write, the part which my friend played is not sufficiently accentuated; and yet the whole train of circumstances is so remarkable that I cannot bring myself to omit it entirely from this series."
Friday, October 8, 1886	"The Adventure of the Noble Bachelor." "I feel that no memoir [of Sherlock Holmes] would be complete without some little sketch of this remarkable episode."
Saturday, October 9, 1886	The Case of the Fishmonger ("The Adventure of the Noble Bachelor").

[1] A pastiche of this adventure, titled "The Adventure of the Wax Gamblers," appears in *The Exploits of Sherlock Holmes* (see Appendix II).

[2] A pastiche of this adventure, titled "The Adventure of the Red Widow," appears in *The Exploits of Sherlock Holmes*.

Monday, October 11, 1886	The Case of the Tide-Waiter ("The Adventure of the Noble Bachelor").
Tuesday, October 12–Friday, October 15, 1886	"The Adventure of the Second Stain." "The most important international case which [Holmes] has ever been called upon to handle." "It is a case, my dear Watson, where the law is as dangerous to us as the criminals are. Every man's hand is against us, and yet the interests at stake are colossal. Should I bring it to a successful conclusion it will certainly represent the crowning glory of my career."
Monday, November 1, 1886	Watson married Miss Constance Adams of San Francisco. Shortly thereafter he purchased a small practice in Kensington.

III. From Dr. Watson's First Marriage to the Death of the First Mrs. Watson: Monday, November 1, 1886– Late December 1887

| November 1886–January 1887 | The Summons to Odessa in the Case of the Trepoff Murder ("A Scandal in Bohemia").[3] The Delicate Affair of the Reigning Family of Holland ("A Scandal in Bohemia," "A Case of Identity"). The Singular Adventure of the Atkinson Brothers at Trincomalee ("A Scandal in Bohemia"). |

It was some time before the health of my friend, Mr. Sherlock Holmes, recovered from the strain caused by his immense exertions in the spring of '87.—John H. Watson, M.D., "The Reigate Squires."

| February–early April 1887 | The Netherland-Sumatra Company and the Colossal Schemes of Baron Maupertuis ("The Reigate Squires"). |

[3] A pastiche of this adventure, titled "The Adventure of the Seven Clocks," appears in *The Exploits of Sherlock Holmes.*

Thursday, April 14–Tuesday, April 26, 1887	"The Reigate Squires." "A singular and complex problem . . ."
April 1887	About this time Sherlock Holmes became a "self-poisoner by . . . cocaine."
April–December 1887	The Adventure of the Paradol Chamber ("The Five Orange Pips"). The Adventure of the Amateur Mendicant Society ("The Five Orange Pips"). The Loss of the British Barque *Sophy Anderson* ("The Five Orange Pips"). The Singular Adventure of the Grice Patersons in the Island of Uffa ("The Five Orange Pips)" The Camberwell Poisoning Case ("The Five Orange Pips").[4] The Death of Mrs. Stewart, of Lauder ("The Adventure of the Empty House"). The Case of Bert Stevens, the Terrible Murderer ("The Adventure of the Norwood Builder").
Friday, May 20–Sunday, May 22, 1887	"A Scandal in Bohemia." "It is quite a pretty little problem."
Saturday, June 18–Sunday, June 19, 1887	"The Man with the Twisted Lip." "I cannot recall any case within my experience which looked at first glance so simple, and yet which presented such difficulties."
Before September 1887	The Saving of Colonel Prendergast in the Tankerville Club Scandal ("The Five Orange Pips"). The Three Occasions on Which Holmes Was Beaten by Men ("The Five Orange Pips").

[4] A pastiche of this adventure, titled "The Adventure of the Gold Hunter," appears in *The Exploits of Sherlock Holmes.*

Thursday, September 29–Friday, September 30, 1887

"The Five Orange Pips." "I think, Watson, that of all our cases we have had none more fantastic than this."

Before October 1887

The Missing Mr. Etherage ("A Case of Identity").
The One or Two Little Skirmishes and Scores to Settle with Mr. John Clay ("The Red-Headed League").

Mid-October 1887

The Dundas Separation Case ("A Case of Identity").
The Rather Intricate Matter from Marseilles ("A Case of Identity").

Tuesday, October 18–Wednesday, October 19, 1887

"A Case of Identity." "There was never any mystery in the matter, though . . . some of the details are of interest."

Saturday, October 29–Sunday, October 30, 1887

"The Red-Headed League." "This rather fantastic business."

Shortly before Saturday, November, 19, 1887

The Fate of Victor Savage ("The Adventure of the Dying Detective").

Saturday, November 19, 1887

"The Adventure of the Dying Detective." "Malingering is a subject upon which I have sometimes thought of writing a monograph."

Tuesday, December 27, 1887

"The Adventure of the Blue Carbuncle." "A most singular and whimsical problem, and its solution is its own reward."

Late December 1887

Death of the first Mrs. Watson.

IV. From Dr. Watson's Return to Baker Street to His Marriage
to Mary Morstan: Late December 1887–Wednesday
May 1, 1889

Before Saturday, January 7, 1888

The Two Cases in Which Holmes Helped Inspector MacDonald (*The Valley of Fear*).

Saturday, January 7–Sunday, January 8, 1888	*The Valley of Fear.* "I can hardly recall any case where the features have been more peculiar."
Tuesday, April 3, 1888	The Murder of Emma Elizabeth Smith, Streetwalker, on Osborn Street, Whitechapel.
Saturday, April 7, 1888	"The Yellow Face." "Now and again, however, it chanced that . . . he erred." "If it should ever strike you that I am getting a little overconfident . . . kindly whisper 'Norbury' in my ear."
Late April–early May 1888	The Curious Case of Dr. Watson's Second Wound. The Little Affair of the Vatican Cameos (*The Hound of the Baskervilles*).[5]
Tuesday, August 7, 1888	The Murder of Martha Tabram, Streetwalker, at Grove-yard Buildings, Whitechapel.
Friday, August 31, 1888	The Murder of Mary Ann Nichols, Streetwalker, in Bucks Row, Whitechapel.
Before September 1888	The Little Domestic Complication of Mrs. Cecil Forrester (*The Sign of the Four*).[6] The Case of the Most Winning Woman Holmes Ever Knew (*The Sign of the Four*). The Bishopgate Jewel Case (*The Sign of the Four*). The Little Case of Messenger-Manager Wilson (*The Hound of the Baskervilles*).
Week of Monday, September 3–Saturday, September 8, 1888	The Manor House Case ("The Greek Interpreter").

[5] Was *this* the case in which Watson received his second wound?

[6] For an interesting speculation on the identity of *Mr.* Forrester, see "Who Was Cecil Forrester?" by Robert Keith Leavitt in *The Baker Street Journal*, Vol. I, No. 2, April 1946, pp. 201–4. See also "The Camberwell Poisoner," by Ruth Douglass, in *Ellery Queen's Mystery Magazine* for February 1947.

Saturday, September 8, 1888	The Murder of Annie Chapman, Streetwalker, on Hanbury Street, Whitechapel.
Week of Monday, September 10–Saturday, September 15, 1888	The French Will Case (*The Sign of the Four*).
Wednesday, September 12, 1888	"The Greek Interpreter." "A singular case . . . the explanation of which is still involved in some mystery."
Tuesday, September 18–Friday, September 21, 1888	*The Sign of the Four*. "An extremely interesting case."
Tuesday, September 25–Saturday, October 20, 1888	*The Hound of the Baskervilles*. "I am not sure that of all the five hundred cases of capital importance which I have handled there is one which cuts so deep."
Wednesday, September 26, 1888	The Blackmailing Case (*The Hound of the Baskervilles*).[7]
Sunday, September 30, 1888	The Murder of Elizabeth Stride, Streetwalker, on Berner Street, Whitechapel, and the Murder of Catherine Eddowes, Streetwalker, in Mitre Square, Aldgate.
Friday, November 9–Sunday, November 11, 1888	The Murder of Mary Jane Kelly, Streetwalker, at No. 26 Dorset Street, Whitechapel, and the taking of Jack the Ripper.
Between Saturday, October 20 and late November, 1888	The Atrocious Conduct of Colonel Upwood in Connection with the Famous Card Scandal at the Nonpareil Club (*The Hound of the Baskervilles*).[8] The Unfortunate Mme. Montpensier (*The Hound of the Baskervilles*).[9]

[7] A pastiche of this adventure titled "The Adventure of the Two Women," appears in *The Exploits of Sherlock Holmes*.

[8] A pastiche of this adventure, titled "The Adventure of the Abbas Ruby," appears in *The Exploits of Sherlock Holmes*.

[9] A pastiche of this adventure, titled "The Adventure of the Black Baronet," appears in *The Exploits of Sherlock Holmes*.

Late 1888 or early 1889	The Abbas Parva Tragedy ("The Adventure of the Veiled Lodger").
Friday, April 5–Saturday, April 20, 1889	"The Adventure of the Copper Beeches." "Your little problem promises to be the most interesting which has come my way for some months. There is something definitely novel about some of the features."
Wednesday, May 1, 1889	Watson married Mary Morstan, daughter of the late Captain Arthur Morstan of the 34th Bombay Infantry, at Saint Mark's, Camberwell. He soon bought a connection in the Paddington district from old Mr. Farquhar, and "for three months . . . saw little of Holmes" ("The Stockbroker's Clerk"). Watson's practice "increased steadily" ("The Adventure of the Engineer's Thumb").

V. From Dr. Watson's Second Marriage to the Disappearance
of Sherlock Holmes: Wednesday, May 1, 1889–
Monday, May, 4, 1891

Saturday, June 8–Sunday, June 9, 1889	"The Boscombe Valley Mystery." "One of those simple cases which are so extremely difficult."
Saturday, June 15, 1889	"The Stockbroker's Clerk." "It is a case . . . which . . . presents those unusual and *outré* features which are as dear to you as they are to me."
July 1889	The *Second* Adventure of the Second Stain. ("The Naval Treaty"). "I still retain an almost verbatim report of the interview in which [Holmes] demonstrated the true facts of the case to Monsieur Dubuque, of the Paris police, and Fritz von Waldbaum, the well-known specialist of Danzig . . ."

July 1889	The Adventure of the Tired Captain ("The Naval Treaty").
Tuesday, July 30, 1889	The Very Commonplace Little Murder ("The Naval Treaty").
Tuesday, July 30–Thursday, August 1, 1889	"The Naval Treaty." "It is a most insoluble mystery." "Well, it would be absurd to deny that the case is a very abstruse and complicated one."
Before Saturday, August 31, 1889	The Bogus Laundry Affair ("The Cardboard Box").
Saturday, August 31–Monday, September 2, 1889	"The Cardboard Box." "A strange, though a peculiarly terrible, chain of events." "Simple as the case is, there have been one or two very instructive details in connection with it."
Saturday, September 7–Sunday, September 8, 1889	"The Adventure of the Engineer's Thumb." "So strange in its inception and so dramatic in its details . . . even if it gave my friend fewer openings for those deductive methods of reasoning in which he achieved such remarkable results."
Wednesday, September 11–Thursday, September 12, 1889	"The Crooked Man." "One of the strangest cases which ever perplexed a man's brain."
Late 1889	The Locking-Up of Colonel Carruthers ("The Adventure of Wisteria Lodge").
March 1881–December 1889	The *Third*[10] Adventure of the Second Stain ("The Yellow Face"). "Now and again, however, it chanced that even when [Holmes] erred the truth was still discovered."

[10] Actually, chronologically, it may have been the *first* or *second*. Since Holmes erred, it is probably an earlier rather than a later case.

Late 1886, 1887, or May–December 1889	Colonel Warburton's Madness ("The Adventure of the Engineer's Thumb").[11]
Probably before December 1889	The Capture of Archie Stamford, the Forger ("The Adventure of the Solitary Cyclist").
Monday, March 24–Saturday, March 29, 1890	"The Adventure of Wisteria Lodge." "A chaotic case, my dear Watson."
Thursday, September 25, and Tuesday, September 30, 1890	"Silver Blaze." "There are points about this case which . . . make it . . . absolutely unique."
Before December 1890	The Case of Morgan, the Poisoner ("The Adventure of the Empty House"). Merridew of Abominable Memory ("The Adventure of the Empty House"). The Case of Mathews ("The Adventure of the Empty House").
Friday, December 19–Saturday, December 20, 1890	"The Adventure of the Beryl Coronet." "A very sweet little problem, and I would not have missed it for a good deal."
Late December 1890	The Service to the Royal Family of Scandinavia ("The Final Problem").
Late December 1890–March 1891	The Matter of Supreme Importance to the French Government ("The Final Problem").
Sunday, January 4–late April 1891	The Napoleon of Crime ("The Final Problem").
Friday, April 24–Monday, May 4, 1891	"The Final Problem." "It is with a heavy heart that I take up my pen to write these the last words in which I shall ever record the singular gifts by which my friend Mr. Sherlock Holmes was distinguished."

[11] A pastiche of this adventure, titled "The Adventure of the Sealed Room," appears in *The Exploits of Sherlock Holmes*.

VI. The Great Hiatus: Monday, May 4, 1891–Thursday, April 5, 1894

June 1891	Dr. Watson sold his Paddington practice and repurchased his former practice in Kensington to give himself more time for his writing. Holmes, as Sigerson, met Irene Adler in Cettigne, Montenegro.
July 1891	The first of Dr. Watson's shorter accounts of the adventures of Sherlock Holmes appeared in *The Strand Magazine*.
Late 1891–September 1893	The remarkable explorations of "a Norwegian named Sigerson."
Late 1891 or early 1892	Mary Morstan Watson died, probably, as Mr. T. S. Blakeney notes, "of heart-trouble, inherited from her father. Twice in *The Sign of the Four* she turned faint on very slight provocation."
Late 1892	Birth of a son to Irene Adler at her girlhood home near Hoboken, New Jersey.
September–November 1893	Holmes passed through Persia, looked in at Mecca, visited the Khalifa at Omdurman.
November 1893–March 1894	Holmes conducted researches into the coal-tar derivatives at a laboratory in Montpellier, France.

VII. From Holmes's Return on Thursday, April 5, 1894 to Dr. Watson's Third Marriage on Saturday, October 4, 1902

When I look at the three massive volumes which contain our work for the year 1894, I confess that it is very difficult for me, out of such a wealth of material, to select the cases which are most interesting in themselves and at the same time the most conducive to a display of those peculiar powers for which my friend was famous.—John H. Watson, M.D., "The Adventure of the Golden Pince-Nez."

From the years 1894 to 1901 inclusive, Mr. Sherlock Holmes was a very busy man. It is safe to say that there was no public case of any difficulty in which he was not consulted during those eight years, and there were hundreds of private cases, some of them of the most intricate and extraordinary character, in which he played a prominent part. Many startling successes and a few unavoidable failures were the outcome of the long period of continuous work. As I have preserved very full notes of all those cases, and was myself personally engaged in many of them, it may be imagined that it is no easy task to know which I should select to lay before the public. I shall, however, preserve my former rules, and give the preference to those cases which derive their interest not so much from the brutality of the crime as from the ingenuity and dramatic quality of the solution.—John H. Watson, M.D., "The Adventure of the Solitary Cyclist."

Thursday, April 5, 1894

"The Adventure of the Empty House." "The crime was of interest in itself, but that interest was nothing . . . compared to the inconceivable sequel."

Early May 1894

"I . . . sold my practice and returned to share the old quarters at Baker Street. A young doctor named Verner . . . purchased my small Kensington practice, and [gave] with astonishingly little demur the highest price that I ventured to ask—an incident which only explained itself some years later, when I found that Verner was a distant relation of Holmes's and that it was my friend who had really found the money." ("The Adventure of the Norwood Builder.")

Wednesday, November 14–Thursday, November 15, 1894

"The Adventure of the Golden Pince-Nez." "A simple case, and yet in some ways an instructive one."

April–December 1894

The Repulsive Story of the Red Leech and the Terrible Death of Crosby the Banker ("The Adventure of the Golden Pince-Nez").

The Addleton Tragedy and the Singular Contents of the Ancient British Barrow ("The Adventure

continued

of the Golden Pince-Nez").[12]

The Famous Smith-Mortimer Succession Case ("The Adventure of the Golden Pince-Nez").

The Tracking and Arrest of Huret, the Boulevard Assassin ("The Adventure of Wisteria Lodge").

The Shocking Affair of the Dutch Steamship *Friesland* (The Adventure of the Norwood Builder").

Friday, April 5–Saturday, April 6, 1895

"The Adventure of the Three Students." "Your discretion is as well known as your powers, and you are the one man in the world who can help me. I beg of you, Mr. Holmes, to do what you can."

Mid-April 1895

The Very Abstruse and Complicated Problem Concerning the Peculiar Persecution of John Vincent Harden, the Well-Known Tobacco Millionaire ("The Adventure of the Solitary Cyclist").

Saturday, April 13, and Saturday, April 20, 1895

"The Adventure of the Solitary Cyclist." "It is true that the circumstances did not permit of any striking illustration of those powers for which my friend was famous but there were some points about the case which made it stand out in those long records of crime from which I gather the material for these little narratives."

May or June 1895

The Famous Investigation of the Sudden Death of Cardinal Tosca ("The Adventure of Black Peter").[13]

---

[12] A pastiche of this adventure, titled "The Adventure of the Faulkes Rath," appears in *The Exploits of Sherlock Holmes*. See also Poul Anderson's "Time Patrol" in *The Science-Fiction Sherlock Holmes* or Mr. Anderson's *Guardians of Time;* New York: Ballantine Books, 1960.

[13] A pastiche of this adventure by Mr. Isaac S. George appears in *The Baker Street Journal,* Vol. III, No. 1, January 1948, pp. 73–82.

continued	The Arrest of Wilson, the Notorious Canary-Trainer ("The Adventure of Black Peter").[14]
Wednesday, July 3–Friday, July 5, 1895	"The Adventure of Black Peter." "No record of the doings of Mr. Sherlock Holmes would be complete which did not include some account of this very unusual affair." "Dear me, it is certainly a very interesting case."
Early July 1895	The Summons to Norway ("The Adventure of Black Peter").
Tuesday, August 20–Wednesday, August 21, 1895	"The Adventure of the Norwood Builder." "I don't mind saying . . . that this is the brightest thing you have done yet, though it is a mystery to me how you did it. You have saved an innocent man's life, and you have prevented a very grave scandal . . ."
Probably before November 1895	The Case of Victor Lynch, the Forger ("The Adventure of the Sussex Vampire"). The Remarkable Case of the Venomous Lizard ("The Adventure of the Sussex Vampire"). The Case of Vigor, the Hammersmith Wonder. ("The Adventure of the Sussex Vampire"). The Case of Vittoria, the Circus Belle ("The Adventure of the Sussex Vampire"). The Case of Arthur H. Staunton, the Rising Young Forger ("The Adventure of the Missing Three-Quarter"). The Case of Henry Staunton, Whom Holmes Helped to Hang ("The Adventure of the Missing Three-Quarter").

[14] A pastiche of this adventure, titled "The Adventure of the Deptford Horror," appears in *The Exploits of Sherlock Holmes*.

Thursday, November 21–Saturday, November 23, 1895	"The Adventure of the Bruce-Partington Plans." "It's a vital international problem that you have to solve. . . . In all your career you have never had so great a chance of serving your country."
Late 1895–late 1896	Called by many Sherlockian commentators "The Missing Year," and the subject of much learned speculation. It was during this period that Sherlock Holmes cleared his brother Sherrinford of the charge of murder, an investigation that led him in turn to "a cesspool of ancient horrors," black magic abroad in the twentieth century.
October 1896 (one day)	"The Adventure of the Veiled Lodger." "The most terrible human tragedies were often involved in . . . cases which brought [Holmes] the fewest personal opportunities, and it is one of these which I now desire to record."
Thursday, November 19–Saturday, November 21, 1896	"The Adventure of the Sussex Vampire." "It has been a case for intellectual deduction, but when this original deduction is confirmed point by point by quite a number of independent incidents, then the subjective becomes objective and we can say confidently that we have reached our goal."
Tuesday, December 8–Thursday, December 10, 1896	"The Adventure of the Missing Three-Quarter." "I don't think that among all our cases I have known one where the motives were more obscure."
Before Saturday, January 23, 1897	The Four Other Cases in Which Holmes Helped Inspector Stanley Hopkins.[15]

15 See Chapter XXII, Footnote 6.

Saturday, January 23, 1897	"The Adventure of the Abbey Grange." "We have got our case —one of the most remarkable in our collection." "But dear me, how slow-witted I have been, and how nearly I committed the blunder of my lifetime."
Before Tuesday, March 16, 1897	The Dramatic Introduction to Dr. Moore Agar ("The Adventure of the Devil's Foot").
Tuesday, March 16–Saturday, March 20, 1897	"The Adventure of the Devil's Foot." "Strangest case I have handled." "A problem . . . more intense, more engrossing, and infinitely more mysterious than any of those which had driven us from London."
Wednesday, July 27–Wednesday, August 10?, and Saturday, August 13, 1898	"The Adventure of the Dancing Men." "A most interesting and unusual case." "A very pretty case to add to your collection, Watson."
July 1898	The Case of the Two Coptic Patriarchs ("The Adventure of the Retired Colourman").[16]
Thursday, July 28–Saturday, July 30, 1898	"The Adventure of the Retired Colourman." "I must admit to you that the case, which seemed to me to be so absurdly simple as to be hardly worth my notice, is rapidly assuming a very different aspect." "It's as workmanlike a job as I can remember."
Thursday, January 5–Saturday, January 14, 1899	"The Adventure of Charles Augustus Milverton." "An absolutely unique experience in the career of Mr. Sherlock Holmes and myself."
c. Saturday, May 20, 1899	The Disappearance of the Famous Black Pearl of the Borgias ("The Adventure of the Six Napoleons").

[16] For a pastiche of this adventure by Mr. John A. Wilson, see *The Baker Street Journal*, Vol. IV, No. 1, January, 1949, pp. 74–85.

Friday, June 8–Sunday, June 10, 1900	"The Adventure of the Six Napoleons." "This business . . . presents some features which make it absolutely original in the history of crime."
Early June 1900	The Conk-Singleton Forgery Case ("The Adventure of the Six Napoleons").
September 1900	"A month of trivialities and stagnation ("The Problem of Thor Bridge").
Thursday, October 4–Friday, October 5, 1900	"The Problem of Thor Bridge." "I fear, Watson, that you will not improve any reputation I may have acquired by adding this case . . . to your annals. I have been sluggish in mind and wanting in that mixture of imagination and reality which is the basis of my art."
Early May 1900	The Case of the Ferrers Documents ("The Adventure of the Priory School").[17]
Early May 1901	The Abergavenny Murder ("The Adventure of the Priory School").[18]
Thursday, May 16–Saturday, May 18, 1901	"The Adventure of the Priory School." "This case deserves to be a classic."
January–December 1901	The Simple Affair of Mr. Fairdale Hobbs ("The Adventure of the Red Circle").
Shortly before May 1902	The Case of the Coiner ("The Adventure of Shoscombe Old Place").
Tuesday, May 6–Wednesday, May 7, 1902	"The Adventure of Shoscombe Old Place." "These are deep waters, Mr. Mason, deep and rather dirty."

[17] A pastiche of this adventure, titled "The Adventure of the Demon Angels," appears in *The Exploits of Sherlock Holmes.*

[18] For a possible outline of this affair, see "A Plot for a Sherlock Holmes Story" in *A Baker Street Four-Wheeler.*

Early June 1902	The Services Which May Perhaps Some Day Be Described ("The Adventure of the Three Garridebs").
Thursday, June 26–Friday, June 27, 1902	"The Adventure of the Three Garridebs." "It cost one man his reason, it cost me a blood-letting, and it cost yet another man the penalties of the law. Yet there certainly was an element of comedy."
Late June 1902	The Mortal Terror of Old Abrahams ("The Disappearance of Lady Frances Carfax").
Tuesday, July 1–Friday, July 18, 1902	"The Disappearance of Lady Frances Carfax." "Should you care to add the case to your annals, my dear Watson, it can only be as an example of that temporary eclipse to which even the best-balanced mind may be exposed. Such slips are common to all mortals, and the greatest is he who can recognize and repair them. To this modified credit I may, perhaps, make some claim."
Late July 1902	Watson moved to his own rooms on Queen Anne Street ("The Adventure of the Illustrious Client").
Before September 1902	The Hammerford Will Case ("The Adventure of the Illustrious Client").
Wednesday, September 3–Tuesday, September 16, 1902	"The Adventure of the Illustrious Client." "[It] was in some ways the supreme moment of my friend's career."
Wednesday, September 24–Thursday, September 25, 1902	"The Adventure of the Red Circle." "This is an instructive case. There is neither money or credit in it, and yet one would wish to tidy it up."

| Saturday, October 4, 1902 | Dr. John H. Watson married for the third time. Shortly thereafter he returned to the practice of medicine, and by September 1903 his practice was "not inconsiderable" ("The Adventure of the Creeping Man"). |

VIII. The Partnership's Last Period: January–October 1903

The relations between us in those latter days were peculiar. He was a man of habits, narrowed and concentrated habits, and I had become one of them. As an institution I was like the violin, the shag tobacco, the old black pipe, the index books, and others perhaps less excusable. When it was a case of active work and a comrade was needed upon whose nerve he could place some reliance, my role was obvious. But apart from this I had uses. I was a whetstone for his mind. . . . It had become in some way helpful that I should register and interject.—John H. Watson, M.D., "The Adventure of the Creeping Man."

| Before January 1903 | The Professional Service for Sir James Saunders, the Great Dermatologist ("The Adventure of the Blanched Soldier"). |

| January 1903 | The Return of "James Wilder" ("The Adventure of the Blanched Soldier"). |

| January 1903 | The Commission for the Sultan of Turkey ("The Adventure of the Blanched Soldier"). |

| Wednesday, January 7–Monday, January 12, 1903 | "The Adventure of the Blanched Soldier." "Elementary as it was, there were points of interest and novelty about it which may excuse my placing it on the record." |

| Before Tuesday, May 26, 1903 | The Killing of Young Perkins Outside the Holborn Bar ("The Adventure of the Three Gables"). |

| Tuesday, May 26–Wednesday, May 27, 1903 | "The Adventure of the Three Gables." "Well, well, I suppose I shall have to compound a felony, as usual." |

Before Summer 1903	The Case of Old Baron Dowson ("The Adventure of the Mazarin Stone").
Summer 1903 (one day)	"The Adventure of the Mazarin Stone." "We give you best, Holmes. I believe you are the devil himself."
Sunday, September 6; Monday, September 14; Tuesday September 22, 1903	"The Adventure of the Creeping Man." "It is certainly a very curious and suggestive case." "In all our adventures I do not know that I have ever seen a more strange sight than this impressive and still dignified figure crouching frog-like upon the ground and goading to a wilder exhibition the maddened hound."
April 1895–October 1903	The Striking Results of Some Laborious Research in Early English Charters ("The Adventure of the Three Students").
Before October 1903	The Adventure of the Politician, The Lighthouse and the Trained Cormorant ("The Adventure of the Veiled Lodger"). The Remarkable Affair of the Cutter *Alicia* ("The Problem of Thor Bridge"). The Disappearance of James Phillimore ("The Problem of Thor Bridge").[19] The Case of Isadora Persano, the Well-Known Journalist and Duelist ("The Problem of Thor Bridge").[20] The Saving of Count Von und Zu Grafenstein ("His Last Bow").

[19] A pastiche of this adventure by the late Edgar W. Smith appears in *A Baker Street Four-Wheeler*. Another, titled "The Adventure of the Highgate Miracle," appears in *The Exploits of Sherlock Holmes*.

[20] Mr. Stuart Palmer has written a pastiche stemming from this reference of Dr. Watson's which Ellery Queen has called "utterly delightful and satisfying." See *The Misadventures of Sherlock Holmes*. For other ingenious explanations, see *The Baker Street Journal*, Vol. II, No. 2, April 1947, pp. 161, 212.

Thursday, October 8, 1903	Death of Irene Adler in Trenton, New Jersey.
Late October 1903	Sherlock Holmes retired to beekeeping and his books at his villa at "Fulworth" (Cuckmere Haven) five miles from Eastbourne on the southern slopes of the Sussex Downs.

IX. The Later Cases: 1909, 1912–14, 1920, 1939–45

At this period of my life the good Watson had passed almost beyond my ken. An occasional week-end visit was the most that I ever saw of him. . . . My house is lonely. I, my old housekeeper, and my bees have the estate all to ourselves.—Sherlock Holmes, "The Adventure of the Lion's Mane."

Tuesday, July 27–Tuesday, August 3?, 1909	"The Adventure of the Lion's Mane." "In all my chronicles the reader will find no case which brought me so completely to the limit of my powers."
1912–13	Mr. Altamont of Chicago ("His Last Bow").[21]
Sunday, August 2, 1914	"His Last Bow." "Strong pressure was brought upon me to look into the matter. . . . The matter was complex."
1920	". . . at Constantinople, during 1920—according to the London *Times*—the Turks were certain that the great English detective was at work behind the scenes." —Vincent Starrett in his "Explanation" (Introduction) to *221B: Studies in Sherlock Holmes.*
Wednesday, July 24, 1929	Death of Dr. John H. Watson.

[21] Mr. Donald Hayne has done a fascinating job of sketching out the first few months of Holmes's visit to the United States in 1912. See *The Baker Street Journal*, Vol. I, No. 2, April 1946, pp. 189–90.

1939–45	The adventures of Mr. Sherlock Holmes, formerly of 221B Baker Street, London, during the Second World War.[22]
Tuesday, November 19, 1946	Death of Mycroft Holmes.
Sunday, January 6, 1957	Death of Sherlock Holmes of Baker Street.

[22] See the contributions of Mr. Manly Wade Wellman and Mr. Anthony Boucher, herein noted.

THE BIBLIOGRAPHICAL HOLMES:
A SELECTIVE COMPILATION

"Let me recommend this book—one of the most remarkable ever penned."

SHERLOCK HOLMES

A. The Writings of John H. Watson, M.D.

The following writings—fifty-six short stories and four long stories —are all from the pen of John H. Watson, M.D., with the exception of two short stories in the *Case Book* ("The Adventure of the Blanched Soldier" and "The Adventure of the Lion's Mane") which were written by Sherlock Holmes himself; another short story in the *Case Book* ("The Adventure of the Mazarin Stone") which is of doubtful authorship; and a short story in *His Last Bow* ("His Last Bow") which has been attributed to Mycroft Holmes.

1. First and Other Important Appearances, in Magazine and Book Form

A Study in Scarlet.

> *Beeton's Christmas Annual* for 1887 (London: Ward, Lock & Co.)
> London: Ward, Lock & Co., 1888.
> Philadelphia: J. B. Lippincott Co., 1890.

The Sign of the Four.

> *Lippincott's Magazine* for February 1890 (Philadelphia: J. B. Lippincott Co., and London: Ward, Lock & Co.).
> London: Spencer Blackett, 1890.
> New York: P. F. Collier, 1891.

The Adventures of Sherlock Holmes.

> London: George Newnes, Ltd., 1892.
> New York: Harper & Bros., 1892.
> > Contains:
> > "A Scandal in Bohemia" (*The Strand Magazine*, July 1891).

"The Red-Headed League" (*The Strand Magazine,* August 1891).

"A Case of Identity" (*The Strand Magazine,* September 1891).

"The Boscombe Valley Mystery" (*The Strand Magazine,* October 1891).

"The Five Orange Pips" (*The Strand Magazine,* November 1891).

"The Man with the Twisted Lip" (*The Strand Magazine,* December 1891).

"The Adventure of the Blue Carbuncle" (*The Strand Magazine,* January 1892).

"The Adventure of the Speckled Band" (*The Strand Magazine,* February 1892).

"The Adventure of the Engineer's Thumb" (*The Strand Magazine,* March 1892).

"The Adventure of the Noble Bachelor" (*The Strand Magazine,* April 1892).

"The Adventure of the Beryl Coronet" (*The Strand Magazine,* May 1892).

"The Adventure of the Copper Beeches" (*The Strand Magazine,* June 1892).

The Memoirs of Sherlock Holmes.

London: George Newnes, Ltd., 1894.

New York: Harper & Bros., 1894.

Contains:

"Silver Blaze" (*The Strand Magazine,* December 1892; *Harper's Weekly,* February 25, 1893).

"The Cardboard Box" (*The Strand Magazine,* January 1893; *Harper's Weekly,* January 14, 1893).

"The Yellow Face" (*The Strand Magazine,* February 1893; *Harper's Weekly,* February 11, 1893).

"The Stockbroker's Clerk" (*The Strand Magazine,* March 1893; *Harper's Weekly,* March 11, 1893).

"The *Gloria Scott*" (*The Strand Magazine,* April 1893; *Harper's Weekly,* April 15, 1893).

"The Musgrave Ritual" (*The Strand Magazine,* May 1893; *Harper's Weekly,* May 13, 1893).

"The Reigate Squires" (U.S.: "The Reigate Puzzle") (*The Strand Magazine,* June 1893; *Harper's Weekly,* June 17, 1893).

"The Crooked Man" (*The Strand Magazine,* July 1893; *Harper's Weekly,* July 8, 1893).

"The Resident Patient" (*The Strand Magazine,* August, 1893; *Harper's Weekly,* August 12, 1893).

"The Greek Interpreter" (*The Strand Magazine,* September 1893; *Harper's Weekly,* September 16, 1893).

"The Naval Treaty" (*The Strand Magazine*, October and November 1893; *Harper's Weekly*, October 14, October 21, 1893).

"The Final Problem" (*The Strand Magazine*, December 1893; *McClure's Magazine*, December 1893).

NOTE: "The Cardboard Box" was omitted from the Newnes edition of 1894 and from the second Harper edition in America.

The Hound of the Baskervilles.

The Strand Magazine, August 1901–April 1902.
London: George Newnes, Ltd., 1902.
New York: McClure, Phillips & Co., 1902.

The Return of Sherlock Holmes.

London: George Newnes, Ltd., 1905.
New York: McClure, Phillips & Co., 1905.
Contains:
"The Adventure of the Empty House" (*The Strand Magazine*, October 1903; *Collier's Weekly*, September 26, 1903).

"The Adventure of the Norwood Builder" (*The Strand Magazine*, November 1903; *Collier's Weekly*, October 31, 1903).

"The Adventure of the Dancing Men" (*The Strand Magazine*, December 1903; *Collier's Weekly*, December 5, 1903).

"The Adventure of the Solitary Cyclist" (*The Strand Magazine*, January 1904; *Collier's Weekly*, December 26, 1903).

"The Adventure of the Priory School" (*The Strand Magazine*, February 1904; *Collier's Weekly*, January, 30, 1904).

"The Adventure of Black Peter" (*The Strand Magazine*, March 1904; *Collier's Weekly*, February 27, 1904).

"The Adventure of Charles Augustus Milverton" (*The Strand Magazine*, April 1904; *Collier's Weekly*, March 26, 1904).

"The Adventure of the Six Napoleons" (*The Strand Magazine*, May 1904; *Collier's Weekly*, April 30, 1904).

"The Adventure of the Three Students" (*The Strand Magazine*, June 1904; *Collier's Weekly*, September 24, 1904).

"The Adventure of the Golden Pince-Nez" (*The Strand Magazine*, July 1904; *Collier's Weekly*, October 29, 1904).

"The Adventure of the Missing Three-Quarter" (*The Strand Magazine*, August 1904; *Collier's Weekly*, November 26, 1904).

"The Adventure of the Abbey Grange" (*The Strand Magazine*, September 1904; *Collier's Weekly*, December 31, 1904).

"The Adventure of the Second Stain" (*The Strand Magazine*, December 1904; *Collier's Weekly*, January 28, 1905).

The Valley of Fear.

The Strand Magazine, September 1914–May 1915.
London: Smith, Elder & Co., 1915.
New York: George H. Doran, 1915.

His Last Bow.

London: John Murray, 1917.
New York: George H. Doran, 1917.
Contains:
"The Adventure of Wisteria Lodge" (magazine titles: "The Singular Adventure of Mr. John Scott Eccles," "The Tiger of San Pedro") (*The Strand Magazine,* September and October 1908; *Collier's Weekly,* August 15, 1908).
"The Adventure of the Bruce-Partington Plans" (*The Strand Magazine,* December 1908; *Collier's Weekly,* December 18, 1908).
"The Adventure of the Devil's Foot" (*The Strand Magazine,* December 1910; *The Strand Magazine*—U.S., January and February 1911).
"The Adventure of the Red Circle" (*The Strand Magazine,* March and April 1911; *The Strand Magazine*—U.S., April and May 1911).
"The Disappearance of Lady Frances Carfax" (*The Strand Magazine,* December 1911; *The American Magazine,* December 1911).
"The Adventure of the Dying Detective" (*The Strand Magazine,* December 1913; *Collier's Weekly,* November 22, 1913).
"His Last Bow: The War Service of Sherlock Holmes" (*The Strand Magazine,* September 1917; *Collier's Weekly,* September 22, 1917).
NOTE: Both the Murray and the Doran edition also include "The Cardboard Box."

The Case Book of Sherlock Holmes.

London: John Murray, 1927.
New York: George H. Doran, 1927.
Contains:
"The Adventure of the Mazarin Stone" (*The Strand Magazine,* October 1921; *Hearst's International,* November 1921).
"The Problem of Thor Bridge" (*The Strand Magazine,* February and March 1922; *Hearst's International,* February and March 1922).
"The Adventure of the Creeping Man" (*The Strand Magazine,* March 1923; *Hearst's International,* March 1923).
"The Adventure of the Sussex Vampire" (*The Strand Magazine,* January 1924; *Hearst's International,* January 1924).

"The Adventure of the Three Garridebs" (*The Strand Magazine,* January 1925; *Collier's Weekly,* October 25, 1924).

"The Adventure of the Illustrious Client" (*The Strand Magazine,* February and March 1925; *Collier's Weekly,* November 8, 1924).

"The Adventure of the Three Gables" (*The Strand Magazine,* October 1926; *Liberty Magazine,* September 18, 1926).

"The Adventure of the Blanched Soldier" (*The Strand Magazine,* November 1926; *Liberty Magazine,* October 16, 1926).

"The Adventure of the Lion's Mane" (*The Strand Magazine,* December 1926; *Liberty Magazine,* November 27, 1926).

"The Adventure of the Retired Colourman" (*The Strand Magazine,* January 1927; *Liberty Magazine,* December 18, 1926).

"The Adventure of the Veiled Lodger" (*The Strand Magazine,* February 1927; *Liberty Magazine,* January 22, 1927).

"The Adventure of Shoscombe Old Place" (*The Strand Magazine,* April 1927; *Liberty Magazine,* March 5, 1927).

2. Collections and Omnibus Editions

Sherlock Holmes: The Complete Short Stories; London: John Murray, 1929.

Sherlock Holmes: The Complete Long Stories; London: John Murray, 1929.

The Complete Sherlock Holmes; Garden City, N.Y.: Doubleday, Doran & Co., 1930.

The two-volume omnibus, with the classic introduction, "In Memoriam Sherlock Holmes" by the late Christopher Morley.

The Complete Sherlock Holmes; Garden City, N.Y.: Doubleday, Doran & Co., 1936.

The one-volume omnibus.

Sherlock Holmes and Dr. Watson: A Textbook of Friendship; edited by Christopher Morley; New York: Harcourt, Brace & Co., 1944.

Five of the tales, copiously and instructively annotated by the late Gasogene and Tantalus of The Baker Street Irregulars, Inc.

The Blue Carbuncle; New York: The Baker Street Irregulars, Inc., 1948.

The first separate appearance of this "Christmas story without slush," with an introduction by the late Christopher Morley and a bibliographical note by the late Edgar W. Smith.

A Treasury of Sherlock Holmes, edited by Adrian Conan Doyle; Garden City, N.Y.: Hanover House, 1955.

A Study in Scarlet, The Hound of the Baskervilles, and twenty-seven of the short stories, with an introduction by the editor.

The Heritage Sherlock Holmes; New York: The Heritage Press, 1957.

An incomparable edition of the tales, definitively edited by the late Edgar W. Smith and with a long introduction by Vincent Starrett. In three volumes, made from the plates of the Limited Editions Club, Profusely illustrated by Sidney Paget, Frederic Dorr Steele, many others.

B. The Writings of Mr. Sherlock Holmes.

"Upon the Dating of Documents," *The British Antiquarian*, Vol. XXIII, No. 9, September 1877.

Deals in the main with the problem of handwritings from the sixteenth century onward.

Upon Tattoo Marks; London: Privately printed, 1878.

Includes one of the first scholarly examinations of the pigments used extensively by Japanese and Chinese artists.

Upon the Tracing of Footsteps; London: Privately printed, 1878.

Includes the master detective's often-quoted remarks upon the uses of plaster of Paris as a preserver of impresses.

Upon the Distinction Between the Ashes of the Various Tobaccos; London: Privately printed, 1879.

A monograph enumerating 140 forms of cigar, cigarette, and pipe tobaccos, with plates in color, illustrating the difference in the ash.

"The Book of Life," *The Fortnightly Magazine*, Vol. XXI, No. 3, March 1881.

Referred to in the present volume. First published anonymously.

A Study of the Influence of a Trade upon the Form of the Hand; London: Privately printed, 1886.

Illustrated by lithotypes of the hands of slaters, sailors, cork cutters, compositors, weavers, and diamond polishers.

Malingering; London: Privately printed, 1888.

A monograph Holmes was inspired to write by his experiences in "The Adventure of the Dying Detective."

"On the Variability of Human Ears," *The Anthropological Journal*, Vol. XL, Nos. 8 and 9, September and October 1888.

Two short monographs, mentioned by Holmes during the gruesome case of "The Cardboard Box."

The Typewriter and Its Relation to Crime; London: Privately printed, 1890.

Secret Writings; London: Privately printed, 1896.

A monograph in which the master detective analyzes 160 separate ciphers.

Upon the Polyphonic Motets of Lassus; London: Read, Allen, Simon, 1896.

A work which experts in medieval music declare to be definitive.

A Study of the Chaldean Roots in the Ancient Cornish Language; London: Keun and Sons, 1898.

As definitive a work in its field as Holmes's *Upon the Polyphonic Motets of Lassus.*

The Use of Dogs in the Work of the Detective; London: Amery-Thompson, 1905.

This, the first monograph published by Holmes after his retirement, will form a part of his *The Whole Art of Detection* (see below).

Practical Handbook of Bee Culture, with Some Observations Upon the Segregation of the Queen; London: Beach & Thompson, 1910.

Holmes called it "the fruit" of his "leisured ease," "the *magnum opus*" of his "latter years."

"The Adventure of the Blanched Soldier," *The Strand Magazine,* November 1926; *Liberty Magazine,* October 16, 1926.

A reminiscence, noted above.

"The Adventure of the Lion's Mane," *The Strand Magazine,* December 1926; *Liberty Magazine,* November 27, 1926.

A second reminiscence, also noted above.

The Whole Art of Detection; New York: Clarkson N. Potter, Inc.

Forthcoming, to be published in four volumes.

C. The Writings of Dr. Conan Doyle.

While these writings of Dr. Watson's distinguished friend, literary agent, and occasional collaborator, Dr. (later Sir Arthur) Conan Doyle, are not eligible for subsumption into the Sherlockian canon, they are nonetheless deserving of respectful study and analysis by the thoughtful student.

"The Field Bazaar: A Short Travesty."

The Student, Edinburgh University, November 1896. First book publication in *221B: Studies in Sherlock Holmes;* New York: The Macmillan Co., 1940.

Issued separately in pamphlet form by The Pamphlet House (Summit, N.J.), 1947.

The Speckled Band: A Play in Three Acts; London and New York: Samuel French, 1912.

Sherlock Holmes: A Drama in Four Acts, in collaboration with William Gillette; London and New York: Samuel French, 1922.

"The Lost Special."

"The Man with the Watches."

Two short tales in *Round the Fire Stories;* London: Smith, Elder & Co., 1908; New York: The McClure Co., 1908. These tales contain the text of letters identified in *Letters from Baker Street* (Maplewood, N.J.: The Pamphlet House, 1942) as having been written by Sherlock Holmes and Mycroft Holmes.

"How Watson Learned the Trick."

A parody in Volume II of *The Book of the Queen's Doll's House Library;* London: Methuen & Co., Ltd., 1924; reprinted in *The Incunabular Holmes;* Morristown, N.J.: The Baker Street Irregulars, Inc., 1958.

Memories and Adventures: The Autobiography of Sir Arthur Conan Doyle; London: Hodder & Stoughton, 1924; Boston: Little, Brown & Co., 1924.

D. The Higher Criticism

1. Chronological Surveys

Baring-Gould, William S.
The Chronological Holmes; New York: Privately printed, 1955.
The most recent attempt to date (by day of the week, date of the month, and year) all of Holmes's cases, both recorded and unrecorded; by the author of the present volume.

Bell, H. W.
Sherlock Holmes and Dr. Watson: The Chronology of Their Adventures; London: Constable & Co., 1932; reissued in paperbound format by The Baker Street Irregulars, Inc., 1953.
The first attempt to date (mostly by month and year) all of Holmes's adventures, both recorded and unrecorded.

Blakeney, T. S.
Sherlock Holmes: Fact or Fiction?; London: John Murray, 1932; reissued in paperbound format by The Baker Street Irregulars, Inc., 1954.
Much more than a chronology, this landmark in Sherlockian criticism also contains essays entitled "Mr. Sherlock Holmes," "Holmes and Scotland Yard," "The Literature Relating to Sherlock Holmes," as well as valuable appendices.

Brend, Gavin
My Dear Holmes; London: George Allen & Unwin, Ltd., 1951.
Primarily a chronology, this volume is also a touchingly written tribute, to Holmes, Watson and Doyle by a late- and much-lamented member of The Sherlock Holmes Society of London. Mr. Brend also submitted a new identification of the site of 221 Baker Street.

Christ, Jay Finley
An Irregular Chronology of Sherlock Holmes of Baker Street; Ann Arbor, Mich.; The Fanlight House, 1947.
One of the most scholarly and certainly the most daring of the volumes written by the six chronologists whom Brend once dubbed The Six Napoleons.

Zeisler, Ernest Bloomfield
Baker Street Chronology: Commentaries on the Sacred Writings of Dr. John H. Watson; Chicago: Alexander J. Isaacs, 1953.
A volume of prodigious scholarship by a man who is a celebrated doctor, lawyer, mathematician, Shakespearean scholar, and social and political commentator—as well as an esteemed Sherlockian.

2. Collected Essays

Baker Street Studies, edited by H. W. Bell; London: Constable & Co., 1934; reissued in paperbound format by The Baker Street Irregulars, Inc., 1955.

> Contains eight essays by Dorothy L. Sayers, Helen Simpson, Vernon Rendall, Vincent Starrett, Ronald A. Knox, A. G. MacDonell, S. C. Roberts, and H. W. Bell.

221B: Studies in Sherlock Holmes, edited by Vincent Starrett; New York: The Macmillan Co., 1940; reissued in paperbound format by The Baker Street Irregulars, Inc., 1956.

> The first American anthology, containing sixteen pieces by H. W. Bell, Frederic Dorr Steele, Christopher Morley, *et al.*

Profile by Gaslight: An Irregular Reader about the Private Life of Sherlock Holmes; edited by Edgar W. Smith; New York: Simon & Schuster, 1944.

> Twenty-eight essays and ten verses by various hands, also including a Sherlockian bibliography, the Constitution and Buy-Laws of The Baker Street Irregulars, Inc., and an article on the Irregulars by the late Alexander Woollcott.

A Baker Street Four-Wheeler, edited by Edgar W. Smith; Maplewood, N.J.: The Pamphlet House, 1944.

> Sixteen pieces of Sherlockiana.

The Second Cab, edited by James Keddie, Jr.; Boston: Stoke Moran, 1947.

> Fifteen Sherlockian essays, a sonnet, and a quiz by members of The Speckled Band of Boston, one of the oldest and most active of the Scion Societies of The Baker Street Irregulars.

Sherlockian Studies, edited by Robert A. Cutter; Jackson Heights, N.Y.: The Baker Street, 1947.

> Seven pieces of Sherlockiana by well-known hands, sponsored by The Three Students of Long Island, another Scion Society.

Client's Case-Book, edited by J. N. Williamson; Indianapolis: The Illustrious Clients, 1947.

> A collection of essays and verse in the best tradition, with an introduction by Vincent Starrett.

Sherlock Holmes: Master Detective, edited by E. W. McDiarmid and Theodore C. Blegen; La Crosse, Wisc.: The Sumac Press, 1952.

> A collection of five essays and a Salute to Sherlock Holmes, sponsored by The Norwegian Explorers of Minneapolis and St. Paul.

Client's Second Case-Book, edited by J. N. Williamson; Indianapolis: The Illustrious Clients, 1951.

> Nine essays, four pastiches, three poems, two quizzes, a letter, and a song. All this and an introduction by Ellery Queen.

Illustrious Client's Third Case-Book, edited by J. N. Williamson and H. B. Williams: Indianapolis: The Illustrious Clients, 1953.

> Eighteen essays, four quizzes, three tales-in-verse, and more, with an introduction by the late Christoper Morley.

The Best of the Pips, sponsored by Richard W. Clarke; New York: The Five Orange Pips of Westchester County, 1955.

A collection of the writings of the members of the Scion Society that the late Edgar W. Smith called "the most erudite"—much of it in the lighter vein.

Exploring Sherlock Holmes, edited by E. W. McDiarmid and Theodore C. Blegen; La Crosse, Wisc.: The Sumac Press, 1957.

A second fine collection of seven essays by members of The Norwegian Explorers of Minneapolis and St. Paul.

The Incunabular Holmes, edited by Edgar W. Smith; Morristown, N.J.: The Baker Street Irregulars, Inc., 1958.

Essays and critical comment published between 1902 and 1944, all of it hard to find elsewhere.

Leaves from The Copper Beeches, edited by H. W. Starr; Philadelphia: The Sons of the Copper Beeches, 1959.

Rollicking essays and commentary by well-known Sons of this prominent Scion Society.

Introducing Mr. Sherlock Holmes, edited by Edgar W. Smith; Morristown, N.J.: The Baker Street Irregulars, Inc., 1959.

A collection of essays and commentary, all originally in the forms of introductions, by Vincent Starrett, S. C. Roberts, Dr. Joseph Bell, Howard Haycraft, Dr. John H. Watson, Rex Stout, Fletcher Pratt, Anthony Boucher, Elmer Davis, Dr. Conan Doyle, Christopher Morley, and others.

The Third Cab, sponsored by the Executive Committee of The Speckled Band of Boston; Boston: Stoke Moran, 1960.

A second anthology by this Scion Society, and possibly even better than the first.

3. Criticism by Individual Authors

Douglass, Ruth

"The Camberwell Poisoner," *Ellery Queen's Mystery Magazine,* February 1947.

In which Mrs. Douglass advances a most interesting theory.

Grazebrook, O. F.

Studies in Sherlock Holmes; London: Privately printed, n.d. (*c.* 1949).

A set of six pamphlets, each treating of an aspect of the Saga in a lively and scholarly fashion: I. Oxford or Cambridge; II. Politics and Premiers; III. Royalty; IV. Dr. Watson and Rudyard Kipling; V. The Author of the *Case Book;* VI. Something of Dr. Watson.

Harrison, Michael

In the Footsteps of Sherlock Holmes; London: Cassell & Company, Ltd., 1958; New York: Frederick Fell, Inc., 1960.

The standard guide to the London, and to the England, that Holmes and Watson knew so well.

Holroyd, James Edward
  Baker Street By-Ways; London: George Allen & Unwin, Ltd., 1959.
  A wholly charming commentary on the Baker Street scene and
  on the London in which Holmes and Watson flourished, by the
  chairman of the Sherlock Holmes Society of London.
Morgan, Robert S.
  *Spotlight on a Simple Case, or, Wiggins, Who Was That Horse
  I Saw With You Last Night?;* Wilmington, Delaware: The Cedar
  Tree Press, 1959.
  In brief, a tour-de-force—simply not to be missed.
Roberts, S. C. (later Sir Sydney)
  *Doctor Watson: Prolegomena to the Study of a Biographical
  Problem;* London: Faber & Faber, Ltd., 1931.
  The standard life of Watson, with a bibliography of Sherlock
  Holmes.
  Holmes and Watson: A Miscellany; London: Oxford University
  Press, 1953.
  A collection of writings by the dean of British Sherlockians—
  some old, some new.
Simpson, A. Carson
  Simpson's Sherlockian Studies; Philadelphia: International Print-
  ing Company, 1953–60.
  There are, to date, eight *Studies* by a man who, like Dr. Ernest
  Bloomfield Zeisler, combines prodigious scholarship with wit.
  The first four *Studies* comprise Sherlock Holmes's *Wanderjahre:*
  I. Fanget An! II. Post Huc Nec Ergo Propter Huc Gabetque.
  III. In Fernen Land, Unnahbar Ruren, Schritten. IV. Auf Der
  Erde Rücken Ruhrt' Ich Mich Viel. Studies V, VI, VII com-
  prise *Numismatics in the Canon:* V. Full Thirty Thousand
  Marks of English Coin. VI. A Very Treasury of Coins of Divers
  Realms. VII. Small Titles and Orders. Study VIII is in a class
  by itself. It is titled *I'm Off for Philadelphia in the Morning.*
Smith, Edgar W.
  The Napoleon of Crime; Summit, N.J.: The Pamphlet House,
  1953.
  The standard life of Professor James Moriarty, Sc.D.
Starrett, Vincent
  The Private Life of Sherlock Holmes; New York: The Macmil-
  lan Co., 1933; London: Nicholson & Watson, 1934. Revised and
  enlarged edition published by The University of Chicago Press,
  1960.
  An authoritative and wholly charming presentation of the life
  and times of the master detective.
Van Lier, Edward J., M.D.
  A Doctor Enjoys Sherlock Holmes; New York: The Vantage Press,
  1960.
  A collection of delightful essays which interpret the master
  detective for the layman's enjoyment as well.

Warrack, Guy
Sherlock Holmes and Music; London: Faber & Faber, Ltd., 1957.
The standard guide to Holmes the Musician.

4. Periodicals

The Baker Street Journal, edited by Edgar W. Smith; New York:
Ben Abramson for The Baker Street Irregulars, Inc.
Publication of this, the official journal of the Baker Street Ir-
regulars, Inc., began in 1946, and thirteen issues appeared in all.
The Baker Street Journal (New Series), edited by Edgar W. Smith;
Morristown, N.J.: The Baker Street Irregulars, Inc.
In more modest format, this quarterly has, since January 1951,
carried on the tradition as the official medium for Irregulars
everywhere. The present editor is Dr. Julian Wolff, of 33 River-
side Drive, New York 23, N.Y.
The Baker Street Journal Christmas Annual, edited by Edgar W.
Smith; Morristown, N.J.: The Baker Street Irregulars, Inc.
The *Annual*—to all intents and purposes a fifth issue of the
quarterly *Journal*—was published in 1956, 1957, 1958, 1959, and
1960.
The Sherlock Holmes Journal, edited by the Marquess of Donegall;
London: The Sherlock Holmes Society of London; 3, Deanery
Street, London, W.1.
This today-handsome publication began as a mimeographed,
twice-a-year effort in May 1952.
The Baker Street Gasogene, edited by P. A. Ruber, 330 East 79th
Street, New York 21, N.Y.
A new—in 1961—Sherlockian quarterly, ably edited by one of
the youngest of Sherlockians. Mr. Ruber has recently expressed
his intention to enlarge the scope of the *Gasogene* by making it
the only publication currently devoted to commentary on the entire field of detective fiction.

5. Reference Works and Miscellanies

Bigelow, S. Tupper
*An Irregular Anglo-American Glossary of More or Less Un-
familiar Words, Terms and Phrases in the Sherlock Holmes Saga;*
Toronto: Castalotte & Zamba, 1959.
An invaluable reference work for the American student un-
versed in British speech mannerisms.
Christ, Jay Finley
An Irregular Guide to Sherlock Holmes of Baker Street; pub-
lished jointly by Argus Books (New York) and The Pamphlet
House (Summit, N.J.), 1947.
A concordance of the Holmesian writings, indispensable to
every true student of the Saga. Two supplements have been
added since the *Guide's* first publication.

Montgomery, James
  A Study in Pictures: Being a "Trifling Monograph" on the Iconography of Sherlock Holmes; Philadelphia: International Printing Company, 1954.
    The standard guide to the subject, containing also two reference tables and an index, as well as thirty-two illustrations from the Sherlockian Canon.
Officer, Harvey
  A Baker Street Song Book; Maplewood, N.J.: The Pamphlet House, 1943.
    Thirteen Leider (with words) about the Baker Street scene, together with the Baker Street Suite for Violin and Piano, in five movements.
Petersen, Svend
  A Sherlock Holmes Almanac; Washington, D.C.: Privately printed, 1956.
    January 1 to December 31 with Holmes and Watson.
Smith, Edgar W.
  Appointment in Baker Street; Maplewood, N.J.: The Pamphlet House, 1938; reprinted, complete, in *221B: Studies in Sherlock Holmes.*
    A repertory of the characters, one and all, who walked and talked with Sherlock Holmes.
  Baker Street and Beyond; Maplewood, N.J.: The Pamphlet House, 1940; reissued (1957) as *Baker Street and Beyond: Together with Some Trifling Monographs;* Morristown, N.J.: The Baker Street Irregulars, Inc.
    A Sherlockian gazetteer, with five detailed and illuminated maps by Dr. Julian Wolff. The reissue includes a selection of the late Mr. Smith's essays on other Sherlockian fields, some not previously published.
  Baker Street Inventory: Summit, N. J.: The Pamphlet House, 1945.
    A listing of the first and other important editions of the Sherlockian Saga, and of the writings about the writings, together with an analysis of various titlings, and a note on the illustrators. Periodically updated in the pages of *The Baker Street Journal.*
  (as by "Helene Yuhasova") *A Lauriston Garden of Verses;* Summit, N.J.: The Pamphlet House, 1946.
    Six Sherlockian sonnets and a ballade, with six line drawings by the author.
Wolff, Julian, M.D.
  Practical Handbook of Sherlockian Heraldry; New York: Privately printed, 1955.
    The standard guide to the subject.
  The Sherlockian Atlas; New York: Privately printed, 1952.
    Thirteen of Dr. Wolff's detailed and illuminated maps, some not previously published.

E. Parodies, Pastiches, and the Tales-in-Verse

Derleth, August

"In Re: Sherlock Holmes": The Adventures of Solar Pons; Sauk City, Wisc.: Mycroft & Moran, 1945.

Twelve adventures of perhaps the nearest approach to the master detective, with an introduction by Vincent Starrett.

The Memoirs of Solar Pons; Sauk City, Wisc.: Mycroft & Moran, 1951.

Eleven more adventures of Solar Pons, with an introduction by Ellery Queen.

Three Problems for Solar Pons; Sauk City, Wisc.: Mycroft & Moran, 1952.

An interim trilogy. All three problems were later included in *The Return of Solar Pons.*

The Return of Solar Pons; Sauk City, Wisc.: Mycroft & Moran, 1958.

Thirteen tales of Solar Pons, with an introduction by the late Edgar W. Smith.

Doyle, Adrian Conan, and Carr, John Dickson

The Exploits of Sherlock Holmes; New York: Random House, 1954.

Twelve "simulacra," six by the agent's son alone, six by Mr. Doyle in collaboration with Mr. Carr.

Fish, Robert L.

"The Adventure of the Ascot Tie": *Ellery Queen's Mystery Magazine,* February 1960.

The first in a series of parodies, appearing irregularly in *EQMM,* about which Anthony Boucher has written: "It seems to me at least possible that Robert L. Fish is writing the very best Holmesian parodies in all the long history of the Misadventures."

Fisher, Charles

Some Unaccountable Exploits of Sherlock Holmes; Philadelphia: privately printed, 1956.

Eight short pastiches, in the lighter vein, which appeared originally in the Philadelphia *Record* in 1939 and 1940.

Heard, H. F.

A Taste for Honey; New York: The Vanguard Press, Inc., 1941.

The first in a series of novels and short stories featuring a certain "Mr. Mycroft," an elderly gentleman who keeps bees in a quiet English village of prewar vintage.

Metcalf, Norman (editor)

The Science-Fictional Sherlock Holmes; Lowry Air Force Base, Colo.: The Council of Four, 1960.

A collection of nine stories, by Anthony Boucher, Poul Anderson, August Derleth, and others, which bring the master detective to the very brink of the unknown.

Muusmann, Carl
Sherlock Holmes at Elsinore: Skjern, Denmark: for The Baker Street Irregulars, Inc., 1956.

> A third-person pastiche, set in the Hamlet country, by a noted Danish author. Translated by Paul Ib Liebe, with illustrations by Corsten Rian and an introduction by Tage La Cour.

Queen, Ellery (editor)
The Misadventures of Sherlock Holmes; Boston: Little, Brown & Co., 1944.

> By detective story writers, famous literary figures, humorists, devotees, and others, and including Vincent Starrett's "The Adventure of the Unique Hamlet," the single greatest Sherlockian pastiche ever written.

Smith, Edgar W.
A Baker Street Quartette; New York: The Baker Street Irregulars, Inc., 1950.

> Four tales-in-verse: "A Case of Identity," "The Speckled Band," "The Adventure of the Solitary Cyclist," and "The Final Problem," with illustrations by the author.

Titus, Eve
Basil of Baker Street; New York: Whittlesey House, 1958.

> The adventures of a mouse who emulated the master detective. An indispensable book for the children of Irregulars. Deliciously illustrated by Paul Galdone.

(Whitaker, Arthur)
"The Case of the Man Who Was Wanted"; *Cosmopolitan Magazine,* August 1948.

> A pastiche, unfortunately cover-billed by the editors of the Hearst magazines as: "The Last Adventure of Sherlock Holmes/ A hitherto unpublished story by Sir Arthur Conan Doyle."

F. Books, Articles, and Short Stories of Related Interest

Barnard, Allan (editor)
The Harlot Killer: The Story of Jack the Ripper in Fact and Fiction; New York: Dodd, Mead & Co., 1953.

> Includes in great detail the reports of the killings by the *Times* of London, as edited by Richard Barker.

Boucher, Anthony
"The Adventure of the Illustrious Impostor," in *The Misadventures of Sherlock Holmes;* Boston: Little, Brown & Co., 1944.
Blood on Baker Street; New York: Mercury Books, 1953.

> A detective story in which certain real-life Irregulars are easily identifiable. A completely rewritten version, constituting a new edition, of the author's famous (1940) *Case of the Baker Street Irregulars;* New York: Simon & Schuster, Inc.

Far and Away; New York: Ballantine Books, 1953.

Contains the short story, "The Anomaly of the Empty Man," about Holmes's cousin, Dr. Horace Verner.

Carr, John Dickson

The Life of Sir Arthur Conan Doyle; New York: Harper & Brothers, 1949.

The standard life of Dr. Watson's friend, literary agent and occasional collaborator.

De Voto, Bernard

"The Easy Chair."

A department. The article of special interest here appeared in *Harper's Magazine,* July 1954, pp. 8–15.

Doyle, Adrian Conan

The True Conan Doyle; London: John Murray, 1945; Coward-McCann, 1946.

A short biography of Sir Arthur by his son, with frequent and illuminating references to Mr. Sherlock Holmes of Baker Street.

Haycraft, Howard

The Art of the Mystery Story: A Collection of Critical Essays; New York: Simon & Schuster, 1946.

Contains, with much other material of interest, Rex Stout's scandalous essay, "Watson Was a Woman."

Murder for Pleasure: The Life and Times of the Detective Story; New York and London: D. Appleton-Century Company, 1941.

The standard guide to the subject, with a fine chapter, "Profile by Gaslight," on Mr. Sherlock Holmes.

Queen, Ellery

In the Queens' Parlor; New York: Simon & Schuster, 1957.

Contains "The Great O-E Theory," noted in this volume, and much other material of interest.